OOPS!

THEY DID IT AGAIN!

More Movie Mistakes
That Made the Cut

Matteo Molinari
and
Jim Kamm

CITADEL PRESS
Kensington Publishing Corp.
www.kensingtonbooks.com

CITADEL PRESS BOOKS are published by

Kensington Publishing Corp.
850 Third Avenue
New York, NY 10022

First printing: October 2002

10 9 8 7 6 5 4 3 2

Printed in the United States of America

Library of Congress Control Number: 2002104522

ISBN 0-8065-2320-4

CONTENTS

LET'S SAY THANKS TO . . .

Once again, our families and friends, first and foremost. As you know (and fear), all inspiration stems from you. We're talking Kamms, Molinaris, Struzzieros, yadda yadda yadda.
  Many of you also keep "tipping us off" to bloopers. And so, to all of these great minds—but mostly eyes—THANKS!

Carlo Alberini, Jim Anderson, Justin Anderson, Sha Asad, Sean Astin, George Barker, Brad Bernstein, Lorenzo Bertacchi, Dave "Kennedy" Beyer, Elisa Bozzo, Charlotte Breeze, Carrie Brunn, Bill Bryan, Jenni Calcara, Fabrizio Campelli, Michelle Chang, Mick Crowley, Chris Cuomo, Louie "LSD" Daidone, Benjamin DeLeon, Rachel DeLeon, Domenico "Dom" Del Zotto, Allison Donnelly, Leonid Doroschenko, Dave Edison, Holly Ellwood, Bevis Faversham, Jesse Felsot, Maggie Fish, Lyzz Forsyth, Michael French, Don Friedman, Silvia Gasparini, Alberto Ghè, Piero and Marina Girotti, Max Greggio, Gregponce, Charlotte Gurganus, Matt Haas, Sam Hanes, Jesica Kents, Joe and Chris, Mike Kirwan, Dale Kryska, Courtney Langdon, Bill LeBoeuf, Ryan Lewis, Erik Lichtenfeld, Rhea Lindsay, Giuseppe Macchion, Dave Marklinger, Francesco Mattarelli, Marco Mazzocchi, Mike Mendez, Andrea Molinari, Nicoletta Molinari, Mike Montes, Manuel Nardi, Paul Navidad, Paolino T. Orsini, Jeff W. Owens, Francesco Pannacciulli, Tito Parodi, Jacopo and Valerio Peretti Cucchi, Michael Plimmer, Emilio Pozzolini, Ryan Prince, Justin Prinze, Tim Ramage, Riccardo Recchia, Vincent Reyes, Carlo Romanò, Arthur Rose, John Rotan, Stefano Ruscitti, Alessandro Sgorbati, Pat Shannon, Larry Sher, Eric Sibelius, Todd Sibelius, Simona and Stefano Sordi, Laurent Soriano, Daniel Sotelo, the Stantons (Chris, Karen, Joel, Patricia, Sam, and Philip), DeWitte Stewart, Elle Struzziero, Phil Struzziero (Jr. and Sr.), Josh Tundra, Pietro Vezil, Stephen Voss, Graham

Winick, Marty Zied . . . and if we forgot anyone, it's a blooper. So strap us to the underbelly of a car and go over speedbumps.

A double thanks (one was for the previous volume, we forgot—how embarrassing!!) to the Two Men Who Believed In Us: Bruce Bender and Richard Ember. It's because of them that you can read what you're reading right now. So they have to be blamed for it (tee hee hee).

Also, thanks to Dave's Video, Laser Blazer, Toshiba, Matsushita, Philips, Sony, and others, and to the still much-abused Netflix.com.

And last, but certainly not least, as always a special thanks to everyone who makes movies, for using your amazing talents to make us laugh, cry, and dream. The world is a better place because of you. Keep plying your craft, if only so we can write more obnoxious books!

P.S.: A very big thanks to whoever can come up with more movies with titles starting with Q and X. We'd like to have at least one movie per letter, but boy is it a tall order!

INTRODUCTION

We're baaaack!!

Gaffe geeks here, comin' at ya again. And we just keep on collecting thousands and thousands of mistakes in the final cuts of movies—just like we did the first time—so we could bring you the SECOND best movie-blooper guide available (after the first, of course, which was still ours . . . but then maybe this will surpass it . . . but we digress).

Again, every blooper you can find in this book we have seen with our very own eyes—in other words, no rumors have gone unchecked, no "secret satanic messages" have slipped through the cracks, no international conspiracies . . . If you have the first *OOPS!* book, then you already know what we're talking about. If you don't have it . . . WELL, WHAT ARE YOU WAITING FOR?!?

First, a few regrets . . .

Yes, we're sorry about a few things: a) that as soon as we "locked" the first book, more mistakes from the movies we covered popped up before our very eyes, but it was too late to squeeze them in; b) that people were disappointed because they didn't find their favorite movie (we're working on this); c) for our own bloopers, which many of you have pointed out, and that we promptly corrected (we are, after all, at *your* service); and d) that so far nobody has been able to locate and film a giant squid (*Architeuthis dux*) alive.

We also want to reiterate that we wrote the *OOPS!* books because we absolutely love movies, not because we're trying to bust the filmmakers.

The *OOPS!* books are for anyone who has a movie or two in their possession and wants to have a little fun. You just pop in the movie, fast-forward or skip to the minute we specify, and find cheap, silly entertainment.

We hope that you'll find our neurotic little obsession as absorbing as we do.

Tally Ho!

Matteo Molinari and Jim Kamm
The Picky, Picky, Picky Folks Who Wrote the Book

Do let us know your favorite bloopers, and we'll guarantee you a full <u>16</u> minutes of fame!

Oops!
P.O. Box 24174, Los Angeles, CA 90024-0174 or dotell@oopsmovies.com

HOW TO USE THIS BOOK

Oops!: They Did It Again is a listing of thousands of amusing mistakes and tidbits in the final cuts of movies. But before you dig in, we offer some simple guidelines.

Note: This book isn't meant to be read cover to cover. It's a reference book; and like any other reference book, to be consulted when needed. (All right, heck, if you really want to read the darned thing straight through, go right ahead—we won't come knocking at your door to poke you in the liver because you did. For all we care, you can also plow through the Oxford English Dictionary. *Nerd!)*

Let's Say You Want to See if a Particular Movie Has Bloopers . . .

Proceed as follows:

A. Grab the movie (e.g., *American Pie 2*).
B. Flip the book open to the letter *A*.
C. Look up *American Pie 2*.
D. Find *American Pie 2*.
E. Read the first blooper.
F. Incredulously cry, "I can't believe it!"
G. Pop *American Pie 2* into your player.
H. Fast-forward to the minute of the blooper.
I. Press Play.
J. Enjoy.
K. Repeat steps A through J.
L. When you reach step E again, make sure to move on to the second blooper, and then the third, and so on. Otherwise, you'll find yourself quite stuck.

LEGEND

TITLE (number of bloopers)
  also Additional Release (SE—special edition, DC—director's cut, etc.)
  year released, color specification, length in minutes

Director(s): The insufferable fools behind the camera.

Cast: The insufferable fools in front of the camera.

  The "blurb," or a very quick take on the content of the movie written by the insufferable fools behind this book.

Blooper: The main course. It's an error, a mistake, a faux pas that you can easily spot in the final cut of a movie. Wrong positions, colors, names, suits, sounds . . . anything that you can actually snicker at, and which we're totally sure is wrong.

DVD Blooper: These can only be seen on those shiny little discs that go in the players with all the bells and whistles. Technology marches on, and the *OOPS!* team is there to scrutinize, as usual: subtitles, special features, etc.

Non-Blooper: Rare, but as powerful as any urban legend, hence very hard to eradicate. There are tons of incorrectly identified non-bloopers in the naked city (the Internet, in particular) and here we focus on the most persistent and widespread false accusations. We've tried to research as thoroughly as possible in order to bring you the truth, the whole truth, and nothing but the truth. Well, all right, maybe with a little embellishment.

Question: A tricky part of our quest. A question is not quite a blooper, but is something that, uh, smells fishy. Not necessarily plot holes (we tend to leave those for movie critics and such), but certain situations that don't sound quite right. You can have your own opinion, your friend can see it from a totally different point of view . . . discuss amongst yourselves.

Fun Fact: A little-known tidbit of juicy trivia, just to amaze friends and family (not so much ours as yours; our friends and families threw in the towel long ago).

Pan & Scan: Sometimes when a movie is "Formatted to fit your TV screen," bloopers that were outside of the frame in the cinema (or the widescreen version) come into view. Darned good reason for them not to "pan & scan" movies.

Sequel Blooper: A blooper that only exists because some filmmakers didn't pay close enough attention to an earlier movie in a series. Or maybe they did, but figured they could just "fudge it a little." Fine, but we cry, "OOPS!"

ICONOGRAPHY

 Must-See: The most astounding and hilarious mistakes.

 Will They Never Learn? Mistakes made again, and again, and again . . . but which are still a kick in the pants.

 Ignorant: Do a little research, folks!

 For Maniacs Only: You have to be a major-league blooper hound to appreciate it. Picky, picky, picky!

 Spoiler: If you haven't seen the movie, beware!

They Did It Again!

A

ABOVE THE LAW (5)
1988, color, 96 min.

Director: Andrew Davis

Cast: Steven Seagal (Nico Toscani), Pam Grier (Delores Jackson), Henry Silva (Zagon), Ron Dean (Lukich), Daniel Faraldo (Salvano), Sharon Stone (Sara Toscani), Miguel Nino (Chi Chi), Nicholas Kusenko (Agent Neeley), Joe Greco (Father Gennaro), Chelcie Ross (Nelson Fox), Gregory Alan Williams (Agent Halloran), Jack Wallace (Uncle Branca).

Nico is in town, and with a wham wham here, and a wham wham there . . .

Bloopers

1. After the party, Nico and Delores drive in her car. The window behind Nico is halfway rolled down, but when they stop the car it's completely up. And when Nico gets out, the window is again rolled halfway down. (00:11, 00:12)

2. At the morgue, Delores picks up Alan Singletary's ID: she holds it from the top right corner, then from the bottom right in the detail. (00:44)

3. Nico meets with Delores, who hands him a picture of Singletary's belongings. The photo Nico holds is different from the one Delores passes to him from her file. (00:54, 00:55)

4. As Nico passes by a marketplace, the camera is reflected in the external rearview mirror. And, just for the record, he also happens to be running a red light. (00:57)

5. After a street assault, Nico has a fight inside a store with four hit men. Nico is wearing low-cut black boots. But when he jumps through the window of the store, he lands on the sidewalk wearing a pair of black sneakers. (00:59, 01:00)

ABSOLUTE POWER (7)
1997, color, 121 min.

Director: Clint Eastwood

Cast: Clint Eastwood (Luther Whitney), Gene Hackman (President Richmond), Ed Harris (Seth Frank), Laura Linney (Kate Whitney), Scott Glenn (Bill Burton), Dennis Haysbert (Tim Collin), Judy Davis (Gloria Russell), E. G. Marshall (Walter Sullivan), Melora Hardin (Christy Sullivan), Kenneth Welsh (Sandy Lord), Penny Johnson (Laura Simon), Richard Jenkins (Michael McCarty).

The president does a bad bad thing, and there's a witness. Sound familiar?

Bloopers

1. Luther steps out of the two-way mirror room and walks by the lifeless body of Christy Sullivan: her mouth is slightly open, showing her teeth. When he picks up the bag with the knife, Christy's mouth is closed. (00:26)
2. In order to create an alibi for himself, Luther asks a friend to videotape a football game. When Luther inserts the tape into the VCR, it needs to be rewound. But Luther presses Play, and the game is on right at the beginning. (00:39)
3. Kate opens a copy of *The Washington Times* and spots, underneath the "Walter Sullivan's wife murdered" article, a second article titled "Jewel thief sought." The first three paragraphs of this article begin with, "An immediate . . ." "Future plans . . ." and "A suggestion . . ." And so does almost every single paragraph on the page. (00:47)
4. The passport Polaroids Valerie is taking of Luther change position on her desk after the second flash. (00:48)
5. The first time that Bill Burton meets Seth Frank, they are in the parking lot of the Metropolitan Police HQ. The shadow of a lamppost reaches the "Headq" part of "Headquarters" on the wall, but less than 30 seconds later, when Bill leans against a parked car, it's much lower. 30 seconds later, when Seth reenters the building, the shadow is even lower on the wall. (00:51, 00:52)
6. During President Richmond's news conference with Walter Sullivan, Richmond says, "If we had not met, I would not be president today. If Christine . . . had not taken ill . . . she would be with you in Barbados even now. Walter, you've been like a father to me . . ." During the breaking news of the president's "suicide," a portion of this conference is replayed. President Richmond says, " . . . I would not be president. If Christine . . . had not taken ill . . . she would be with you in Barba-

dos even now. Walter, you've been like a f—like a father to me." (01:04, 01:53)

7. When Seth goes to the meeting with Kate, she closes a beige folder, places an azure folder on top of it, and grabs them both with her right hand, which is also holding a pen. As she walks away from her desk, the azure folder has jumped inside the beige one, and the pen seems to have disappeared. (01:09)

Question
President Richmond rips Christy's dress during their fight, yet when Luther steps into the room, the dress seems perfect. Did the secret service agents mend it? (00:18, 00:26)

AIR FORCE ONE (2)
1997, color, 124 min.

Director: Wolfgang Petersen

Cast: Harrison Ford (President James "Jim" Marshall), Gary Oldman (Egor Korshunov), Glenn Close (Vice President Kathryn Bennett), Wendy Crewson (Grace Marshall), Liesel Matthews (Alice Marshall), Paul Guilfoyle (Chief of Staff Lloyd "Shep" Shepherd), Xander Berkeley (Agent Gibbs), William H. Macy (Major Caldwell), Dean Stockwell (Defense Secretary Walter Dean), Tom Everett (N.S.A. Advisor Jack Doherty), Jürgen Prochnow (General

Ivan Radek), Donna Bullock (Press Secretary Melanie Mitchel).

The president fights for his life as if he were Indiana Jones.

Bloopers
1. President Marshall is about to enter the conference room when a terrorist fires a couple of shots at him—hitting the door. Later on, when Ivan steps into the room through the same door, the bullet holes are gone. In later shots they're back—and in one shot, there are no less than three. (00:45, 00:49, 01:13)

2. President Marshall uses a cellular phone to call the White House from Air Force One. The actual plane has the safest vocal transmission center and eighty-seven phones that can call anywhere, including the space shuttle, but a cellular phone, at least at the time the movie was made, would never have worked at 30,000 feet over Europe. (00:54)

Question
Reality Check: Is there an escape pod on Air Force One or not? According to Wolfgang Petersen, there is one. According to Bill Clinton (president at the time the movie was released) there is not. And White House spokesmen denied it. But director John Carpenter also suggests there's one (see *Escape from New York*).

Fun Facts

1. The plane conference room we see in the movie has some fifty seats. The real one has only eight. (00:19)
2. It's really hard for a civilian to jump from a plane, even if the height is optimal; jumping from a 747 is almost impossible because of the speed of the plane. (01:14, 01:22)
3. The real Air Force One doesn't carry parachutes and doesn't have a launch platform like the one in the movie. (01:14)

ALADDIN (12)

1993, color, 90 min.

Directors: John Musker and Ron Clements

Cast: Scott Weinger (Aladdin—speaking), Robin Williams (Genie), Linda Larkin (Jasmine—speaking), Jonathan Freeman (Jafar), Frank Welker (Abu), Gilbert Gottfried (Iago), Douglas Seale (Sultan), Bruce Adler (Merchant / Narrator—singing), Brad Kane (Aladdin—singing), Lea Salonga (Jasmine—singing).

Disney's animated version of The Arabian Nights is a lot of fun; the Genie is a scene-stealer, Aladdin and Jasmine are vanilla.

Bloopers

1. The thief Gazeem has one half of the beetle, and he shows it to Jafar: the half has an out-curve. Iago the parrot steals the half and deposits it into Jafar's hand—but now the part has changed and it's the half with the in-curve. (00:03)
2. The patch on Aladdin's pants vanishes and comes back all through the picture (e.g., the first time, a guard tries to slice Al, but instead he smashes a large fish barrel). (00:07, 00:08)
3. At the sultan's palace, Jasmine's tiger, Rajah, rips Prince Ahmed's pants, revealing his heart-covered boxers. The tiger has, in her mouth, a piece of ripped cloth decorated with little hearts. But the pants Rajah ripped were purple, and the boxer shorts seemed to be intact. (00:12)
4. Holding the piece of Ahmed's pants, the Sultan doesn't pay any attention to the fact that the number of hearts varies between close-ups and long shots. (00:12)
5. Jasmine is sitting on the edge of a fountain filled with nothing but water. But when the scene cuts to the princess' close-up, a few flowers appear in the water. (00:13)
6. The sultan has a ring on his left hand that appears only when Jafar refers to it; otherwise, you never see the ring at all. (00:14)
7. Jafar unrolls a scroll in front of the sultan and reads from

it. However, since it appears to be written in Arabic, Jafar should move his eyes from right to left, and not from left to right—which is what he does. (00:47)

8. During the flight on the magic-carpet ride, Aladdin passes a flower to Jasmine, and she puts it in her hair, on the left side. When she pets a little horse the flower is gone, and when she looks into the stream they're sailing on, the reflection shows a flower on her right side—but right after, she has a flower on her left side. (00:58, 00:59, 01:00)

9. During the magic-carpet ride, Aladdin and Jasmine pass in front of a full moon, which becomes a half moon a few seconds later. (00:58, 01:00)

10. When the sultan tells Jasmine that he has chosen Jafar as her future husband, the feather on the sultan's turban changes color from azure to gray (when Jafar says, "He's obviously lying.") to azure again (the Sultan yells "Guards! Guards!") and to gray again, and to azure . . . (01:04, 01:05)

11. Turned into a slave by Jafar, Jasmine wears a red dress and a golden armband on her right arm. When Jafar finds out that Aladdin is in the palace, he throws Jasmine to the floor—and the armband has jumped to her left arm. When she stands up again, the armband has returned to her right arm. (01:15, 01:17)

12. When the spell changes Jasmine from a princess into a slave, she is wearing a beautiful white dress. When the spell's broken, Jasmine becomes a princess again, except now she's wearing the blue dress we saw her wearing in the beginning of the story. (01:15, 01:21)

Questions

1. If Jasmine is so rich, how come she wears only two dresses all through the picture?

2. Aladdin, disguised as Prince Ali Ababwa, visits Jasmine, landing on her balcony. Rajah growls at him as he says, "Good kitty . . ." Then, on Jasmine's close-up, does he or does he not add "Take off your clothes!"? NOTE: The Closed Captioning says, "Good kitty . . . Take off." (00:56)

Set Free for the Hiatus

Because of the third wish, the Genie is free. His wrist bands snap open and vanish (01:23). But in the direct-to-video sequel, *The Return of Jafar*, the bands are back.

Fun Facts

1. If you prick up your ears, you'll notice a slight differ-

ence in the opening song "Arabian Nights." It goes, "Oh I come from a land, from a faraway place, where the caravan camels roam, *where it's flat and immense, and the heat is intense*—It's barbaric but hey, that's home!" The original lyrics were "... camels roam, where they cut off your ear if they don't like your face ..." It was changed after protests from the Arab community, but you can still hear the original lyrics on the soundtrack. (00:00)

2. There are two men in the crowd who are pushed by Aladdin: these men are caricatures of the directors, John Musker and Ron Clements. (00:24)

3. The sultan is piling up a series of action figures—among them is a fairly recognizable Beast, from Disney's *Beauty and the Beast*. (00:46)

AMERICAN GRAFFITI (10)
1973, color, 110 min.

Director: George Lucas

Cast: Richard Dreyfuss (Curtis "Curt" Henderson), Ron Howard (Steve Bolander), Paul Le Mat (John Milner), Charles Martin Smith (Terry "The Toad" Fields), Cindy Williams (Laurie Henderson), Candy Clark (Debbie Dunham), MacKenzie Phillips (Carol), Wolfman Jack (The Wolfman / XERB Disc Jockey), Bo Hopkins (Joe Young), Harrison Ford (Bob Falfa), Terence McGovern (Mr. Bill Wolfe), Kathleen Quinlan (Peg), Flash Cadillac and the Continental Kids (Herby and the Heartbeats), Jana Bellan (Budda, Carhop at Mel's Drive-in).

The documentary-style coming-of-age movie is born.

Bloopers
1. As Toad arrives at Mel's Diner with his Vespa, he can't stop it and he runs into a trash can. As Curtis reaches Toad and Steve, the top of the trash can is no longer on the ground and the Vespa has backed up about a foot, apparently all by itself. (00:01)

Actor Charles Martin Smith later admitted that he had no idea how to drive a Vespa, and even less of an idea how to stop it. The scene is an actual accident that wound up in the movie.

---

2. While driving, John engages in a conversation with Zudo, a guy in another car. In the last shot of John, when he says, "Yeah, all right, thanks a lot!" someone briefly appears sitting next to him. But at that point, he was still alone in the car ... so who is this guy?! (00:11)

3. The license plate of the car of the girls from Turlock is JPM 351. And so is Steve's.

Hmmm... (00:14, 00:49, 01:41)

4. During the performance of "At the Hop" by Herby and the Heartbeats, in the shot that moves away from the band ("You can rock it, you can roll it...."), at least three extras stare directly into the camera—for example, the yellow-shirted kid. (00:18)

5. While talking with Curt outside the dance, Mr. Wolfe smokes a cigarette. When he says that he mostly was scared, he's holding the cigarette with his left thumb and index finger, middle and ring fingers from the front, and between the index and middle fingers from the back. In addition, when he says, "Now don't be stupid..." he has the cigarette in his left hand. As he adds, "... experience life!" The cigarette has suddenly jumped back into his right hand. (00:24, 00:25)

6. John and Carol are cruising in his hot rod: John's trademark pack of Camels is rolled up his left sleeve, and it's possible to see, through the fabric of the shirt, the back of the packet. But when Carol sprays him with some shaving cream, the packet has turned and now the camel on the front of the packet can be seen. (00:26)

7. Producer Francis Ford Coppola's 1963 movie *Dementia 13* is listed on the cinema marquee behind the cop car when it loses its rear axle. However, *American Graffiti* is set in 1962. (01:19)

Early Career Schlock Homage

Producer Francis Ford Coppola: "It's an issue of period. What would have been playing [in that theater]? And George [Lucas] gave me the honor of putting my movie up on the marquee."

---

8. When Steve is sitting alone at Burger City, he has a coffee cup in front of him: the handle of the cup is at "twelve o'clock" for him. But as Budda, the roller-skate waitress, arrives, the cup's handle has moved to "nine o'clock" without him touching it. (01:21)

9. John's hot rod's front license plate vanishes when he makes a U-turn to go help Toad and Debbie by Steve's car. The plate is back after this brief soujourn. (01:31)

10. The race between John and Bob ends with the black '55 Chevy flipping over: the trunk pops open, but as the car explodes, the trunk is perfectly closed. (01:43, 01:44)

Question
If the Wolfman's radio broadcasting station is supposedly clandestine, how come his radio antenna is more well-lit than the Washington Monument? (01:36)

Fun Facts

1. The breathtaking sunset at the beginning of the DVD is fake. Lucas "retouched" the film for its digital debut. (00:00)

2. The license plate number on John's yellow hot rod is "THX 138," which is an homage to director George Lucas' previous films *THX 1138* (1970) and *THX 1138:4EB* (1967). It is most clearly visible right before Carol first steps into John's car and he discovers how young she is. (00:14, 00:46, 01:13)

> Walter Murch (Sound Montage and Rerecording): "In those days—which is 1962, when the movie is supposed to be happening—you weren't allowed to have personalized license plates. You got whatever they gave you. And at that time there were three letters and three digits on a California license plate. Nonetheless, George wanted to have something that indicated the existence of his previous film."

AMERICAN HISTORY X (5)
1998, black & white, 117 min.

Director: Tony Kaye

Cast: Edward Norton (Derek Vinyard), Edward Furlong (Danny Vinyard), Beverly D'Angelo (Doris Vinyard), Jennifer Lien (Davina Vinyard), Ethan Suplee (Seth), Fairuza Balk (Stacey), Avery Brooks (Principal Bob Sweeney), Elliott Gould (Murray), Stacy Keach (Cameron Alexander), William Russ (Dennis), Guy Torry (Lamont), Tommy L. Bellissimo (Cop #2).

Neo-nazi grows a conscience . . . and his hair back.

Bloopers

1. As Principal Sweeney is talking to Murray, the boom mike is visible, reflected in the glass door of the cabinet behind the desk. (00:06)

2. While watching the basketball players, Danny stands by a metal fence. The straps of his backpack are on his shoulder, then around his arm, falling from the shoulder, and back up again. (00:16)

3. Seth enters the Vinyard's home with a videocamera. On its viewfinder there's a REC in red on the top right corner. A few minutes later, when Seth's taping Danny, there's not only REC, but also two other lines (white) with numbers on the screen. And, as Danny says "I hate Tabitha Soren and her Zionist MTV f***ing pigs," the viewfinder is totally clear: no REC, no nothing. (00:25, 00:27, 00:28)

4. When Derek gets arrested, a cop places his left arm around Derek, over the

swastika. The cop lifts Derek up by putting his right arm around his neck, and then walks him away—with his left arm around his neck. (00:55)

5. While refusing to talk to Lamont, Derek gets "mad at the damn sheets" and tosses a bunch of them on a shelf. During the whole sequence, the sheets on the shelf change position behind Derek. (01:17)

AMERICAN PIE 2 (9)
also Unrated Version
2001, color, 104 min. / UV 111 min.

Director: James B. Rogers

Cast: Jason Biggs (James "Jim" Levenstein), Shannon Elizabeth (Nadia), Alyson Hannigan (Michelle Flaherty), Chris Klein (Chris "Oz" Ostreicher), Natasha Lyonne (Jessica), Thomas Ian Nicholas (Kevin Myers), Tara Reid (Victoria "Vicky" Lathum), Seann William Scott (Steve Stifler), Mena Suvari (Heather), Eddie Kaye Thomas (Paul Finch), Eugene Levy (Jim's Dad), Chris Owen (Chuck Sherman), Denise Faye (Danielle), John Cho (John), Justin Isfeld (Justin).

New year, new pies, same old embarrassing moments.

Bloopers
1. John, the peeing guy, knocks down a vase (which knocks Stifler's partner unconscious) from the handrail of the second-floor verandah. But right after Stifler says, "Actually, I can't," the vase is back up in place. And when John zips his pants up, the vase is missing again. (00:15, 00:16 / 00:17, 00:18 UV)
2. Stifler interrupts Finch's tantric moment while holding a Mountain Dew bottle

KA-BOOM MIKES

If a sound technician falls in the forest, and nobody is around to film him, does he still wind up in the movie? Lets check . . .

American History X	Blooper No. 1
The Empire Strikes Back	Blooper No. 1
The Fugitive	Blooper No. 11
Rudy	Blooper No. 1
A View to a Kill	Blooper No. 6

horizontal; in the following shot, he's holding it vertically, by its neck. (00:24 / 00:26 UV)

3. When Jim meets Michelle at band camp for the first time, she takes him aside: the tag she's wearing is around the T-shirt's collar (from the side) and then around her neck (from the front). (00:26 / 00:28 UV)

4. The girls on the beach whom Stifler sends Oz to "fish" for have a bottle of Pepsi standing in the middle of a towel. When Oz falls flat in the middle of the group, the bottle appears to be already flat, crushed and empty—even if Oz doesn't get near it. Can anyone say, "second take?" (00:34 / 00:36, 00:37 UV)

5. When Stifler proclaims that the guys are painting the house of two lesbians, Finch (on the second floor) is painting the top of the handrail, yet in the matching cut he's painting one side, and in the next matching cut the top again. (00:37 / 00:40 UV)

6. The pillow behind Oz the first time he attempts phone sex with Heather keeps changing positions by itself, literally moving up and down throughout the sequence. (00:39 / 00:42 UV)

7. Danielle, the alleged lesbian with longer hair, removes her dress in her room then, when Kevin looks through the window, she removes it again. (00:43 / 00:46 UV)

8. Michelle lowers Jim's pants and boxer shorts, and they go all the way down. In the following shot, they are at Jim's calves, and in the next shot they're up to his knees. (00:56, 00:57 / 01:01 UV)

9. Before the gang leaves the house, Oz opens the door of the truck: the crew can be seen reflected in it. (01:37 / 01:43 UV)

Question
While driving to the house by the lake, Stifler stands up in the truck and yells, "That's right, baby, we're here! Woo-hoo-hoo!" Do they run a red light? (00:22 / 00:24 UV)

Easter Egg Au Naturale

On the *American Pie 2* DVD, go to the Special Features menu, and select the second page (the one with Kevin Myers and Vicky Lathum). Nudge up on the screen until "Special Features" is highlighted. Press Enter. You'll find a quite amusing Easter Egg.

AMERICAN PSYCHO—Unrated Version **(3)**
  2000, color, 103 min.

Director: Mary Harron

Cast: Christian Bale (Patrick Bateman), Willem Dafoe (Detective Donald Kimball),

Jared Leto (Paul Allen), Josh Lucas (Craig McDermott), Samantha Mathis (Courtney Rawlinson), Matt Ross (Luis Carruthers), William Sage (David Van Patten), Chloë Sevigny (Jean), Cara Seymour (Christie), Justin Theroux (Timothy Bryce), Guinevere Turner (Elizabeth), Reese Witherspoon (Evelyn Williams).

N.Y. yuppie mixes business and slaughter.

Bloopers
1. Patrick is talking on the phone with Courtney while looking at the cover of a porno video. When he says, "Pumpkin, you're dating a tumbling, tumbling dickweed," the spine of the tape is to Patrick's right (as if he were examining the back cover), yet the detail shows he's looking at the front cover. (00:15)
2. Patrick is examined by Det. Kimball. Patrick's secretary brings Kimball a bottle of water and a glass. After Patrick asks, "Do you have any witnesses or fingerprints?" a large ashtray suddenly appears behind the bottle and glass. (00:35)
3. During Kimball's second visit to Patrick's office, right after the detective says, "How about lunch in a week or so?" you can see the reflection of a moving boom mike

on the CD behind Patrick's right arm. (00:51)

AMERICAN WEREWOLF IN PARIS, AN (4)
1997, color, 98 min.

Director: Anthony Waller

Cast: Tom Everett Scott (Andy McDermott), Julie Delpy (Sérafine), Vince Vieluf (Brad), Phil Buckman (Chris), Julie Bowen (Amy), Pierre Cosso (Claude), Tom Novembre (Inspector LeDuc), Thierry Lhermitte (Dr. Pigot), Maria Machado (Chief Bonnet), Ben Salem Bouabdallah (Detective Ben Bou).

Love bites, even in France.

Bloopers
1. On the train going toward Paris, Andy's close-up shows a different background from the window than on the close-up on Brad and Chris. (00:04)
2. Andy is attacked by a big guy in a bar. Brad and Chris, in the background, stand up three times in a row. (00:22)
3. Sérafine raises her left hand to touch Andy's face (in front), but both hands are raised from behind. (00:23)
4. A woman's bag falls on the floor of the train: its position changes from the wide shot to the detail. (01:26, 01:27)

Question
How come so many Parisians converse with one another in fluent English? (00:29, 01:11, 01:19)

ARACHNOPHOBIA (4)
1990, color, 103 min.

Director: Frank Marshall

Cast: Jeff Daniels (Doctor Ross Jennings), Harley Jane Kozak (Molly Jennings), John Goodman (Delbert McClintock), Julian Sands (Doctor James Atherton), Stuart Pankin (Sheriff Parsons), Brian McNamara (Chris Collins), Mark L. Taylor (Jerry Manley), Henry Jones (Doctor Sam Metcalf), Peter Jason (Henry Beechwood), James Handy (Milton Briggs), Roy Brocksmith (Irv Kendall), Kathy Kinney (Blaire Kendall).

Deadly spider takes a holiday and decimates an American town.

Bloopers
1. Dr. Metcalf is killed by a spider and lies on his side on the left side of the bed, his arms on his chest. Yet after Ross checks for spider marks, Henry is in a totally different position in the middle of the bed. Nobody moved him. (00:56, 00:57)
2. When they check the bodies of the first three victims again, the last victim's face is gray, while the other two bodies are fleshy pink. (01:06, 01:07)
3. Dr. Atherton walks to the barn and Sheriff Parsons slams his car door and walks to the barn, too (four or five steps at least). As Dr. Atherton opens the door, Sheriff Parsons has just slammed his door in the background. (01:23)
4. Trying to kill the spider general, Ross grabs a bottle of red wine. In the following shot, not only has the bottle turned 180 degrees in his hands, but it has turned into a bottle of white wine. (01:37)

Question
When Ross comes back home and sees his daughter leaving with a friend, he doesn't turn the headlights of his BMW off. Huh? (01:00)

AROUND THE FIRE (4)
1999, color, 105 min.

Director: John Jacobsen

Cast: Devon Sawa (Simon Harris), Bill Smitrovich (Matt Harris), Tara Reid (Jennifer), Eric Mabius (Andrew), Colman Domingo (Trace), Charlayne Woodard (Kate Matthews), Lisa Burgett (Lauren), Henri Lubatti (Kevin), John Pirruccello (Joe), Stephen Tobolowsky (Doc), Steve Anthony Jones (N.Y. Policeman).

The life and times of a pot-smoking, drug-dealing,

shoplifting kid just like everyone else.

Bloopers

1. Simon's hair keeps jumping in front of his eyes and behind his ears while the policeman tells Simon's parents about his shoplifting at Patrick & Co. (00:07)
2. While having breakfast in rehab, Simon is given a package: he opens it, and out come two pictures and one wildly colored card. The detail, however, doesn't show the card at all; the following shot shows the card on the pictures, to the right side, and the following details have the card right in the middle of the frame. (00:49)
3. Doc explains the similarity between *Maple Leaf Rag* and "Brown-Eyed Girl" to Simon. Meanwhile, the bloody mary and the remote, both of which Doc places on the table on the side of the couch, keep changing positions back and forth without him touching them once. (01:12)
4. The wad of money Simon spreads on the dinner table in front of his parents keeps shifting position. (01:21)

ARRIVAL, THE (3)
1996, color, 109 min.

Director: David N. Twohy

Cast: Charlie Sheen (Zane Zaminsky), Lindsay Crouse (Ilana Green), Richard Schiff (Calvin), Shane (JPL Guard #1), Ron Silver (Phil Gordian / Mexican Guard), Teri Polo (Char), Phyllis Applegate (Mrs. Roosevelt), Alan Coates (Terraformer), Leon Rippy (DOD #1), Buddy Joe Hooker (DOD #2), Javier Morga (Co-worker), Tony T. Johnson (Kiki).

Charlie Sheen unmasks the alien conspiracy . . . and we're not talking about the one keeping him away from respectable films.

Bloopers

1. At the NASA entrance, a guard places a clipboard on the roof of Zane's car. When Zane backs up, the clipboard is gone. (00:15)
2. Zane hits an alien with his car . . . an alien who looks like his boss. The alien hits the ground, lying in front of the car: head to the left, feet to the right. As Zane runs over him one more time, the alien has rotated 180 degrees on the ground, for his head is now to the right and his feet are to the left. (01:15, 01:16)
3. A van bursts through a door that was locked by Zane using a red axe. As the door shatters, the head of the axe falls to the ground . . . but after a few seconds, it flies through the air and hits a computer only inches away from Zane's head. (01:40)

B

BABE (2)
1995, color, 89 min.

Director: Chris Noonan

Cast: Christine Cavanaugh (Babe), Miriam Margolyes (Fly), Danny Mann (Ferdinand), Hugo Weaving (Rex), Miriam Flynn (Maa), Russi Taylor (Cat), Evelyn Krape (Old Ewe), Michael Edward-Stevens (Horse), Charles Bartlett (Cow), Paul Livingston (Rooster), Roscoe Lee Browne (Narrator), James Cromwell (Farmer Hoggett).

Talking pig wins the hearts of millions: or, The Rush Limbaugh Story.

Bloopers
1. Two sheep thieves drop the truck ramp before Farmer Hoggett arrives. But as the old man reaches the area, the ramp is nowhere to be seen. (00:35)
2. During the final contest, Babe has three sheep with collars marching out of the white-ringed area. The sheep obey and take their places in front of the three sheep who are already in the ring, so that they're facing one another. As Farmer Hoggett opens the fence, the sheep are all facing the Farmer, and as they begin walking, they all come out of the ring. (01:24)

Fun Facts
1. When stealing the alarm clock, Babe awakens the cat. What follows is a long shot of the house, a lot of noise . . . and two ducks savagely mating in the pond outside the house. (00:21)
2. Babe tries to talk to the sheep at the contest. Only one is facing him, while two more are facing away. When the pig says "Are they feeding you well?" and, a little later, ". . . out in the field with all this rain we've been having," the sheep to the far left poops twice. (01:13, 01:15)

BACK TO SCHOOL (3)
1986, color, 96 min.

Director: Alan Metter

Cast: Rodney Dangerfield (Thornton Melon), Sally Kellerman (Dr. Diane Turner), Burt Young (Lou, Melon's Chauffeur), Keith Gordon (Jason Melon), Robert Downey, Jr. (Derek Lutz), Paxton Whitehead (Dr. Phillip Barbay), Terry Farrell (Valerie Desmond), M. Emmet Walsh (Coach Turnbull), Adrienne Barbeau (Vanessa Melon), William Zabka (Chas Osborn), Ned Beatty (Dean Martin), Kurt Vonnegut, Jr. (Kurt Vonnegut, Jr.).

A dad follows his son to college . . . and it's even more humiliating than you'd expect.

Bloopers
1. When Valerie gets her note-books knocked down, she picks them up, placing the red binder on top of the blue one and holding on to them. After the Bruce Springsteen stunt, the red binder has moved to the bottom. (00:23, 00:25)
2. Dr. Barbay and Dr. Turner talk about creating a merger while walking to Barbay's car. The boom mike is reflected in the car parked behind Barbay's. (00:37)
3. In order to connect with his son, Thornton performs a

 dive from a platform . . . but if you look carefully, you'll see that the diver is not Thornton at all: it's a stunt double with a bald head and a wig that flaps way too much. (00:39)

Fun Facts
1. Writer and philosopher Kurt Vonnegut, Jr., appears as himself. (00:55)
2. Soundtrack composer Danny Elfman appears as leader of his band, Oingo Boingo. (01:05)

BACK TO THE FUTURE PART II (20)
1988, color, 108 min.

Director: Robert Zemeckis

Cast: Michael J. Fox (Marty McFly, Jr. / Marty McFly, Sr. / Marlene McFly), Christopher Lloyd (Dr. Emmett "Doc" L. Brown), Lea Thompson (Lorraine Baines / McFly), Thomas F. Wilson (Biff Tannen / Griff), Elisabeth Shue (Jennifer Parker), James Tolkan (Principal Strickland), Jeffrey Weissman (George McFly), Casey Siemaszko (3-D), Billy Zane (Match), Jeffrey Jay Cohen (Skinhead), Charles Fleischer (Terry), Harry Waters, Jr. (Marvin Berry), Joe Flaherty (Western Union Man).

The trilogy continues in the future . . . and the present . . . and the past.

Bloopers

1. When the DeLorean backs up from the driveway of McFly's home, it stops in the middle of the road: the camera can be seen reflected in the car's license plate. (00:02)

2. Once in the future, en route to Hill Valley, Doc announces, "Here's our exit!" and he proceeds to steer to the left. But the DeLorean swerves to the right. (00:05)

3. Marty wears a jacket that is too big for him. The left pocket's "retractable" flap is shorter than it appears just before Doc pushes the self-adjusting command on the jacket. (00:08)

4. When Doc shows an issue of *USA Today*, Marty grabs it in the middle of its shorter sides—but in the opposite shot, he's holding it from the bottom. (00:09)

5. Inside Café 80s, Old Biff stands up to approach Marty: the Pepsi bottle that Marty is working on appears by him on the table in the over-the-shoulder shot, and back in his hands in the next. (00:13)

6. Marty walks to the video-game kids to show them how to play; from the back, he's a few feet away from them, but from the front, he has zapped right behind them. (00:15)

7. When he's by the video-game, Marty takes off his hat and places it on top of the machine. But when Marty, Jr. enters the café, Marty ducks behind the counter: he never takes it, yet the hat is gone from the videogame. (00:15)

8. Marty dries his hair and it's all messy. In the next shot, it's dry and perfect. (00:21)

9. In the alternate 1985, during a discussion about their son and Switzerland, Lorraine takes a long sip of whiskey from a glass she's holding with her left hand, but as she walks to her husband, she's holding the glass with her right hand. (00:47)

10. Lorraine is wearing slippers with pink taffeta, but when Biff shoves her to the floor, she isn't anymore. However, when she reacts to a punch Marty receives in his stomach, she's wearing the pink slippers again. (00:47, 00:48)

11. Marty distracts Biff, then throws a round ashtray at his head, but Biff leans over and the ashtray gets stuck in a chair. But it somehow manages to turn upside down in mid-flight. (00:59)

12. In 1955, Biff's car sports a rearview mirror in the middle of the windshield's center divider. But when old Biff drives Biff home, the rearview mirror has moved up along the center divider, and now is at the same height as the shades. When Biff leaves for the dance, while he's pulling the car out of the drive-

way, the rearview mirror zaps back to its original place. (01:05, 01:09, 01:11)

13. When principal Strickland grabs the almanac from Biff, he rolls it up and whacks Biff with it. The almanac keeps rotating in Strickland's hand. Check the letters ALMA on the cover and their position during the dialogue. (01:18)

14. While Biff is knocked out, Marty makes everyone back up, then proceeds to unzip Biff's jacket. But the jacket, almost unzipped when Marty grabs it, is then almost completely zipped up in the following shot (and Marty's hands are nowhere near it). Also, just for fun, check the position of Marty's legs. (01:22)

15. Chasing Biff to get the almanac from him, Marty places his left foot into the hoverboard strap. But once inside the tunnel, it's his right foot that's in the strap. And when Marty tries to reach the opposite end of the tunnel, the right foot is pushing, the left foot is on the hoverboard, but there's no strap at all. After Biff's car skids toward Marty, the left foot appears to be in the strap, but as Biff's car is approaching, no strap can be seen. (01:30, 01:32, 01:33)

16. In the last shot before Marty moves via hoverboard from the DeLorean to Biff's Ford,

it's possible to catch a glimpse of the real wheels of the "flying" time machine. Also, on the bottom of the screen is the shadow of the camera car. Oh, the wheels of the DeLorean can also be spotted after the thumbs-up and the machine steers to the left. (01:30)

17. The camera crew is visible in the Ford's hubcap when the wheel peels out on the road at the end of the tunnel. (01:33)

18. Marty receives a seventy-year-old letter from Western Union. It's a large brown envelope with a knot on top. Marty turns the envelope in his hands, but when he unties the knot, he does it from the top. (01:38)

19. The Western Union man presents a clipboard to Marty with a receipt to sign: the man holds the clipboard with his four fingers underneath it—but in the matching shot, he's holding it with the five fingers over it. (01:39)

20. In the final shot of the trailer for BTTF III, Marty has his hands along his sides, but as they snap a picture of him and Doc by the Hill Valley clock, Marty has his hands folded together. (01:42)

Question

If Biff from 2015 steals the sports almanac and gives it to himself in 1985, shouldn't he return to a different future than the one he came from? (00:32, 00:37)

Remember the Desk, Marvin!

During Marty's performance of "Johnny B. Goode," Marvin Berry rushes to the phone to call his cousin. He dials the number from the front of the desk, but in *Back to the Future* he did it from *behind* the desk. (01:26)

Fun Facts
1. Among all the inside jokes of the movie, probably the cutest is that the movie *Jaws 19* has been directed by Max Spielberg—one of Steven's sons. (00:11)
2. The red-shirted kid who is able to turn on the video-game *Wild Gunner* is a very, very, very, very, very young Elijah Wood. (00:15)

BASEKETBALL (4)
1998, color, 103 min.

Director: David Zucker

Cast: Trey Parker (Joe Cooper), Matt Stone (Doug Remer), Dian Bachar (Kenny "Squeak" Scolari), Yasmine Bleeth (Jenna Reed), Jenny McCarthy (Yvette Denslow), Ernest Borgnine (Ted Denslow), Robert Vaughn (Baxter Cain), Trevor Einhorn (Joey), Al Michaels (Al), Bob Costas (Bob).

Slackers invent hybrid of two popular sports and fi-
nally get some attention from the opposite sex.

Bloopers
1. Squeak opens the window of his new room: blinds are lowered halfway down the window, but from the outside they're gone. They'll be back when the dog jumps into the room. (00:15)
2. When Mr. Denslow approaches Cooper, a bunch of guys in the background are doing the wave on the roof. They begin to fall down, and a guy with a leather jacket and white pants falls twice. (00:17)
3. The sports commentators Bob and Al wear red and yellow polos, respectively. However, while watching the cheerleaders in the first game after Ted Denslow's death, there's a close-up that shows Al with a blue shirt and tie, and Bob with a white shirt and tie. Then the polos come back a little later. (00:33)
4. Jenna picks up a picture from a table with her right hand. In the reverse shot, she's holding it in her left. (00:54)

Question
What are the odds that Cooper's car stereo looks *exactly* like the cab's car stereo? (01:16, 01:29)

BATMAN FOREVER (9)
1995, color, 122 min.

Director: Joel Schumacher

Cast: Val Kilmer (Bruce Wayne / Batman), Tommy Lee Jones (Harvey Dent / Two-Face), Jim Carrey (Edward Nygma / The Riddler), Nicole Kidman (Dr. Chase Meridian), Chris O'Donnell (Dick Grayson / Robin), Michael Gough (Alfred Pennyworth), Pat Hingle (Commissioner Gordon), Drew Barrymore (Sugar), Debi Mazar (Spice), Elizabeth Sanders (Gossip Gerty), Rene Auberjonois (Dr. Burton), Joe Grifasi (Bank Guard), Ed Begley, Jr. (Fred Stickley).

Third adventure and second face for the superhero.

Bloopers
1. While retrieving the safe from the chopper, Batman tells the bank guard to "hang on." The guard holds on to the chain to which the safe is attached. But as the safe comes back into the vault, the guard is holding on to one of the tubular structures of the safe itself. (00:09)

2. When checking a tape that shows a (fake) suicide, Bruce is handed a "good-bye cruel world" letter, which was folded in three parts. The detail shows a clean sheet of paper, with no wrinkles or folds. (00:26)

3. Dick grabs Two-Face's bomb when its timer reads 0:12, and throws it away when the timer reads 0:07 . . . twenty seconds later. (00:39, 00:40)

4. To escape from an ambush that Two-Face prepared for him, Batman tilts the Batmobile onto its rear wheels, and thanks to a bat-hook, he's able to use the vertical facade of a building as an alternate route. However, when Two-Face looks up to see this amazing escape, the sparks coming out of the Batmobile fall *toward the wall* (and not toward the ground, as they should). (00:50)

WHAT'S YOUR FAVORITE COLOR?

Anything that (mis)matches.

Prince Ahmed's pants in *Aladdin*	Blooper No. 4
A bottle of wine in *Arachnophobia*	Blooper No. 4
Al Michaels and Bob Costas's shirts in *BASEketball*	Blooper No. 3
Michelle Joyner's jacket in *Cliffhanger*	Blooper No. 1
R2-D2's dome in *The Empire Strikes Back*	Blooper No. 10

5. During their first buddy-buddy robbery, the Riddler smashes a glass cabinet to take a very large diamond—but in the following shot, he's holding a very small diamond. Two-Face will then produce the very large diamond. Talk about sleight of hand. (00:56)

6. The Riddler shows Two-Face a small tube with Bruce Wayne's thoughts inside. He holds the tube with his left hand in the long shot, and with his right hand in the close-up. (01:24)

7. Young Bruce Wayne runs away holding his dad's diary. As he falls into a pit, he lets the red book go—but he lands holding on to it. (01:30)

8. In order to enter the Wayne mansion with Two-Face, the Riddler knocks out Alfred ("Trick!"). The butler falls to the ground, then, while unconscious, moves a tray to allow Riddler to easily open a closet door. (01:31)

9. Robin is kept prisoner in the Riddler's secret lair and duct tape is wrapped around his mouth. When he falls into a pit, and when Batman saves him, the duct tape has mysteriously slipped down the Boy Wonder's mouth and around his neck. Lousy brand. (01:49, 01:51)

Question
The Riddler enters Two-Face's secret lair, holding only his golden cane. But a few minutes later, while explaining his plan, the Riddler grabs two of his "boxes" from Two-Face's furniture. When did he place them there, and, since they're not exactly small, how come Two-Face didn't notice them? (00:52, 00:54)

Billy Dee's Not *That* Light-Skinned!

Harvey Dent's story is presented on TV station GNN (00:24). Dent is a tall, white man—but in *Batman*, he was played by African-American actor Billy Dee Williams.

BATMAN & ROBIN (9)
1997, color, 126 min.

Director: Joel Schumacher

Cast: Arnold Schwarzenegger (Mr. Freeze / Dr. Victor Fries), George Clooney (Batman / Bruce Wayne), Chris O'Donnell (Robin / Dick Grayson), Uma Thurman (Poison Ivy / Dr. Pamela Isley), Alicia Silverstone (Batgirl / Barbara Wilson), Michael Gough (Alfred Pennyworth), Pat Hingle (Commissioner Gordon), John Glover (Dr. Jason Woodrue), Elle Macpherson (Julie Madison), Vivica A. Fox (Ms. B. Haven), Jeep Swenson (Bane), Coolio (Banker).

Fourth adventure and third face for the super hero.

Bloopers
1. At the Gotham Museum of Art, in order to fight the

"hockey team from hell," Batman and Robin click their heels and ice blades appear on their soles. But as they skate on the ice, it's easy to see that the two heroes (and the thugs) are wearing Rollerblades, not ice blades. (00:06, 00:07)

2. When Barbara is trying the passwords to access her uncle's secret program, she looks at the picture of Alfred's wife we saw before. The picture is clean—yet in the next shot it has a signature that reads "Love, Peg" like it was the first time we saw it. (00:32, 01:31)

3. Poison Ivy wears a wig while going to the observatory in her red Mercedes. Once there, the wig she's wearing is a different style. (00:34, 00:36)

4. After she's "helped with the reporters," Julie smiles—yet in the matching wide-shot she's passing one hand through her hair. (00:35)

5. Bruce Wayne gives Dr. Isley's proposal back. She grabs it, the printed part toward her—but in the following shot, she's holding the paper so we can see the printed part, which now faces away from her. (00:37)

6. During her breathtaking entrance at the charity convention, Poison Ivy dives backwards into the arms of five men. Yet when she lands, she seems to have made a 180-degree spin in midair, for now her head is where her feet should have been. (00:43)

7. Just before decorating her new hideout, Poison Ivy mentions to Bane that "It took God seven days to create Paradise." Well, not really. It took God six days to create the Universe, and He rested on the seventh day. (00:58)

8. Right before Batman produces a circular saw to cut a few trapping vines, Robin is fighting underwater. The boy emerges for a gasp of air and submerges almost instantly. Well, perhaps *too* instantly: the shot is stopped and reverse-played (notice the water's drip going away and then toward Robin's head). (01:39)

9. Mr. Freeze uses his device to freeze half of Gotham, including two police cars. The first car smashes through a store window, and the icicles on top wobble considerably. Later on, when Batman defreezes the town, a cop exits the second car: again, the icicles on the door wobble as if made of rubber. (01:42, 01:52)

Questions

1. If Barbara has arrived "all the way from England," where she's studied at the Oxbridge Academy (sic), how come she doesn't have, like, an English accent? (00:29, 00:30)

2. Barbara finally breaks into

Alfred's computer and discovers the Wayne Mansion secrets. The computer projects colored images all over her face—why? Especially since it didn't do anything like that earlier, when Alfred used it. (01:31)

BEAN—THE MOVIE (4)
1997, color, 90 min.

Director: Mel Smith

Cast: Rowan Atkinson (Mr. Bean), Peter MacNicol (David Langley), John Mills (Chairman), Pamela Reed (Alison Langley), Harris Yulin (George Grierson), Burt Reynolds (General Newton), Larry Drake (Elmer), Danny Goldring (Security Buck), Johnny Galecki (Stingo Wheelie).

Mr. Bean jumps from the small to the big screen . . . with the same catastrophic results.

Bloopers
1. At the airport, Mr. Bean is chased by a few policemen. He enters the second pedestrian walkway with his coat on his left arm, but as he frantically zigzags through the people, the coat jumps onto his right arm, then back onto his left. (00:13)
2. When David's wife leaves him for the first time, it is

during the magic hour—the light is really low on the horizon. The matching close-ups in the same place shows an even lower light. You know the old saying, "Time flies when you're shooting a movie." (00:27, 00:28)

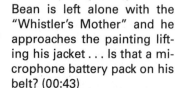

3. Bean is left alone with the "Whistler's Mother" and he approaches the painting lifting his jacket . . . Is that a microphone battery pack on his belt? (00:43)
4. On a mission to save the painting he's damaged, Bean enters the museum and distracts the guard by calling for help. Bean is wearing cow-and-frog slippers. When he enters the guard's room to put the laxative in his coffee, Bean is wearing regular shoes. The cow-and-frog slippers will return when he's contemplating the safe in which "Whistler's Mother" is kept. (00:56, 00:58)

Question
When Bean sneezes on the "Whistler's Mother" painting, in the background, a vase with red flowers is to the right of the door. When Bean comes back into the room, the vase and several flowers are now lying on the ground. But apparently no one ever touched this vase, so what happened in the room when no one was there? (00:43, 00:47)

BEDAZZLED (7)
2000, color, 93 min.

Director: Harold Ramis

Cast: Brendan Fraser (Elliot Richards), Elizabeth Hurley (The Devil), Frances O'Connor (Alison Gardner), Miriam Shor (Carol), Orlando Jones (Daniel), Paul Adelstein (Bob), Toby Huss (Jerry).

Loser strikes a deal with the devil, who happens to be a sexy supermodel.

Bloopers

1. Elliot (as Jefe, the drug lord) is in the middle of a firefight, and he throws a brick of cocaine into the air and shoots it to create a "smoke screen." The cocaine emits flames when it explodes... yeah, right. (00:35)

2. Elliot slam-dunks the ball for the last shot of the game. The final score is Diablos 135, Shirts 85. However, as he's soaring for the dunk (both the first and second time they show it), the hanging scoreboard at the top of the Forum already credits 135 to the Diablos before he makes the shot... official scorer getting a little ahead of himself? And then the third time they show the dunk, Elliot shatters the glass; as the glass rains down, the Diablos' total increases to 137. Then as he does his dance

and spits glass, it has increased to 138. Two points for breaking the backboard, and one for celebrating? (00:49, 00:52)

3. Elliot the basketball star has a game in which he breaks the NBA single-game records for points (104), rebounds (45), assists (32), steals (37), and blocks (28). However, the *real* NBA record for most rebounds in a game is 55, set by Wilt Chamberlain on November 24, 1960. What, you say there's no proof that this was actually an NBA game? Fine, but later the interviewer mentions that Elliot broke Wilt's scoring record of 100 points in a game. So there. (00:49, 00:52)

4. While we're at it, let's talk about Elliot's assist record (32). Just so we're clear, one is credited with an assist when one passes the ball to a teammate, and that teammate scores either 2 or 3 points. Even if every assist resulted in only 2 points, that still means at least 64 points for another teammate. Considering that Elliot scored 104, that means at least 168 for the Diablos. Unfortunately, their point total was 135. Oops. (00:49)

5. The second time they show Elliot slam the winning dunk, the glass shatters after he lets go of the rim. The third

time they show it, the glass shatters while he's still hanging on. (00:51)

6. When Bob interviews Elliot courtside after the game, a good portion of the crowd in the background are cardboard cutouts. (00:51)

7. As the teacher, the Devil erases the algebra at the top of the blackboard. When we see the blackboard after she erases the history homework, it's back, then gone. After the bell rings, it's back again. And then gone again. (01:04)

Fun Fact
Sensitive Elliot is about to kiss Alison on the beach when they're interrupted by two vicious Dobermans that the Devil is walking on the beach. She calls them off by their names: Dudley and Peter. These are the first names of the stars of the original *Bedazzled*: Dudley Moore and Peter Cook. (00:42)

BEDKNOBS AND BROOMSTICKS—Restored Version **(8)**
1972, color, 129 min.

Director: Robert Stevenson

Cast: Angela Lansbury (Eglantine Price), David Tomlinson (Prof. Emelius Browne), Roddy McDowall (Mr. Jelk), Sam Jaffe (Bookman), Ian Weighill (Charlie Rawlin), Roy Smart (Paul Rawlin), Cindy O'Callaghan (Carrie Rawlin), Lennie Weinrib (Secretary Bird / Lion), John Ericson (Colonel Heller), Bruce Forsyth (Swinburne), Tessie O'Shea (Mrs. Hobday).

A good witch helps three kids and all of England during wartime.

Bloopers
1. Mrs. Hobday leaves the children in the museum, steps outside, and closes the door twice. (00:05)

2. When Miss Price tries to fly with the broom, but falls flat, the "flying" cables are visible (particularly just before she falls to the floor). (00:19)

3. During the song "The Age of Not Believing," Carrie says, "That's Charlie to a T." and she pulls up the beige blanket twice. (00:33)

4. In the Bookman's pad, Miss Price is holding one half of *The Book of Astoroth* in her right hand, the left hand on top of it. The detail shows her holding the book with her left hand. (01:12)

5. The Ruddy Cup that Miss Price and Professor Browne win dancing in the lagoon doesn't cast a shadow like everything else does (check out the shadow of Miss Price's hands on Browne's vest). (01:21)

6. "Referee" Browne examines the Star of Astoroth on the lion's necklace for the first

time, then lets go of the necklace. Browne's hand moves right through the lion's body, as if it weren't there. Wait a second! . . . (01:27)

7. During the soccer game, Professor Browne is trampled by the players. The king lifts him up and dusts him with his tail. Check out the shadow on the ground: the lion's shadow is missing, and you can see Browne's jersey lifted up . . . by nothing. (01:30, 01:32)

8. Professor Browne juggles three green apples, but one falls into a bowl of soup, splashing his face and his shirt collar. He begins cleaning his face, but when Mrs. Hobday arrives, his collar is spotless. (01:48, 01:49)

Question
The animals are playing a soccer game, and in the end the rhino pokes a hole in the ball, which flies away. When it comes back, deflated . . . doesn't it look suspiciously like a football—rather than a soccer ball? (01:26, 01:34)

BEING JOHN MALKOVICH (6)
1999, color, 112 min.

Director: Spike Jonze

Cast: John Cusack (Craig Schwartz), Cameron Diaz (Lotte Schwartz), John Malkovich (John Horatio Malkovich), Charlie Sheen (Charlie), Ned Bellamy (Derek Mantini), Mary

Kay Place (Floris), Orson Bean (Dr. Lester), Catherine Keener (Maxine), K. K. Dodds (Wendy), Gregory Sporleder (Drunk at bar).

A portal to Malkovich's mind is discovered and exploited for money.

Bloopers
1. At a payphone, Craig explains to Lotte why he's late when he sees Maxine walking by. Craig holds the phone with his left hand—but in the close-up it jumps into his right. (00:18)

2. When we first see his face, John Malkovich is looking at himself in the mirror—at an angle—so he shouldn't be able to see himself directly, right? (If you're picky, picky, picky, this also happens when John is in his bathroom.) (00:30, 00:37)

3. While still in front of the mirror, John passes one hand over his head. The "real" hand is slower coming down than the "reflected" hand. (00:30)

4. When Lotte first enters Dr. Lester's John Malkovich shrine, there is a prominently displayed diploma from Northwestern University. The real John Malkovich never attended Northwestern, nor was he ever given an honorary degree. (00:40)

5. When Lotte experiences being John Malkovich, she

finds him reading aloud from a book. The actor is holding the book from the middle, with his left hand above the spine. But John's point of view reveals only two fingers holding the book. (00:44)

6. In a crowded bar, John denies he's Malkovich to an insistent drunk man. John holds and sips from a glass in his left hand, but the drink swaps to his right hand after one shot. (01:40)

BEVERLY HILLS COP (4)
1984, color, 105 min.

Director: Martin Brest

Cast: Eddie Murphy (Axel Foley), Judge Reinhold (Detective Billy Rosewood), John Ashton (Sergeant Taggart), Lisa Eilbacher (Jenny Summers), Ronny Cox (Lieutenant Bogomil), Steven Berkoff (Victor Maitland), James Russo (Mikey Tandino), Jonathan Banks (Zack), Stephen Elliott (Chief Hubbard), Gilbert R. Hill (Inspector Todd), Bronson Pinchot (Serge), Paul Reiser (Jeffrey), Damon Wayans (Banana Man).

Detroit cop goes out of his jurisdiction to L.A., destroys tons of property, and somehow doesn't get thrown in jail.

Bloopers
1. Inside Victor Maitland's office, Axel is shown the door

by five henchmen. The one with the sunglasses enters the room with his jacket buttoned, but when he marches to the door, he buttons it one more time. (00:29)

2. The bananas Axel gets at the hotel are straight. When he places them in the exhaust pipe of Rosewood's car, they're curved. (00:39, 00:40)

3. Axel and Victor Maitland both pull into the Harrow Club from a road where you can easily read "POTS" (the upside-down image of "STOP") written on the asphalt. (01:01)

4. When the police enter Maitland's villa, two henchmen flee ("You hanging around here?" "F***, no!"). The first one is carrying a gun in a belt holster, the second one has a shoulder holster. When they're running down the stairs, the holsters are gone. As they jump into the van, the holsters are back. (01:32, 01:33)

BILLY ELLIOT (4)
2000, color, 110 min.

Director: Stephen Daldry

Cast: Julie Walters (Mrs. Wilkinson), Jamie Bell (Billy Elliot), Jamie Draven (Tony Elliot), Gary Lewis (Dad / Jackie Elliot), Jean Heywood (Grandma), Stuart Wells (Michael), Mike Elliot (George Watson), Janine Birkett (Billy's Mum), Nicola

Blackwell (Debbie Wilkinson), Billy Zane (Mr. Braithwaite), Colin MacLachlan (Mr. Wilkinson), Joe Renton (Gary Poulson), Adam Cooper (Billy, age 25).

A kid decides that dancing is better than boxing.

Bloopers
1. Young Billy has blue eyes; older Billy has green-brown eyes. (00:01, 01:43)
2. During boxing practice, Billy's dad keeps an eye on his son from a balcony over the gym entrance. When Billy "dances" around the ring, his dad is not in the background, but one second later he's there, yelling, "Billy! Hit him!" (00:07)
3. The boxing trainer calls Billy's father "Jackie," (00:22) and he even gives the name "Jackie Elliot" when he decides to go back to work despite the strike (01:13). Yet, on Billy's mom's gravestone, it says "Wife of Peter." [Note: the gravestone has been "vandalized" to cover the name.] (00:13)
4. After slapping Billy, Mrs. Wilkinson places her hands in front of her face, as if she were praying. In the following shot, she has them folded one over the other. (00:47)

BIO-DOME (4)
1995, color, 95 min.

Director: Jason Bloom

Cast: Pauly Shore (Bud MacIntosh), Stephen Baldwin (Doyle Johnson), William Atherton (Dr. Noah Faulkner), Joey Adams (Monique), Teresa Hill (Jen), Denise Dowse (Olivia Biggs), Dara Tomanovich (Mimi Somkins), Kevin West (T. C. Romulus), Kyle Minoguee (Petra Von Kent), Henry Gibson (William Leaky).

Two dudes devastate and then restore an ecological experiment.

Bloopers
1. Bud hits Doyle with a book, whereupon Doyle flies into a bookshelf, and the shelves fall to the ground. But when Monique and Jen get to the apartment, the bookshelf is up in place. (00:04, 00:06)
2. Supposedly, the two dudes get trapped in the Bio-Dome facility with the clothes they were wearing and nothing more. However, Bud's checkered pants are long when he enters, then short when he and Doyle offer a drink to the two female doctors, long again when he pulls up the flypaper to capture the insects, short again when he meets the entomologist to show what they've just done... (00:14, 00:39, 00:44)
3. Doyle kills a fly on his shoul-

der with his left hand, yet he licks it off of his right hand. (00:16)

4. The perfect, state-of-the-art LCD clock above the door sucks. Bud and Doyle want to get out, and they talk with Dr. Biggs. Meanwhile, the clock reads "Day 363—16:28:49" and counting. Then it reads "16:29 . . ." then "16:28 . . ." and "16:29 . . ." and finally it goes "16:28:02 . . . 01 . . . 00 . . . 16:30:00 (!!!) . . . 16:29:59 . . ." (00:26)

Questions

1. A frustrated Monique says to Jen, "Face it: we're dating primates." Doesn't she know that men *are* primates? (00:07)

2. Dr. Romulus is upset because the two dudes are using his toothbrush. Yet, later on, he isn't afraid to share it with them anymore. However, if he's a scientist, didn't he know that the average life of a toothbrush is three months, so inside Bio-Dome he should have had at least four of them? (00:23, 01:14)

3. Right after Bio-Dome has been resealed, all the scientists except for Dr. Faulkner form a conga line. However, the first one in the front of the line is a little person, neither a scientist nor Bud nor Doyle. Where did he come from? (01:14)

BIRDS, THE (2)
1963, color, 120 min.

Director: Alfred Hitchcock

Cast: Rod Taylor (Mitch Brenner), Jessica Tandy (Lydia Brenner), Suzanne Pleshette (Annie Hayworth), "Tippi" Hedren (Melanie Daniels), Veronica Cartwright (Cathy Brenner), Ethel Griffies (Mrs. Bundy), Charles McGraw (Sebastien Sholes), Ruth McDevitt (Mrs. MacGruder), Joe Mantell (Traveling Salesman), Malcolm Atterbury (Sheriff Al Malone), Karl Swenson (Drunken Man), Elizabeth Wilson (Helen Carter).

The first FOX special: When Volatiles Attack.

Bloopers
1. Trying to prevent another bird attack, the kids flee from the school: their shadows on the ground keep changing directions, most notably during the two details of "kids' running legs." (01:10)

2. When the pupils are chased by the same flock, none of the birds cast shadows on the ground. (01:10)

Fun Fact
HITCHWATCH: The director can be spotted walking two dogs out of a pet store. (00:02)

BLACK HOLE, THE (7)
1979, color, 97 min.

Director: Gary Nelson

Cast: Maximilian Schell (Dr. Hans Reinhardt), Anthony Perkins (Dr. Alex Durant), Robert Forster (Captain Dan Holland), Joseph Bottoms (Lieutenant Charles Pizer), Yvette Mimieux (Dr. Kate McCrae), Ernest Borgnine (Harry Booth), Tommy McLoughlin (Captain S.T.A.R.), Roddy McDowall (V.I.N.Cent), Slim Pickens (Bob).

Spacecraft parked on the edge of a black hole has more than one secret to tell.

NOTE: Take out 2:32 of overture at the beginning if you don't like the score.

Bloopers

1. As the *Palomino* makes the second pass underneath the *Cygnus,* Alex says, "Activating the macro beam." A powerful light beam hits the deck of the *Cygnus* as the *Palomino* travels left to right. The light "follows" the *Palomino.* In the following shot, the *Palomino*'s still traveling left to right, but the light is now at the opposite angle from the ship. Even if it's clear there's only one macro beam coming from the *Palomino,* as Alex looks out of the window, he still sees the light at its original angle. (00:11)

2. When Harry is talking to

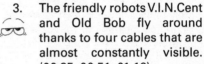

Captain Reinhardt and leaning on the console ("The authority would still consider that an act of piracy, Doctor"), the number on the computer zaps from 4177685 to 4333185 during the cut. (00:33)

3. The friendly robots V.I.N.Cent and Old Bob fly around thanks to four cables that are almost constantly visible. (00:35, 00:51, 01:16)

4. While sharpshooting with the other robots, V.I.N.Cent says "Nice shooting, Bob," even if Bob hasn't yet identified itself ("My name is B.O.B."). (00:47, 00:51)

5. During the rescue of Dr. McCrae, Captain Holland has a shootout with several robots. A few of these fire back, but at least a couple of their shots make neither the "laser noise" nor the impact noise. (01:08)

6. The meteorites that smash against the starship are transparent. (01:16)

7. As the group flees on the vehicle along one of the spacecraft's transport conduits, a meteor snaps the tube in two. The vehicle our heroes are on slows down and stops on the edge of the broken tube ... but it goes too far, and part of the matte "eats" the tip of the car. (01:17)

THE NAME GAME

Fama, Fama, Fo-fanano-mama, mo ...

A tombstone in *Billy Elliot*	Blooper No. 3
Alicia Silverstone's name in *Clueless*	Blooper No. 1
Todd Field's band in *Eyes Wide Shut*	Blooper No. 8
Tom Cruise's name in *Days of Thunder*	Blooper No. 4
V.I.N.Cent's partner in *The Black Hole*	Blooper No. 4

BLADE RUNNER (11)

also Director's Cut
1982, color, 117 min.

Director: Ridley Scott

Cast: Harrison Ford (Rick Deckard), Rutger Hauer (Roy Batty), Sean Young (Rachael), Edward James Olmos (Gaff), M. Emmet Walsh (Bryant), Daryl Hannah (Pris), William Sanderson (J. F. Sebastian), Brion James (Leon), Joe Turkel (Eldon Tyrell), Joanna Cassidy (Zhora), James Hong (Hannibal Chew, Eyemaker), Morgan Paull (Holden).

Hunting down renegade artificial humans ... has never been so goshdarned fun!

Bloopers

1. Holden interviews Leon, and then the tape of the session is replayed by Bryant in Deckard's briefing, and also by Deckard while riding in a transport ship. Each time a recording of the scene is re- played, the timing and read- ing of the lines is slightly dif- ferent than the original. (00:05, 00:13, 00:23)

2. A police ship takes off with Deckard in it. You can see the cables that pull the ship up. The cables are also visible when a police ship takes off after Deckard is told about Sebastian. (00:10, 01:28)

3. Bryant tells Deckard that six replicants escaped from an off-world colony and have returned to Earth. Let's see, one was fried running through an electrical field. Bryant shows profiles of (and Deckard later meets up with) Leon, Roy, Pris, and Zhora. There's also Rachael, but she's clearly not an es- capee from off-world ... so what the hell happened to the sixth??? (00:12, 00:14)

4. The Asian woman finds the serial number on the fish scale, and reads it off ... *ex- tremely* inaccurately. The se- quence of numbers she's

speaking are nowhere to be seen in the microscope's viewer. (00:47)

5. Deckard interrogates Abdul Hassan, the snake maker, and we see the conversation though a glass snake cage. This is one of the worst extended mismatched ADR (automated dialogue replacement) scenes we've ever seen. Nothing said matches the movement of the characters' mouths . . . with the possible exception of each other's! (00:48, 00:49)

6. Zhora, dressed in a transparent plastic coat and high-heeled boots, runs away from Deckard. But when he shoots her, and she runs through several windows, a protective shirt appears under the coat, and her boots no longer have heels . . . not to mention that her stunt-double's face is strikingly different. (00:55, 00:58)

7. Deckard's shot leaves a large, bleeding, red exit wound on Zhora's chest. When she gets up to keep running, the wound is totally healed. (00:57, 00:58)

8. Deckard buys a bottle of booze, and his face is covered with blood and bruises . . . but when he chases down Zhora his face is just fine. It's messed up again later while he's beaten up by Leon. (00:59, 01:01)

9. Leon beats up Deckard in the street, and throws him into a windshield . . . which is already shattered before he lands. (01:02)

10. After Roy discovers Pris's dead body and begins howling, Deckard wanders into a room where four spotlights are shining out from behind a wall of chain links and horizontal planks. Look carefully at the wall just before Deckard walks to the lights: we see his shadow . . . preceded by the shadows of the director and the steadicam operator walking backward in front of him. (01:38)

11. Roy says, "Time to die," and releases a dove. Despite the fact that the sky has been dark and rainy (and continues to be so after the dove flies away), the dove flies up into a clear, blue sky. (01:47)

 DVD Blooper

Roy meets Tyrell, and demands, "I want more life . . . Fu**er!" But the DVD subtitles say, ". . . Father!" (01:23)

Question

The first time Roy Batty appears, he is apparently alone in a phone booth . . . so whose hand is on his right shoulder? (Turns out it's Tyrell's hand on Roy's shoulder— this is a flipped shot from when Tyrell is consoling Roy about his impending death later on in the movie.) (00:26)

BLOW OUT (5)
1981, color, 108 min.

Director: Brian De Palma

Cast: John Travolta (Jack), Nancy Allen (Sally), John Lithgow (Burke), Dennis Franz (Manny Karp), Peter Boyden (Sam), Curt May (Frank Donahue), John Aquino (Det. Mackey), John McMartin (Lawrence Henry), Maureen Sullivan (First Murder Victim — Mary Robert), Elaine Filoon (Screamer #1), Robin Sherwood (Screamer #2).

Sound engineer Travolta turns detective in this engaging De Palma thriller.

Bloopers
1. Jack sees a car plow into a creek. As he runs and dives into the water, the car sinks completely. But as he's looking for the car, the trunk is above the surface, then it sinks a second time. (00:11)
2. From the outside of a motel, Jack's head is leaning directly against the window; from the inside, between his head and the window is a blue curtain. (00:27)
3. Burke's first victim (later identified as Mary Robert) still blinks as the killer turns her head to check her face. (00:47)
4. In order to replace an awful scream from an awful B-movie, a director is testing two screamers in a sound booth:

the brunette grabs the blonde's hair with her right hand — but when Jack enters the room, the brunette is using her left hand to pull instead. (01:00)
5. To track Sally down, Jack places the earpiece in his left ear (when he's in the ambulance), then he runs through the crowd with the earplug in his right ear. When Jack finally reaches Sally, surrounded by fireworks, the earplug is gone for good. (01:37, 01:38, 01:42)

BOWFINGER (5)
1999, color, 98 min.

Director: Frank Oz

Cast: Steve Martin (Robert K. "Bobby" Bowfinger), Eddie Murphy (Kit Ramsey / Jiffernson Ramsey), Heather Graham (Daisy), Christine Baranski (Carol), Jamie Kennedy (Dave), Barry Newman (Kit's Agent), Adam Alexi-Malle (Afrim), Kohl Sudduth (Slater), Terence Stamp (Terry Stricter, MindHead Honcho), Robert Downey, Jr. (Jerry Renfro).

Has-been producer desperately tries to make a comeback . . . and almost succeeds.

Bloopers
1. Close to the phone, Bowfinger has a bulletin board: the pamphlet "Learn How to

Act" is there. But then when Bowfinger plays with his dog, it's not. When Dave calls after the first shot scene, the pamphlet is back. And it's gone again when Afrim tells Bowfinger he's writing new scenes. (00:03, 00:13, 00:32, 00:38)

2. Outside of a restaurant, Bowfinger rips off his fake ponytail and sticks it into his left pocket. When he later hands his card to Jerry Renfro, he produces it from his right pocket—along with the ponytail. (00:09, 00:12)

3. After running the script in his computer, Kitt states that the letter *K* appears 1,456 times. "That's perfectly divisible by three." Hence, KKK appears in the script 486 times. Well, almost. If you divide 1,456 by three, you get 485.3333. It is 1,458 that is perfectly divisible by three. (00:13)

4. Bowfinger tells Dave that he's forty-nine years old, and that he's been putting away one dollar every week since he was ten. He then opens a box with $2,184. But in thirty-nine years there are only 2,028 weeks. 2,184 weeks is forty-two years. (00:22)

5. Waiting to shoot one scene with Kitt, Carol says that she would like to "work with someone who had honored their craft." She raises her right hand—but she lowers her left (when Bowfinger is in the shot). (00:33)

Question
Inside the Griffith Observatory, Bowfinger and his crew film one scene that is captured live by the security monitors. Live? So how come the monitor has a tape drop during the "broadcast"? (01:18)

BOYS DON'T CRY (3)
1999, color, 118 min.

Director: Kimberly Peirce

Cast: Hilary Swank (Teena Brandon / Brandon Teena), Chloé Sevigny (Lana Tisdel), Peter Sarsgaard (John Lotter), Brandon Sexton III (Tom Nissen), Alicia Goranson (Candace), Alison Folland (Kate), Jeanetta Arnette (Lana's Mom), Rob Campbell (Brian), Matt McGrath (Lonny), Cheyenne Rushing (Nicole).

She acts like a he; he likes other shes.

Bloopers
1. John sits on the couch next to Brandon/Teena at his/her birthday party. During the dialogue, a cigarette jumps from behind Brandon/Teena's left ear to his/her right ear, and then back to the left. (01:04)

2. Lana convinces John to let Brandon/Teena show his/her private parts to her alone. As Lana and Brandon/Teena get up from the couch and start toward Lana's room, a boom mike's shadow zips away on

the wall behind Tom's head. (01:20)

3. Brandon/Teena is shot through the head by John. In the morning, Lena takes a letter from Brandon's pocket and reads it in tears. In the background, a dead Brandon/Teena keeps breathing normally. (01:52)

BOYS FROM BRAZIL, THE (4)
1978, color, 123 min.

Director: Franklin J. Shaffner

Cast: Gregory Peck (Dr. Josef Mengele), Laurence Olivier (Ezra Lieberman), James Mason (Eduard Seibert), Lilli Palmer (Esther Lieberman), Uta Hagen (Frieda Maloney), Steve Guttenberg (Barry Kohler), Denholm Elliott (Sidney Beynon), Rosemary Harris (Mrs. Doring), John Dehner (Henry Wheelock), John Rubinstein (David Bennett), Anne Meara (Mrs. Curry), Jeremy Black (Jack Curry / Simon Harrington / Erich Doring / Bobby Wheelock), Bruno Ganz (Professor Bruckner).

Unusual gang of Nazis decides to clone Adolf Hitler in order to try the whole thing one more time.

Bloopers
1. Self-proclaimed Nazi investigator Barry finally winds up

stabbed to death; he hits a wall, slides down . . . but, most important, blinks. (00:26)

2. Lieberman arrives at the train station at 11:00 A.M. (a large clock says so when he and his sister walk along the platform). When the duo meet David and agree to go with him, a clock above the stairs says it's 9:50. (00:55, 00:57)

3. Lieberman interviews Frieda Maloney in jail. There's a pack of cigarettes on a table, and a golden lighter sitting on it. When Fräu Maloney takes a cigarette, the lighter has moved to the side of the packet. (01:09)

4. Dr. Brucker circles the word "boy" on his blackboard. When he finds out that Lieberman has left, the circling and other marks on the blackboard look completely different. (01:32)

Question
Since when does everyone in Vienna speak English to one another—with an accent? (00:07)

BRAVEHEART (25)
1995, color, 177 min.

Director: Mel Gibson

Cast: Mel Gibson (William Wallace), Sophie Marceau (Princess Isabelle), Patrick McGoohan (Longshanks—King Edward I), Catherine McCormack (Murron), Angus

ARE THEY REALLY DEAD?

Or is it just a case of deadly discomfort?

Henry Jones in *Arachnophobia*	Blooper No. 1
Maureen Sullivan in *Blow Out*	Blooper No. 3
Steve Guttenberg in *The Boys from Brazil*	Blooper No. 1
Kellye Nahahara in *Clue*	Blooper No. 3
Cassandra Harris in *For Your Eyes Only*	Blooper No. 19

McFadyen (Robert the Bruce), Brendan Gleeson (Hamish), David O'Hara (Stephen), Ian Bannen (The Leper), James Robinson (Young William), James Cosmo (Campbell), Sean McGinley (MacClannough), Brian Cox (Argyle Wallace).

Mel dons a skirt and becomes even more macho.

Bloopers

1. The narrator states that "historians will say I am a liar . . ." Well, maybe that's because he says that Isabella of France's first child was born in 1312—seven years after William Wallace's death. Either she's very slow, or Wallace is not the father of the child. Also, Wallace died in 1305, and Edward I in 1307—and he still led the invasion of Scotland. To top all of that, Isabella never met William Wallace, and even if she did marry Edward, that happened three years after Wallace's death. It also happened in France. (00:01, 01:46, 02:36)

2. Young William Wallace throws rocks with his left arm. Adult William Wallace throws rocks with his right. (00:06, 00:25, 00:34)

3. At the funeral of his dad and brother, young William fakes the sign of the cross—with his left hand. Adult William Wallace makes a perfect right-handed sign of the cross. (00:11, 01:22)

4. Young Murron and her taller sister switch places at the time of the sign of the cross: in the close-up, Murron is to the right and her sister to the left; in the master shot, they're vice versa. (00:11)

5. Young William receives a purple flower from young Murron. He takes the flower twice—the first time as she gets his attention, the second time in the detail. (00:11)

6. At the village, William Wallace stands still while Hamish tosses a boulder at him.

The boulder passes Wallace by his left shoulder—if seen from the front—and by his right shoulder—if from behind. (00:25)

7. Hit by a rock, Hamish collapses to the ground: the blood on his forehead vanishes right after Wallace helps him up. (00:25)

8. Murron waves at Wallace while he's on his horse, making the animal rear up. Murron's mom stares at Wallace and at her sister, and then in Murron's close-up, she stands and repeats the exact same action in the background. (00:36)

9. Wallace disguises himself as an English soldier: he carries a long sword as he flees the village. Running in the forest, he has no sword whatsoever. As he reaches the meeting point where he should have found Murron, the sword is back. (00:44)

10. When he surrenders, Wallace places his hands on his head: from behind they're at the height of the neck. From the front, they're much higher. (00:48)

11. Wallace reveals his weapon from underneath his hair, and hits the soldier who's holding his horse. Twice (once from the front, once from behind). (00:49)

12. At Murron's funeral, Wallace kneels down before her dad, MacClannough. He hesitates, but eventually places his

hand over Wallace's head—and in the master shot, the hand is in a totally different position. (00:55)

13. As he steps into the camp, Steven's hair changes from dry to wet, some of it sticks to his forehead, then on the mouth, back to the forehead ... all through the scene. (01:08, 01:09)

14. During his first entrance, Steven says, "The Almighty says, don't change the subject—just answer the f***ing question." The word "f***" wasn't used until the fifteenth century. (01:09)

15. Wallace is hunting for a deer: he has a bow and an arrow already in place, however he draws a second arrow—without shooting the first. (01:10)

16. Paudren attacks Wallace, but is killed by Steven, who throws his sword. As he's hit, Paudren lets his sword go—but as he falls to the ground, he's still holding it. (01:11)

17. Before the first battle starts, Lochlan lists the king's terms. Wallace reaches him, and aims to Lochlan's right, while riding a horse. In Lochlan's close-up, Wallace is seen passing behind him—to the left. (01:19)

18. After being told by Wallace that his commander has to kiss his own ass, Lochlan turns his horse left and leaves—but in the master shot, he's leaving to the right. (01:21)

19. When Lochlan and his escort leave, Wallace approaches his companions and explains his plan—for a little more than thirty seconds. As Wallace & Co. leave, we see in the wide shot Lochlan and the others who are just leaving—again. Slow, aren't they? (01:21)

20. The cavalry charges away from the infantry and (in slo-mo) attacks the Scottish—but as they gallop downhill, there's no infantry behind them anymore. (01:25, 01:26)

21. Wallace leads his people in an attack on the English: during the charge, he's holding a pickaxe, then nothing, then his sword, the pickaxe again, and then the sword again. (01:28)

22. Wallace meets with Princess Isabelle. The kerchief hanging from her hat moves from underneath her chin to over her chin, to underneath it again, to above . . . (01:47)

23. Wallace finds out that Robert the Bruce betrayed him. He collapses to the ground, and the piece of arrow he had in his chest is no longer protruding from his upper chest. But when Steven arrives, and Robert decides to help Wallace, he pulls him up—and the arrow is back. (02:08, 02:09)

24. When Princess Isabelle goes to visit Wallace in jail, the jailor closes the door almost completely. But in the following shots, the door is wider open, then closed, then open again. (02:31)

25. During the final, slo-mo charge, Hamish's axe wobbles in the wind as if it were made of rubber. By golly, that's what it is!! (02:49)

Questions

1. Just before kneeling down during his marriage, does Mel Gibson take a peek at the camera and then look away??? (00:37)

2. Does the lady to the right of the woman who first yells, "Mercy!!" glance at the camera? And does the red-headed lady in the right, bottom corner of the screen do the same thing in the following shot? (02:43)

BROKEN ARROW (4)
1996, color, 108 min.

Director: John Woo

Cast: John Travolta (Vic Deakins), Christian Slater (Riley Hale), Samantha Mathis (Terry Carmichael), Delroy Lindo (Colonel Max Wilkins), Bob Gunton (Pritchett), Frank Whaley (Giles Prentice), Howie Long (Kelly), Vondie Curtis Hall (Lt. Colonel Sam Rhodes), Jack Thompson (Chairman, Joint Chiefs of Staff), Vyto Ruginis (Johnson), Ousaun Elam (Lt. Thomas).

John Travolta is evil, and Christian Slater has to stop

him. He'll do it, but four he-licopters will be destroyed in the process.

Bloopers

1. Riley jumps out of the stealth bomber, grabbing his trusty army gun. Later in the picture he needs to borrow a gun from Terry the park ranger. At the end of the movie, his faithful gun, which he'd grabbed from the stealth bomber, is back. Huh? (00:16, 00:35, 00:56)

2. Vic's Humvee rams Riley's Humvee. Vic's Humvee loses one of its headlights. Later on, Riley tosses a gasoline can at Vic's Humvee, but now the headlights are both intact. (00:47)

3. Riley reaches the bomb in the cave; the timer reads 22:59—and counting. But when Vic later caresses the same bomb, we briefly see the timer—which now reads 26:00. (00:56, 00:57)

4. Riley and Terry are on the roof of a train car, and an evil guy shoots them. The bullets hit a white rectangular antenna, chipping away a corner. In the following shots, the corner is back, and then it's gone again. (01:28)

Questions

Riley puts a bullet in Vic's arm—the very same arm Vic later uses to shoot down a chopper, arm a nuclear bomb, and beat the crap

out of poor Riley. Huh? (01:27, 01:28, 01:36)

BULLETPROOF (6)
1996, color, 84 min.

Director: Ernest R. Dickerson

Cast: Damon Wayans (Keats / Jack Carter), Adam Sandler (Archie Moses), James Caan (Frank Colton), Jeep Swenson (Bledsoe), James Farentino (Capt. Will Jensen), Kristen Wilson (Traci Flynn), Larry McCoy (Detective Sulliman), Allen Covert (Detective Jones), Bill Nunn (Finch), Mark Roberts (Charles), Mark Casella (Disneyland Cop), Andrew Shaifer (Cop at Airport), Xander Berkeley (Darrel Gentry), Sal Landi (Cole).

Your average two-bucks-a-pound, paint-by-the-numbers, one-is-black-one-is-white, odd-couple, buddy-buddy movie.

Bloopers

1. Keats and Moses steal a Ferrari and back away from a villa, and the car's owner exits with a gun and fires two shots. The first shot emits only a loud *bang,* the second—with the gun barrel not aiming at the thieves—emits a flame and a *bang.* Hmmm . . . (00:01)

2. Moses and Keats are on a plane that runs out of fuel.

First the right prop stops, then the left one. As the plane glides, after Keats moves to sit, a wide shot shows the props spinning as if everything were Okay. (00:29)

3. Moses manages to land the plane on the edge of a cliff, and the duo flee from the rear exit. At that point, the plane falls down the cliff, and explodes in a huge ball of fire. Why such a tremendous explosion if it was carrying no more fuel? (00:31)

4. Keats throws agent Gentry out of the car. Gentry rolls close to the median. The shot from inside the car doesn't show anybody in the middle of the road. (00:58)

5. Keats exits the police station telling his captain, "You ought to be ashamed of yourself." Then he grabs a broom, and before closing the door, says something else—but apparently he just moved his lips, because there's no sound at all. (01:04)

6. In Mexico, the drunk dog stumbles around on the counter because two "helping hands" are pulling him from behind. (01:19)

Question

When Charles helps Keats and Moses run away from the gunmen at the motel, is that the gas pedal that Charles hits to stop his van on the edge of Devil's Drop Off? (00:50)

'BURBS, THE (4)
1989, color, 101 min.

Director: Joe Dante

Cast: Tom Hanks (Ray Peterson), Bruce Dern (Lt. Mark Rumsfield), Carrie Fisher (Carol Peterson), Rick Ducommun (Art Weingartner), Corey Feldman (Ricky), Wendy Schaal (Bonnie Rumsfield), Henry Gibson (Werner Klopek), Brother

SUPERFLY

Bloopers lighter than air.

Adam Sandler and Damon Wayans's plane in *Bulletproof*	Blooper No. 3
The highjacked plane in *Cliffhanger*	Blooper No. 3
Kurt Russell–flown plane in *Executive Decision*	Blooper No. 8
Tim Thomerson's plane in *Iron Eagle*	Blooper No. 1
Roger Moore's hydroplane in *The Man With the Golden Gun*	Blooper No. 15

Theodore (Uncle Reuben Klopek), Courtney Gains (Hans Klopek), Gale Gordon (Walter), Dick Miller (Garbageman), Robert Picardo (Garbageman), Nick Katt (Steve Kuntz).

Life in middle-America is not so boring, after all.

Bloopers

1. Ricky and Art tell Ray the story of a neighbor who allegedly killed his family. Eventually, Ricky scares Ray by yelling in his face, and the can Ricky is holding in his right hand (from the front angle) jumps into his left hand (from behind). (00:24)

2. Ray doesn't want to hear what Art has to say about Satanism, so he places his hands over his ears and starts to perform "unconscious chanting." His left middle finger is in his ear, his ring and little fingers are rolled inside the hand—but in the side shot, it's his index finger in his ear, while his other three fingers are stretched across his cheek. (00:40)

3. Ray's dog digs up a femur bone and holds it in its mouth very close to one of the ends. Yet, when Art retrieves the bone, the dog is now holding it right in the middle. (00:49)

4. After Rick proclaims that he loves the street he lives on, the shot moves away from the 'burbs and goes up, up, up...to show the entire Earth—which somehow spins to the left. (01:37)

Fun Fact

The breathtaking opening sequence places the movie in middle-America. However, when Lt. Rumsfield is on the roof of his home yelling at one of Ricky's "lame-o" friends, in the background we catch a quick glimpse of the Disney Channel building—which is in Burbank, California [the movie was shot in the backlot of Universal Studios Hollywood—a blooper in itself: Universal Studios "Hollywood" is actually in the Burbank-adjacent Universal City, not Hollywood]. (00:00, 01:17)

C

CABLE GUY, THE (8)
1996, color, 91 min.

Director: Ben Stiller

Cast: Jim Carrey (Chip Douglas), Matthew Broderick (Steven M. Kovacs), Leslie Mann (Robin Harris), Jack Black (Rick Legatos), George Segal (Mr. Kovacs), Diane Baker (Mrs. Kovacs), Ben Stiller (Sam Sweet / Stan Sweet), Eric Roberts (Eric Roberts), Misa Koprova (Heather), Janeane Garofalo (Waitress), Andy Dick (Medieval Host), Harry O'Reilly (Steven's Boss).

Sinister Cable Guy fixes everything: TVs, power plants, broken hearts . . . or does he?

Bloopers
1. The Cable Guy tells Steven that his name is Ernie Douglas, but his friends call him "Chip." Later on in jail, the Cable Guy tells Steven that his real name is Larry Tate. When Steven wants his friend Rick to investigate the Cable Guy's past, Steven says "He calls himself Larry Tate but he told me his name is Chip Douglas." That's true, only it's backward: the Cable Guy *calls* himself Chip Douglas, but *told* Steven his name is Larry Tate. (00:17, 01:06, 01:07)

2. One of Steven's pals injures himself while playing basketball. He's helped to one of the courtside seats and is there when Chip warms himself up before playing. One of the guys throws the ball to Chip, asking him to "check it." The injured player has vanished—but he's back, in the same seat, less than ten seconds later. Evidently he's still quite mobile. (00:19, 00:20)

3. Steven's having a *Sleepless in Seattle* evening, and Robin asks him, "How's Hal?" and he replies, "How's Hal? Don't get me started. The guy has no vision. It's like working for Mr. Magoo. Those hair-

plugs . . . (And she says, "I know . . .") He's just an utterly useless person. I think I hate him." When Chip e-mails Steven the taping of that evening, at "How's Hal?" Steven replies "Don't get me started. That man, he has no vision. It's like working for Mr. Magoo. If only somebody at corporate would wise up and dump Hal. Those . . . hairplugs are so awful to look at. . . . Everybody knows that he's utterly useless." (00:25, 01:14)

4. When Steven's having a *Sleepless in Seattle* evening with Robin, he says "I think I hate him," and his arm sits on the sofa headrest. In the over-the-shoulder, the arm zaps behind Steven's head. (00:25)

5. During the battle at Medieval Times, Chip fakes a leg injury then, after saying "I am now," he clobbers Steven, causing his helmet to spin to one side. As Chip bows to the audience, in the background Steven appears with his helmet already straightened out. In the following close-up, he has to straighten it out again. (00:34)

6. During a karaoke night, Chip bursts into a room and snaps a Polaroid still of Steven and Heather: he's kissing her, and she's holding his head with her right hand, while caressing his chest with her left. Later on, Chip shows Steven

the picture: Heather is smiling wildly at the camera, with both her hands on Steven's face. And yep, Chip took only one snap. (00:47, 01:08)

7. In jail, Chip unbuttons his shirt and places his nipple against the glass. Steven says, "Don't do that!" and puts the phone down. In the following shot he has the phone in his hand, and in the next the phone is gone. (01:06)

8. While there, Chip sits down. In the following over-the-shoulder shot, he's suddenly holding the phone, which he wasn't doing before. (01:06)

Question
During visiting hours, after the Oliver Stone remark, Chip addresses the guard who's standing several feet away on the other side of the glass. How could the guard possibly hear what the Cable Guy is saying into a phone whose receiver is in Steven's ear? (01:06)

CANNONBALL RUN, THE (16)
  1981, color, 95 min.

Director: Hal Needham

Cast: Burt Reynolds (J.J. McClure), Roger Moore (Seymour Goldfarb), Farrah Fawcett (Pamela), Dom DeLuise (Victor Prinzim / Captain Chaos), Dean Martin (Jamie Blake), Sammy Davis,

Jr. (Fenderbaum), Jack Elam (Doctor Nicholas Van Helsing), Adrienne Barbeau (Marcia), Terry Bradshaw (Terry), Jackie Chan (First Subaru Driver), Bert Convy (Brad Compton), Jamie Farr (The Sheik), Mel Tillis (Mel), Tara Buckman (Jill), Michael Hui (Second Subaru Driver).

Cars, cars, cars, cars, cars ... and one motorcycle on its rear wheel.

Bloopers

1. Right after the Lamborghini ladies vandalize a 55-mph sign, their car bullets away. And just before the police car passes by the same sign, the dust created by the Lamborghini in the far distance vanishes abruptly. (00:01)
2. On the Cannonball board behind the bookmaker, among the brands of cars is "Porche." Shouldn't it be "Porsche"? (00:06)
3. When J.J.'s plane lands in the middle of the road, you can see a police barricade in the background, blocking off a street. Also, cars suddenly appear behind the plane, along with pedestrians. (00:08)
4. When Mel and Terry jump into a pool with their car (courtesy of a ramp placed conveniently by the pool), they emerge without wearing any shoes. (00:17)
5. As the sheik arrives at the motel and walks by one of his copilots (who's puking), the shadow of a boom mike is visible on the ground. (00:23)
6. Brad tries his motorcycle inside the motel. He's wearing a baseball hat, but as he drives through the Cannonball Pub, he's wearing a helmet. For the final jump on the stairs, he's back to the baseball hat. (00:31)
7. During the speech to the pilots just before the race starts, J.J., Victor, Marcia, and Jill (the Lamborghini team) are standing close to one another. In the following wide shot, they're quite far away from one another. (00:34)
8. Mad Dog brings his truck up to the starting clock. But when Mr. Foyt and Pamela check on the very same spot, the vehicle by the clock is a car, not a truck. And when we go back to the clock, there's Mad Dog's truck again. (00:38)

Director-May-Care Attitude

Talking about continuity problems, Hal Needham wisely said that "if the people are enjoying the film, you can do almost anything you want to, and they don't pay any attention to it. . . . If it's good entertaining, they don't care."

9. When the Lamborghini ladies are stopped by the first cop,

Marcia has her blouse zipped up, then down (when a few cars zoom by), then up again, and finally she zips it down to get her license. (00:46)

10. The doctor checks Pamela's pulse: her wristwatch reads 3:30, but when she asks, "If you guys laid a finger on me . . ." her watch reads 11:15. (00:54)

11. When Fenderbaum and Jamie are driving next to the ambulance, the camera car with the crew is reflected in their Ferrari's door. (00:55)

12. Seymour drives the Aston Martin bare-handed, yet when he prevents his new girl from operating the lighter, he's wearing black gloves. (00:57, 00:58)

13. The sheik stops at a restaurant and pays the waitress with a ring. As he leaves and she leans back, she's holding a wad of money. The Sheik then comes back and hands her . . . a wad of money. (01:09)

14. Surrounded by bikers, Brad hands his business card to their leader. The leader grabs it with his right hand, but in the following shot he's holding it with his left. (01:21)

15. Vincent, as Captain USA, has the back of his mask alternatively outside and inside his jacket collar. (01:30)

16. A drenched Seymour reaches J.J., who's celebrating with champagne. As we move to

an aerial shot, Seymour arrives a second time. (01:31)

Questions
1. Why does the Japanese car, whose drivers are Japanese as well, have a computer that communicates in English? (00:13, 00:46, 01:08)
2. Also, why does Jackie say "Excuse me" in English to the host of the Japanese TV show? (00:14)

Fun Fact
The paramedic on the ambulance carrying J.J. and Victor is played by *Cannonball Run* director Hal Needham. (00:12)

CAPRICORN ONE (3)
1978, color, 123 min.

Director: Peter Hyams

Cast: Elliott Gould (Robert Caulfield), James Brolin (Charles Brubaker), Brenda Vaccaro (Kay Brubaker), Sam Waterston (Peter Willis), O. J. Simpson (John Walker), Hal Holbrook (Dr. James Kelloway), Karen Black (Judy Drinkwater), Telly Savalas (Albain), David Huddleston (Hollis Peaker), David Doyle (Walter Laughlin), Robert Walden (Elliot Whitter).

NASA goes to Mars. Or do they?

Bloopers
1. During the countdown, there's a shot of the NASA mission-control room, and

the timer on the screen goes to 05:24 and counts down. The countdown reaches 05:00 1 minute and 7 seconds later (00:06, 00:07)

2. On March 16, Elliot, one of the NASA technicians, discovers an anomaly in the readout on his computer. He leans his head on his right hand—but in the next shot, he's resting his head against his left hand. (00:27)

3. While fleeing, the three astronauts hijack a small jet and take off, but they lose the left wheel of the landing gear and smash into a car. However, when they push the button to retract the right-side landing gear, well ... it looks suspiciously like the left-side gear is retracted—not the right. (01:00, 01:01)

CAST AWAY (7)
2000, color, 143 min.

Director: Robert Zemekis

Cast: Tom Hanks (Chuck Noland), Helen Hunt (Kelly Frears), Nick Searcy (Stan), Chris Noth (Jerry Lovett), Lari White (Bettina Peterson), Geoffrey Blake (Maynard Graham), Jenifer Lewis (Becca Twig), David Allen Brooks (Dick Peterson), Semion Suradikov (Nicolai), Nan Martin (Kelly's Mother), Peter von Berg (Yuri), Dmitri S. Boudrine (Lev), Wilson (Himself).

Man loves woman, is stranded on desert island, falls for volleyball.

Bloopers

1. Entering the DICK & BETTINA estate, the FedEx van stops exactly at the edge of the shadow projected on the ground by the barn. When the carrier takes the package and brings it to the back of the van, the shadow on the ground has stretched so far that it almost entirely covers the van. (00:02, 00:03)

2. During the family dinner, Chuck has a bandage around his left thumb. But when he raises his left hand to mock Kelly's former husband, in the over-the-shoulder shot the bandage has vanished. It'll be back almost immediately. (00:14, 00:15, 00:16)

3. On the ill-fated FedEx plane, Chuck places the pocketwatch on the armrest, the picture of Kelly facing him. Yet when he goes to the restroom, the watch has rotated 90 degrees (and don't talk to us about vibrations from the turbulence and crap like that, please). (00:21, 00:22)

4. On the island, Chuck spots a FedEx package on the shore, and he walks to it on a beach that, except for two black rocks, is almost entirely sand. Yet after he picks up the package, many many rocks have appeared on the very same beach. (00:33, 00:34)

5. As Chuck is trying to make fire, he cuts his right hand pretty badly. He washes the wound in the sea and bandages it, yet when he contemplates the huge fire he was able to make, he opens his hands wide and his right palm has healed. (01:07, 01:08, 01:12)

6. Right after cutting himself, Chuck blows a fuse and begins to scream and toss everything away: he grabs the volleyball, and some of his blood winds up on the cardboard box. But when he recovers the ball, the box is clean (and the hand-shaped spot is upside down). (01:07, 01:08)

7. At the crossroads, when Chuck is trying to decide what direction to take after delivering the package that saved his life, the shadow on the ground keeps zapping left and right and back. (02:14)

Non-Blooper

At least twice, Chuck indicates that a tooth is aching on the right side of his face. But when he uses the skate to remove the tooth, he *seems* to be "operating" on the left side of his face. Wrongo! He uses the blade of the skate diagonally in his mouth, hence the blade enters the mouth from the left side, but hits the tooth on the right side. (00:16, 01:13, 01:17)

CHAIN REACTION (2)
1996, color, 106 min.

Director: Andrew Davis

Cast: Keanu Reeves (Eddie Kasalivich), Morgan Freeman (Paul Shannon), Rachel Weisz (Dr. Lily Sinclair), Fred Ward (FBI Agent Leon Ford), Kevin Dunn (FBI Agent Doyle), Brian Cox (Lyman Earl Collier), Joanna Cassidy (Maggie McDermott), Chelcie Ross (Ed Rafferty), Nicholas Rudall (Dr. Alistair Barkley), Tzi Ma (Lu Chen), Krzysztof Pieczynski (Lucasz Screbneski), Julie R. Pearl (Emily Pearl).

Chubby Keanu fights double- and triple-chemical crossing.

Bloopers

1. At FBI headquarters, Agent Doyle receives a phone call that informs him that Eddie is being chased; Doyle picks up the phone with his right hand, but after he utters "What?" he's holding the telephone with his left. (00:30)

2. Eddie and Lily emerge after the big explosion thoroughly covered in ash. As they walk away from the plant, they are remarkably clean. (01:37, 01:38)

CHILD'S PLAY (6)
1988, color, 87 min.

Director: Tom Holland

Cast: Catherine Hicks (Karen Barclay), Chris Sarandon (Mike Norris), Alex Vincent (Andy Barclay), Brad Dourif (Charles Lee Ray / Chucky's Voice), Dinah Manoff (Maggie Peterson), Tommy Swerdlow (Jack Santos), Jack Colvin (Dr. Ardmore), Neil Giuntoli (Eddie Caputo), Juan Ramírez (Peddler), Alan Wilder (Mr. Criswell), Richard Baird (News Reporter at Toy Store), Raymond Oliver (Dr. Death).

"A doll! A doll! Andy wants a doll!" Fool!

Bloopers
1. Detective Norris follows Charles Lee Ray into the toy store. Norris is wearing black gloves, but in the first shot of him in the store, he's holding the gun without gloves. When he ducks behind the counter, he's wearing gloves again, which he will remove a few seconds later. (00:00, 00:01, 00:02)
2. Andy fixes breakfast for his mom. He spills Sugar Coated Good Guy cereal all over the table, then he pours milk, increasing the chaos. When he puts the pieces of burnt toast on the plate, there's far less cereal on the counter, but there'll be more when he takes the tray away. (00:07, 00:08)
3. Karen comes home with Chucky, and she drops her coat on the couch. The coat "crawls" up the pillows of the couch a little more when she moves to the kitchen, and even more when she returns to Chucky to check his batteries. (00:42, 00:43)
4. While talking about Charles Lee Ray with Norris after the peddler's incident, Karen's coat's collar keeps flipping up and down. (00:50)
5. Dr. Ardmore wants to inject a sedative into little Andy; the syringe Ardmore is holding in his left hand vanishes for one second when he removes Andy's jacket, but reappears almost immediately in his right hand. (01:06)
6. During the final fight between an almost-melted Chucky and Santos, a basket is knocked off of the TV set, but it's back in place in the following shots. (01:21)

CHILL FACTOR (5)
1999, color, 101 min.

Director: Hugh Johnson

Cast: Cuba Gooding, Jr. (Arlo), Skeet Ulrich (Tim Mason), Peter Firth (Captain Andrew Brynner), David Paymer (Dr. Richard Long), Hudson Leick (Vaughn), Daniel Hugh Kelly (Colonel Leo Vitelli), Kevin J. O'Connor (Telstar), Judson Mills (Dennis), Jordan Mott (Carl), Dwayne Macopson (Burke), Jim Grimshaw

(Deputy Pappas), Richard Todd Aguayo (Gomez), Suzi Bass (Darlene).

. . . or How to Cool Off Your Career.

Bloopers

1. At the diner, Darlene tells Dr. Long, "There's something else, too." She places her towel on her left shoulder, she turns, and the towel has vanished. She'll put it back almost instantly. (00:16)
2. A wounded Dr. Long stumbles into the diner holding a paper bag. He hits the counter, and lets go of the bag. As he hits the floor, he's hugging the bag. (00:29)
3. While fighting on the roof of the truck, Mason hits the bag, and it rolls toward the edge of the roof. The thug jumps to grab it, but when he kicks Mason away and he slams his back onto the roof, the bag lies in the middle of the roof. Then, it's back by the edge. (00:47)
4. Arlo drives the truck dangerously close to the edge of the broken road; so close that he smashes his left sideview mirror against the sheer rock face. But when one of the thugs drops down from above, firing his gun at the truck, the sideview mirror looks fine. (00:55, 00:56)
5. Mason, Arlo, and a rowboat take a dive from a cliff into a river. The boat lands upside down—but after an euphoric moment for Arlo and Mason, it appears to be floating right-side up. (01:00)

CLEAR AND PRESENT DANGER (8)

1994, color, 141 min.

Director: Phillip Noyce

Cast: Harrison Ford (Dr. Jack P. Ryan, Acting Deputy Director of Intelligence CIA), Willem Dafoe (John Clark), Anne Archer (Dr. Cathy Ryan), Joaquim de Almeida (Col. Felix Cortez / Roberto Alonzo Landa), Henry Czerny (Robert Ritter, Deputy Director CIA), Harris Yulin (James Cutter, National Security Advisor), Donald Moffat (President Bennett), Miguel Sandoval (Ernesto Escobedo, Cali Cartel), Benjamin Bratt (Captain Ramirez), Raymond Cruz (Domingo "Ding" Chavez), Dean Jones (Judge Moore), Thora Birch (Sally Ryan), Jorge Luke (Sipo).

Jack Ryan is at it again, this time fighting with drug dealers and . . . colleagues?

Bloopers

1. A shot from above the U.S. Coast Guard ship shows the sun coming from the port side. When three men exit a starboard-side door, the sun appears to have moved to

the starboard side of the ship, and then it's back off of the port side again. (00:02)

2. When Escobedo, playing baseball, speculates that Cortez has met "a woman," a ball passes by Escobedo, but doesn't make any sound when it hits (as all the previous ones did). (00:12)

3. Jack sees the president on TV commenting about his lifelong friendship with a victim. Jack undoes the knot on his tie, but when he hushes his daughter, the tie is perfectly tied around his neck (also, he removes it and he wears ... the same tie? Again?). (00:29)

4. After Escobedo receives the news of another plane being lost, he walks to his family. Sipo leans on Cortez's chair asking him something. In the following shot, Sipo's arm is no longer on the chair. (00:43)

5. Jack tries to print a reciprocity file, but his printer has run out of paper. He opens the tray, dives under the desk, comes back with paper ... and the tray already has paper in it (also, although he doesn't close it properly, the printer works fine). (01:33, 01:34)

6. Escobedo plays a tape from Jack's tape recorder. The tape inside is black. When Escobedo plays the same tape to Cortez, the tape has become silver and red. More than one copy? (01:57, 01:59)

7. After Clark gets rid of two of Cortez's henchmen, Jack's chopper is approaching: in its window it's possible to see the camera-crew chopper, filming the first chopper. (02:05)

8. The *A* tag Jack has on his jacket while in the White House keeps jumping under and over his jacket lapel while he's talking to President Bennett. (02:11)

THE TIE THAT BINDS

These bloopers are the finalists in a neck-to-neck race . . .

Harrison Ford in *Clear and Present Danger*	Blooper No. 3
Rob Brown in *Finding Forrester*	Blooper No. 3
Steve Guttenberg in *Short Circuit*	Blooper No. 1
Xander Berkley in *Volunteers*	Blooper No. 3
Charlie Sheen in *Wall Street*	Blooper No. 3

CLIFFHANGER (4)
1993, color, 118 min.

Director: Renny Harlin

Cast: Sylvester Stallone (Gabe Walker), John Lithgow (Eric Qualen), Michael Rooker (Hal Tucker), Janine Turner (Jessie Deighan), Rex Linn (Travers, Treasury Agent), Caroline Goodall (Kristel, Jetstar Pilot), Leon (Kynette), Craig Fairbrass (Delmar), Gregory Scott Cummins (Ryan), Denis Forest (Heldon), Michelle Joyner (Sarah), Max Perlich (Evan).

Oh, the mountains, the snow, the cold air, the terrorists . . . you know, the usual.

Bloopers
1. Sarah wears a light blue jacket, which turns to gray when she falls to her death, and then turns back to light blue. (00:02, 00:11)
2. Three briefcases get hooked to a cable, which goes from one plane to another. When the first plane blows up, the cable is gone. Then it's back. (00:26, 00:27)
3. When Qualen's plane crash-lands on the hill, it stops with the nose just over the edge of a mountain; in the next shot, the whole plane seems to be safely lying on the mountain. (00:29, 00:30)
4. Hal removes his jacket and, before getting beaten by the Australian henchman, shows a zipped red vest—which becomes unzipped as the villain head butts him. (01:27)

CLUE (7)
1985, color, 96 min.

Director: Jonathan Lynn

Cast: Eileen Brennan (Mrs. Peacock), Tim Curry (Wadsworth), Madeline Kahn (Mrs. White), Christopher Lloyd (Professor Plum), Michael McKean (Mr. Green), Martin Mull (Colonel Mustard), Lesley Ann Warren (Miss Scarlet), Colleen Camp (Yvette), Lee Ving (Mr. Boddy), Jane Wiedlin (The Singing Telegram Girl), Kellye Nahahara (The Cook).

It's not a boardgame anymore, but it's still a lot of fun!!

Bloopers
1. Professor Plum gives Miss Scarlet a lift, and he activates the windshield wipers of his car. But when the car leaves, the wipers are motionless. (00:07)
2. Miss Scarlet moves to a table with her unexpected gift wrapped in a box. When she says "I enjoy getting presents from strangers," she removes the box's purple ribbon twice. (00:25)
3. The cook's body falls in Mr. Green's arms, and the two collapse to the ground. Mr. Green frees himself, and the

cook has both of her arms along her sides—but in the following shot, her right arm is stretched out. (00:34)

4.   The cook's body is dropped in the middle of the studio doorway, leaving Mrs. White side by side with Mrs. Peacock, and Yvette and Miss Scarlet behind them. Mrs. White works her way into the studio, and Mrs. Peacock takes the first step into the same room, but in the (mis)matching cut, Mrs. White is in the studio, Miss Scarlet is just behind her, and Yvette and Mrs. Peacock are still struggling to walk by the cook. (00:36)

5.   The gang clumsily places the two dead bodies on the couch, "trapping" Professor Plum between them. Mr. Boddy's body moves to his right without anybody touching him (just after his close-up, where it also seems like he's opened his mouth by himself). (00:40)

6.   Colonel Mustard pours whiskey into a few glasses on a table, and when he says, "Look: pay attention, everybody!" a glass has jumped into his hand without him picking it up. (00:42)

7.   The singing telegram girl's body is found in front of the main door, her right arm close to her head, her left almost by her hip. But in the body's close-up, both arms are close to her head. (01:07)

Question

Mr. Boddy gives all of his guests a deadly weapon, then he suggests that someone should kill Wadsworth. Boddy flicks the switch and the room is plummetted into complete darkness. Uh . . . what about the gargantuan fire in the fireplace? (00:27)

CLUELESS (5)
1995, color, 97 min.

Director: Amy Heckerling

Cast: Alicia Silverstone (Cher Horowitz), Stacey Dash (Dionne), Brittany Murphy (Tai Fraiser), Paul Rudd (Josh), Donald Adeosun Faison (Murray), Elisa Donovan (Amber), Breckin Meyer (Travis Birkenstock), Jeremy Sisto (Elton), Dan Hedaya (Mel Hamilton . . . or Horowitz?), Aida Linares (Lucy), Wallace Shawn (Mr. Wendell Hall).

Whatever!!!

Bloopers

1.   While giving out report cards, Mr. Hall comes to Cher Horowitz. But when Cher's dad receives her report card in the mail, his name is listed as Hamilton (like in the closing credits). (00:14, 00:19, 01:33)

2.   Elton drives Cher home from a Valley party, and his blue car passes by a very distinctive yellow Hertz sign. Later on, when Josh drives Cher

home from another party, the car shown is Elton's—passing by the very same Hertz sign (which is very far away from Cher's home, as she says that they're in Sun Valley). (00:39, 00:58)

3. After being robbed, Cher calls Josh on a payphone without using coins or making a collect or credit card call. (00:43)

4. While talking about Mexico and El Salvador, Cher argues with Josh. He leans against the fridge. In the long shot nothing is on the metal door, but during his close-up, a magnet has appeared on the door (Josh moved to his left for the close-up). (01:11)

5. During Cher's driving test, she rams a parked car and knocks off the right sideview mirror of her Jeep. As the DMV instructor tells her to stop, the mirror is back in place. (1:12)

Question

During the phone call, Cher asks Josh to pick her up. The last three lines of the conversation, before Josh hangs up, are: "Where are you?" "Sun Valley." "Man, you owe me." How did he manage to find Cher?? (00:43)

COBRA (5)

1986, color, 87 min.

Director: George Pan Cosmatos

Cast: Sylvester Stallone (Marion "Cobra" Cobretti), Brigitte Nielsen (Ingrid), Reni Santoni (Gonzales), Andrew Robinson (Detective Monte), Brian Thompson (Night Slasher), John Herzfeld (Cho), Lee Garlington (Nancy Stalk), Art LaFleur (Captain Sears), Marco Rodríguez (Supermarket Killer), Ross St. Phillip (Security Guard), Val Avery (Chief Halliwell), David Rasche (Dan).

Wrecking-crew cop protects beautiful witness.

Bloopers

1. Cobra comes home after the supermarket shooting, takes his gun from his belt, places it on the desk, then opens a carton of eggs where he keeps bullets. To reload the gun, he takes it from his belt—again. (00:14, 00:15)

2. While escorting Ingrid from the hospital, Cobra winds up chasing a car and is simultaneously chased by a truck. The rearview mirror of Cobra's car vanishes and reappears all through the sequence: it's gone during the first close-ups of Ingrid and Cobra, but it's back when they round a corner, then it vanishes when the shooting begins, it's back when they're on the highway, it's gone when the cars literally fly onto the bridge . . . (00:45, 00:46, 00:49)

3. During the same car chase, Cobra's trunk gets pierced

by three bullets. The holes vanish as soon as Cobra spins the car to fire at the truck behind him. (00:47)

4. In the diner, as Cobra places a giant hamburger down on the counter, the ketchup bottle Ingrid was squeezing jumps into the rack in the middle of the table. (00:57)

5. Even though it's a very sunny morning and it was a clear night, when Cobra and Ingrid flee from the motel chased by the motorcycle gang, the road is thoroughly wet. (01:08)

COMMANDO (21)
1985, color, 90 min.

Director: Mark L. Lester

Cast: Arnold Schwarzenegger (Colonel John Matrix), Rae Dawn Chong (Cindy), Dan Hedaya (Arius), Vernon Wells (Bennett), James Olson (Major General Franklin Kirby), David Patrick Kelly (Sully), Alyssa Milano (Jenny Matrix), Bill Duke (Cooke), Drew Snyder (Lawson, man putting out the garbage), Sharon Wyatt (Leslie), Michael Delano (Forrestal, car salesman), Bob Minor (Jackson, Kirby's Man).

"Let's paa-dee!!"

Bloopers

1. Col. Matrix and his daughter, Jenny, are having ice cream. She pushes hers in Matrix's face holding it with her left hand, her right hand, and then her left again. (00:05)

2. During breakfast, Matrix is distracted by the sound of an incoming chopper. He's holding a sandwich in his hands, but in the following shot the sandwich is on the plate. (00:08)

3. Under attack at his home, Matrix and Jackson lie down on the floor, protecting Jenny. A drop of blood on his forehead keeps coming and going while he's talking to Jackson. (00:12)

4. Matrix returns to his home passing by the roof, opens one screen door and Jackson's dead body falls to the ground. As Matrix enters the house, the screen door slams shut (how, since Jackson was in its way?). But after Matrix kills the unexpected visitor in his daughter's room, he runs outside—but the screen door is now open. (00:13)

5. Trying to chase a few kidnappers, Matrix pushes a broken-down van downhill. As he goes off-road and the van flips, you can see smoke coming out of the exhaust pipe. But the engine was off. (00:14, 00:15)

6. As Matrix regains his senses, he faces four thugs who look at him from up above. Sully, the blond guy, is smoking. In the following shot, he's wearing sunglasses. (00:16)

7. Backing up the car in which

Matrix is hiding, Cindy stops briefly before shifting into drive. Briefly, but long enough to reflect part of the crew—particularly a man who walks slowly and bends down. (00:29)

8. Matrix is run over by Sully's Porsche, which loses its left rearview mirror (yep, it's a mirror, NOT Matrix's wallet, as pointed out somewhere else). The mirror will be back in place just before Matrix and Cindy begin smashing their car into Sully's. (00:37, 00:39)

9. During the car-ramming sequence, the left side of the Porsche is heavily damaged, but it's okay after Sully fires his fourth bullet. The car flips onto its left side, yet is without a scratch once again as Matrix drives away. It'll look damaged one more time, later. (00:39, 00:40, 00:41, 00:43)

10. Matrix brings Sully to a cliff, and holds him by one leg while saying, "But what is important is gravity." At that point, it's possible to see a cable that runs from Sully's left leg to the top of the screen. (00:40)

11. In the motel, Matrix fights with Cooke. They knock down a few glass tiles (two rows from one side, three from the other), and also a lamp next to these tiles... but it's back again in the following shot. (00:46)

12. Cindy and Matrix decide to take Cooke's car. As they get in, the boom mike is reflected in the hood. (00:48)

13. When Matrix goes shopping for weapons, he grabs a rocket launcher and passes it to Cindy. Right after she walks away with it, the launcher is back in place on the wall, where it was before. (00:55)

14. A couple of thugs fire at the amphibious airplane in which Matrix and Cindy are about to take off. The bullets riddle the metal next to the plane's door. As Cindy says good-bye to Matrix after landing, the holes are gone. (01:00, 01:05)

15. Just off the plane, Matrix rows toward the island... but the following close-up shows him rowing toward the open sea. (01:06)

16. Prepping for the attack, Matrix wears his vest, then puts some camouflage make-up on his face. Later on, in a shack, he removes the vest: he has makeup on his chest, too (but he never applied it). (01:07, 01:14)

17. Matrix has to examine the villa he's about to attack: he moves his binoculars right to left, but the image he sees goes left to right. (01:08)

18. As Matrix blows up a few buildings around the villa, it's hard not to notice that the "soldiers" in front of them were blatant dummies, a few even have clearly visible

supports holding them up. (01:11)

19. During the same attack, Matrix throws a couple of grenades that blow up, causing a few soldiers to fly off the ground . . . courtesy of the hydraulic device that throws them up in the air. You can see the ramp on the grass. (01:13)

20. Outside of the shack, Matrix grabs one of the victims' machine guns and fires it, holding the weapon with his right hand. The next shot shows him holding the machine gun with his left hand, the cartridge belt is longer, and he's gained a black strap across his chest. Then the machine gun jumps back to Matrix's right hand. (01:15)

21. Fighting with Bennett, Matrix winds up in front of a roaring furnace. Bennett's hand holds him by the face, then by the neck in the following shot. (01:23)

CON AIR (6)

1997, color, 115 min.

Director: Simon West

Cast: Nicolas Cage (Cameron Poe), Monica Potter (Tricia Poe), John Cusack (U.S. Marshal Vince Larkin), Landry Allbright (Casey Poe), M.C. Gainey (Swamp Thing), Danny Trejo (Johnny "Johnny-23" Baca), Steve Buscemi (Garland "The Marietta Mangler" Greene), Steve Eastin (Guard Falzon), Rachel Ticotin (Guard Sally Bishop), David Chappelle ("Pinball" Parker), Ving Rhames (Nathan "Diamond Dog" Jones), John Malkovich (Cyrus "The Virus" Grissom).

Hero becomes a convict who becomes a hero.

Bloopers

1. Cameron calls his wife, Tricia, after the fight with the bar regular. After the guy is pronounced dead, the blood on Cameron's cheek vanishes. (00:04)

2. The *Spanish for Beginners* book is handed to Cameron by a man who holds it with his left hand in the detail, but with his right in the wide shot. (00:07)

3. During the chaos on board the plane, Guard Bishop goes after "Pinball," who's about to open the cages of the very dangerous prisoners. In the subsequent fight, Bishop loses her hat, but the hat is back in place when "Pinball" opens Cyrus's cage. (00:23, 00:24)

4. After the plane takes off in Carson City, "Diamond Dog" is in the cockpit wearing a sheriff's hat with the star in front. But when they discuss the plane's tracking device, in one shot the hat appears backwards, then is straight again. (00:43)

5. Duncan enters the building where he learns what is going on. As he walks in through the door, two U.S. Marshals walk out: a black guy, and a white guy. In the (mis)matching shot, the Marshals have switched places, and now the black guy is following. (00:44)

6. Duncan's car falls from the sky: Larkin goes from having his arms crossed to having them uncrossed, then crossed and with sunglasses on, then uncrossed without sunglasses, and back. Different every take. (01:28)

Questions

1. It's clearly stated, "No personal possessions on [the] airplane." Notwithstanding, when undercover agent Sims marches up the platform for boarding, the bulge of a wallet in his left back pocket is quite evident. Didn't anyone notice? (00:17, 00:18)

2. Cameron handcuffs both of Johnny 23's wrists to each other around a rail. After the landing, two paramedics escort the body of Johnny 23 out of the plane, the severed arm still swinging from the rail. How so, since the arms were cuffed together? What happened to the handcuffs? (01:26, 01:39)

3. When Duncan goes to check out the wreck that once was his car, he picks up the bent license plate. But when the car landed, the license plate was still firmly bolted to the car—and there's no front license plate, as we clearly saw the first time the car appeared (00:12). So . . . ? (01:28)

4. Cyrus falls from a conveyor belt, headfirst, feet toward the crusher. But in the following shot, he's lying directly underneath the crusher. How did he do that? And how many crushers are there on the Las Vegas strip? Not to mention conveyor belts? (01:44)

CROUCHING TIGER HIDDEN DRAGON (3)

2000, color, 120 min.

Director: Ang Lee

Cast: Yun-Fat Chow (Master Li Mu Bai), Michelle Yeoh (Yu Shu Lien), Ziyi Zhang (Jen Yu [China] / Sha-Long [U.S.]), Chen Chang (Lo [China] / Sha-Hu [U.S.]), Sihung Lung (Sir Te [China] / Be-Lai-Ye [U.S.]), Pei-pei Cheng (Jade Fox / Governess [China] / Bei-Ah-Hui [Jade Fox] / Governess [U.S.]), Fa Zeng Li (Governor Yu), Xian Gao (Bo [China] / Yo-Shi [U.S.]), Yan Hai (Madame Yu), De Ming Wang (Police Inspector Tsai), Li Li (May), Su Ying Huang (Auntie Wu).

"Look, Yu Shu Lien! I can fly! . . ."

Bloopers

1. During Dark Cloud's assault on the caravan, Jen looks outside of her coach, revealing two beautiful blue pendant earrings. When she jumps out of the coach to chase Dark Horse, she loses her left earring—but it's back when she reaches the nomads' camp. (00:54)

2. After racing through the desert, Jen is in desperate need of water. Dark Cloud offers her his canteen. She grabs it, drinks from it, then tosses it back to him and the fight among the two starts over. But as she kicks him, the canteen has vanished. (00:58)

3. By the pond inside the cave, Li Mu Bai is approached by Jen. Li Mu Bai's sword is behind him, but when he picks Jen up, the sword is gone. No *clangs* of the sword hitting the ground, no fancy movements . . . yet the sword has completely vanished. (01:42, 01:43)

JEWEL CASE

Or, the case of the missing earring.

ZiYi Zhang's earrings in *Crouching Tiger, Hidden Dragon*	Blooper No. 1
Kathleen Turner's earrings in *Jewel of the Nile*	Blooper No. 1
Eric Schweig in *The Last of the Mohicans*	Blooper No. 2
Ling Bai's earring in *Wild Wild West*	Blooper No. 8

D

DARK HALF, THE (4)
1992, color, 122 min.

Director: George A. Romero

Cast: Timothy Hutton (Thad Beaumont / George Stark), Amy Madigan (Liz Beaumont), Michael Rooker (Sheriff Alan Pangborn), Julie Harris (Reggie DeLesseps), Robert Joy (Fred Clawson), Kent Broadhurst (Mike Donaldson), Beth Grant (Shayla Beaumont), Rutanya Alda (Miriam Cowley), Tom Mardirosian (Rick Cowley), Glenn Colerider (Homer Gamache), Chelsea Field (Annie Pangborn), Royal Dano (Digger Holt).

Pseudonym of a writer is more real than the writer thinks.

Bloopers

1. Thad double underlines the *s* in "beings" (using two strokes on the second line); later, the *s* is underlined with three lines; yet later, with five lines. (00:08, 00:09)

2. When the sheriff tells Thad how someone died, Tim goes "That's exactly what I said I want to do with him!" Not true. He said "I'll make you suffer . . . before you die." (00:12) Are we clear? (00:43)

3. Thad grabs a pencil with a dull tip; after a few seconds, the pencil has a sharpened tip. (01:14)

4. Thad writes "If I don't I'll die" on a sheet of paper. In the following shot, the line has changed. (01:16)

DAYS OF THUNDER (7)
1990, color, 107 min.

Director: Tony Scott

Cast: Tom Cruise (Cole Trickle), Robert Duvall (Harry Hogge), Nicole Kidman (Dr. Claire Lewicki), Randy Quaid (Tim Daland), Cary Elwes (Russ Wheeler), Michael Rooker (Rowdy Burns), Fred Dalton Thompson (Big John), John C. Reilly (Buck Bretherton), J.C. Quinn (Waddell), Don Simpson

(Aldo Bennedetti), Caroline Williams (Jennie Burns), Donna Wilson (Darlene).

Race-car driver finds both love and an outrageous insurance premium.

Bloopers

1. Harry explains to Cole about tires, and he's wearing a white Georgia hat. A few minutes later, while telling Cole to do fifty laps his way, Harry's wearing a white Florida hat. (00:23, 00:24)

2. Cole and Rowdy race against each other even when on wheelchairs. Just after a doctor crosses in the foreground, Cole's jacket jumps from his shoulders to his elbows, and back up when the racers meet Claire. (00:45)

3. While on the phone, Cole is introduced to Russ. Cole holds the phone with his left hand, with no hands (reverse angle), then he lifts his left hand to grab it, but in the next cut it's his right hand holding the phone. Also, Cole has a pen in his right hand, but it's missing when the shot is from behind him. (00:53)

4. Cole and Claire are walking with Rowdy, and Jennie catches up with them. She says to Cole "Hi, Tom." Oops! (01:02)

5. *Lip 'n sync:* During the race in North Wilkesboro, Cole addresses Russ as a "son of a bi**h!" without moving his lips. In Daytona, Cole yells, "The accelerator is stuck, Harry!" and "Remember me?" —and he performs the same trick: no lip movement. (01:09, 01:36, 01:39)

6. Right after Claire stands up in the Daytona changing room, Cole's collar closes itself without anyone touching it. (01:30)

7. Cole wins Daytona. He gets out of the car, removes his helmet, hugs Buck, then . . . voilà, a pair of earplugs appear in his ears out of nowhere. They vanish when Claire tells Cole, "I lied." (01:41)

Question

While racing in Daytona, Cole's car is hit by Rowdy's. Cole's car spins counterclockwise, but the last spin he does, just before reentering the race, is clockwise. Is that possible, or . . . ? (00:37)

DAZED AND CONFUSED (3)

1993, color, 103 min.

Director: Richard Linklater

Cast: Jason London (Randall "Pink" Floyd), Joey Lauren Adams (Simone), Milla Jovovich (Michelle), Shawn Andrews (Pickford), Rory Cochrane (Slater), Adam Goldberg (Mike), Sasha Jenson (Don Dawson), Deena Martin (Shavonne), Cole Hauser (Benny), Wiley Wiggins (Mitch), Ben Affleck (O'Bannion), Parker

Posey (Darla), Matthew
McConaughey (Wooderson),
Parker Brooks (Stoner), Renée
Zellweger (Senior).

*Texas teens party seventies
style.*

Bloopers

1. While driving around town at
   night getting high in Pickford's orange car, Slater and
   a stoner switch places in the
   backseat—in-between is a shot
   of a young woman jumping
   from a car to a truck. (00:44)
2. While in Pickford's car, Don
   (in a green shirt with rolled-
   up sleeves) stretches out of
   the window, grabs a trash
   can, and tosses it at a mailbox. A few seconds later,
   Pink (in a blue shirt with long
   sleeves) tries the same stunt:
   he leans out of the window,
   gets ready to grab the trash
   can . . . but the hand that grabs
   the can belongs to someone
   with a green shirt with rolled-
   up sleeves. Strange . . . because the following shot
   shows Pink holding the can.
   (00:55)
3. On the football field, Wooderson sits close to Slater. As always, Wooderson carries a
   pack of cigarettes rolled up in
   his left sleeve . . . except when
   Slater says, "Hey, Pink, d'you
   got my papers, man?" In that
   shot, the cigarette pack is
   nowhere to be seen. Don't
   worry—it'll come back. (01:27)

Fun Fact

After being hit by a load of paint,
O'Bannion yells at everyone. Pink
backs up, bumps a car, a beer can
slides down . . . and Pink grabs it
at the last second. Nice save!
(01:05)

DEAD POETS SOCIETY (6)
1989, color, 128 min.

Director: Peter Weir

Cast: Robin Williams (John
Keating), Robert Sean Leonard
(Neil Perry), Ethan Hawke
(Todd Anderson), Josh Charles
(Knox Overstreet), Gale Hansen
(Charles "Newanda" Dalton),
Dylan Kussman (Richard
Cameron), Allelon Ruggiero
(Steven Meeks), Norman Lloyd
(Mr. Nolan), Kurtwood Smith
(Mr. Perry), James Waterston
(Gerard Pitts), Carla Belver
(Mrs. Perry), Alexandra Powers
(Chris Noel).

*Carpe diem: live the
moment, and watch this
movie. It's good!*

Bloopers

1. When Professor Keating
   makes his first entrance in
   class, his arms are along his
   sides. A wide shot instead
   shows him carrying a clipboard underneath his right
   arm, with the right hand
   holding it. And when he
   opens the door to walk out,
   he does it with his right

hand, and the clipboard has flown into his left. (00:11)

2. Just before being asked to read a poem, Mr. Pitts signals his presence by raising his right hand. In the following shot, though, he lowers his left. (00:13)

3. Charlie shows a centerfold to the other poets, then turns it to show a handwritten poem on the back. In the next shot, the centerfold has already turned back as it was, and has been half folded. (00:39)

4. Professor Keating writes on the blackboard "I sound my barbaric yawp over the rooftops of the world," from Walt Whitman's (1819–1892) *Song of Myself*. Whoops! The actual poem reads, "I sound my barbaric yawp over the ROOFS of the world." (00:55)

5. Before going to the theater, Knox talks with Chris outside of the school building. Snow falls down from the sky, then it stops ("You come with me tonight . . ."), but the following shot seems to be footage of a blizzard. But when Chris asks, "What is that?" the snow has stopped again. (01:31, 01:32)

6. Once at home after the show, Neil opens a couple of windows in his room. Snowflakes on the windowsill blow in the breeze like . . . well, fake snowflakes. (01:43, 01:46)

Questions

1. Professor Keating is given his yearbook, and he giggles at his picture in the bottom-right corner. Then, looking at another picture on the same page, he whispers, "Stanley 'The Tool' Wilson." Shouldn't the yearbook be in alphabetical order, with *w* coming way after *k*? (00:28)

2. Neil shows Todd a flier of *A Midsummer Night's Dream*, staged at Henley Hall. But when he walks out of the theater, the name is the Everett Theatre. Was Henley Hall closed for renovations? (00:45, 01:38)

DEMOLITION MAN (5)
1993, color, 110 min.

Director: Marco Brambilla

Cast: Sylvester Stallone (Sgt. John Spartan), Wesley Snipes (Simon Phoenix), Sandra Bullock (Lenina Huxley), Nigel Hawthorne (Dr. Raymond Cocteau), Benjamin Bratt (Alfredo Garcia), Bob Gunton (Chief George Earle), Glenn Shadix (Associate Bob), Denis Leary (Edgar Friendly), Grand L. Bush (Zachary Lamb—Young), Pat Skipper (Helicopter Pilot), Steve Kahan (Captain Healy), Paul Bollen (T.F.R. Officer), Rob Schneider (Erwin).

Cryogenically frozen cop gets thawed out because a

cryogenically frozen criminal has defrosted.

Bloopers

1. Before being frozen, Sgt. John has two monitoring devices placed on him: one on his left breast, one on his left temple. They jump from left to right twice during the main credits. (00:08, 00:10, 00:11)
2. The action zaps to August 3, 2032. Lenina says that "It's a beautiful Monday morning." Well . . . unless in the future our calendar system gets interrupted or changed, August 3, 2032 will be a Tuesday. (00:11, 00:12)
3. Simon's blue eye is the left one, and we have a clear view of it when he's at the compukiosk. But later on, when he pops out of a manhole, the blue eye is briefly on the right. (00:24, 01:30)
4. When Simon fights with a cop, he grabs one with sunglasses, hits him, and the sunglasses fly off, but then are back when the cop collapses to the ground. (00:27)
5. John puts a gun to Cocteau's head: the gun changes between the shot in the monitor and the real thing. (01:18)

Questions

1. Simon threatens John by holding a flaming torch a few inches above a gasoline lake. Nothing happens. But gas fumes are flammable, too. Wouldn't they have ignited? . . . (00:03)
2. There are fines for saying profanities. Yet Simon says more than one (e.g., "Spartan? John Spartan? Oh, sh**, they let anybody into this century!" at the museum), and so does John (e.g., "I'm Betsy f***ing Ross?" in the police car) yet nothing happens. Are some monitors more lenient than others? (00:15, 00:48, 01:16)

COLOR ME BAD

'Cause I cause so many bloopers!

Wesley Snipes's eyes in *Demolition Man*	Blooper No. 3
A radio in *Dr. Seuss's How the Grinch Stole Christmas*	Blooper No. 1
Craig Thomas and Diane Almeida's blanket in *Friday the 13th Part VII: The New Blood*	Blooper No. 7
Little John's fur in *Robin Hood*	Blooper No. 2

DIE HARD WITH A VENGEANCE (12)

1995, color, 123 min.

Director: John McTiernan

Cast: Bruce Willis (Lieutenant John McClane), Jeremy Irons (Simon Peter Gruber / Peter Krieg), Samuel L. Jackson (Zeus Carver), Graham Greene (Joe Lambert), Colleen Camp (Connie Kowalski), Larry Bryggman (Chief Cobb), Anthony Peck (Ricky Walsh), Nicholas Wyman (Targo), Sam Phillips (Katya), Kevin Chamberlin (Charles Weiss), Sharon Washington (Officer Jane), Stephen Pearlman (Dr. Schiller).

In order to get him back, terrorists give McClane a hard time.

Bloopers

1. When the Bonwit Teller's explodes in New York, take a good look at the cars: they have the steering wheels on the right side. (00:01)
2. In front of the 72nd Street payphone, McClane tells Zeus that he's the only one on "official police business." A blond extra, wearing a red T-shirt and with a black bag strapped across his chest walks by, then walks back again (in the opposite direction) when Zeus answers McClane. (00:16)
3. McClane hijacks a cab to go to the Wall Street station. The left rear window is half-rolled down, but as he leaves a skidmark on the street, the window is completely rolled up. (00:27)
4. While driving the cab, McClane says "I didn't say Park Drive," and steers to the left. Yet the cab swerves to the right. (00:28)
5. Plowing through Central Park with the cab, Zeus does the sign of the cross with his left hand. (00:30)
6. In the vault, both Simon and Zeus pick up gold bars with one hand in order to shatter the window of a car. You simply can't hold a gold bar in one hand. Not to mention the trucks that enter the aqueduct and pass over thin boards to go to the exit ramp. Those trucks would have collapsed under the weight of the stolen gold. (00:58, 01:11, 01:22)
7. Arguing in the fountain, John and Zeus hold two jugs: John's is empty, Zeus's contains three gallons of water. They put the jugs down on the brim of the fountain and argue about racism. When they pick the jugs up, John's has two gallon in it. (01:01, 01:02)
8. After they disarm the bomb, McClane gets a cell phone and talks with Simon. The antenna of the phone is down, but when McClane begins to argue, the antenna is up. (01:03)

9. McClane decides to exchange his Yugo for a Mercedes: they stop a businessman who was talking on the phone, and whose window is rolled up. As the Mercedes stops, the window is completely rolled down. (01:12)

10. McClane is literally shot out of a sewer and lands in a puddle of muddy water. A few minutes later, as he crawls along a rope to reach a ship, he reveals his socks, which are whiter than white. (01:27, 01:34)

11. While being chased by a truck, the Mercedes' windshield alternates between being cracked and being in one piece. (01:30)

12. The villain by the helicopter tells Simon that they will be ready in "zwanzig minuten." The subtitles translate that as "ten minutes," but "zwanzig" in German means "twenty." (01:55)

DR. SEUSS' HOW THE GRINCH STOLE CHRISTMAS (6)
2000, color, 104 min.

Director: Ron Howard

Cast: Jim Carrey (The Grinch), Rachel Bailit (Nurse Who), Jeffrey Tambor (Mayor May Who), Taylor Momsen (Cindy Lou Who), Christine Baranski (Martha May Whovier), Bill Irwin (Lou Lou Who), Anthony Hopkins (Narrator), Molly Shannon (Betty Lou Who), Josh Ryan Evans (8-Year-Old Grinch), T.J. Thyne (Stu Lou Who), Rachel Winfree (Rose Who-Biddy), Lacey Kohl (Christina Whoterberry).

"You're a mean one, Mr. Grinch!"

Bloopers

1. One of the two Who girls who go up to the Grinch's lair is carrying a purple radio. Yet when she stops by the entrance of the cave and looks at the two scared Who guys, her radio looks black. (00:04)

2. When Lou discovers Cindy Lou wrapped in gift paper, he passes by the sorting machine: a purple package is about to fall from the conveyor belt—but after the cut, it becomes a silver package. (00:13)

3. Once at home, Lou asks his busy wife, Betty, if what he's holding is the dining room chandelier. When she replies from the roof that it's all for the cause, one green bulb goes off right in front of her. In the following shot, the same bulb is okay. (00:14)

4. Before entering the garbage disposal "Dumpit to Crumpit" to return home from Whoville, Max's collar is gone— but the dog had it one moment before. The collar is back when the dog is sliding with the Grinch along the disposal. (00:16)

5. The Grinch sets a few moths

free to destroy hanging stockings. Actually, it's the larvae of the moths, not the flying ones, which eat clothes. (01:10)

6. Before leaving Whoville on his sled, the Grinch shuts down all of the town's lights. Yet as he tries to take off, the lights are on. When he crashes, they are all off. (01:16, 01:17)

DROWNING MONA (6)
2000, color, 95 min.

Director: Nick Gomez

Cast: Danny DeVito (Chief Wyatt Rash), Bette Midler (Mona Dearly), Neve Campbell (Ellen Rash), Jamie Lee Curtis (Rona Mace), Casey Affleck (Bobby Kalzone), William Fichtner (Phil Dearly), Marcus Thomas (Jeff Dearly), Peter Dobson (Lt. Feege Gruber), Kathleen Wilhoite (Lucinda, Wrecker Service), Tracey Walter (Clarence), Will Ferrell (Cubby the Funeral Director), Paul Ben-Victor (Deputy Tony Carlucci).

Who didn't *do it?*

Bloopers

1. Mona steps out of the house with the car keys in her left hand. After fixing her purse strap, she passes the keys to the right hand, but in the following shot, the keys are back in her left. (00:01)

2. Rona sits on the bed, and a *Wheel of Fortune* gameboard box lies on the edge. When Phil tells Rona that Mona is dead, the box has moved closer to the center of the bed, and when he stands up, the box is on the edge of the bed again. (00:16, 00:17)

3. Ellen uses ketchup on a pickle at a diner while talking with her dad. When she's done, she places the squeeze bottle to her right, but as Rona says, "enjoy your meal," and walks away, the bottle (in the background) has vanished. (00:29, 00:30)

4. Bobby lifts a bag of fertilizer and places it on his shoulder, the red side against him, the white side facing away. As Chief Rash arrives, Bobby turns—and so does the bag: the white side is now against Bobby's shoulder, and the red side is facing away. (00:33)

5. The pile of donuts placed on Mona's grave by Jeff changes from the shot behind the grave to the one in front of it. (00:49)

6. Ellen stops at a gas station and places the gas cap on the roof of her car. She then drives away, upset, leaving the cap on the roof. As she stops at the police station, the cap is back in place. (01:13, 01:14)

Question

At the wedding, Cubby has a string of confetti on his shoulder, way before they begin tossing it on the married couple. Was Cubby ahead of the game, or? . . . (01:29)

DUDE, WHERE'S MY CAR? (5)
2000, color, 83 min.

Director: Danny Leiner

Cast: Ashton Kutcher (Jesse Montgomery III), Seann William Scott (Chester Greenberg), Jennifer Garner (Wanda), Marla Sokoloff (Wilma), Kristy Swanson (Christie Boner), David Herman (Nelson), Hal Sparks (Zoltan), Charlie O'Connell (Tommy), John Toles-Bey (Mr. Pizzacoli), Christian Middlelthon (Alien Nordic Dude #1), David Bannick (Alien Nordic Dude #2), Turtle Lini (Jeff).

A couple of stoners live the day of their lives—but can't remember a thing about it.

Bloopers
1. In Jesse and Chester's living room, the lava lamp is active and "bubbling" as we see it, but when Jesse talks about his dream, the lamp is bubbleless. Then they come back, then they vanish again, and back and forth . . . (00:02, 00:03)

2. When Chester finds the Kitty Kat Club matchbox in his pocket, he holds it in his right hand and motions the left one to open it, but the detail shows the matchbox in his left palm, and he proceeds to open it with his right hand. (00:16)

3. To pick up the Mountain Dew cap that has fallen from the trashbag he's helping Jesse carry, Chester removes his left shoe and sock—yet he grabs the cap with his bare right foot. (00:23)

4. Jesse walks out of a frozen yogurt store and reaches Chester, who's working on a Rubik's Cube. The street behind them is dry as a bone, but as police cars arrive, the entire street is thoroughly wet. (00:30, 00:33)

5. Chester and Jesse reach Zoltan's parents' house, and turn while leaning against a fence: Chester puts his left hand on it and Jesse leans over. In the over-the-shoulder shot, it's Chester who's leaning over the fence, while Jesse has his right hand on it. (00:48)

E

EARTHQUAKE (6)
1974, color, 123 min.

Director: Mark Robson

Cast: Charlton Heston (Stuart Graff), Ava Gardner (Remy Graff), George Kennedy (Lew Slade), Lorne Greene (Sam Royce), Geneviève Bujold (Denise Marshall), Richard Roundtree (Miles Quade), Marjoe Gortner (Jody), Barry Sullivan (Stockle), Lloyd Nolan (Dr. Vance), Victoria Principal (Rosa Amici), Walter Matthau (Drunk), Monica Lewis (Barbara), Bob Gravage (Farmer Mr. Griggs), John Randolph (Mayor), George Murdock (Colonel).

Let's get ready to rumble!

Bloopers
1. Farmer Griggs riding his tractor approaches Dr. Adams. The shadow of the camera is visible on its side. (00:18)
2. Miles, the biker, warms up by trying his stunt track, which begins with a loop. The first time he fails, falling from the loop. The following attempt is successful—but if you check the shot of him doing the loop, it's the same sequence as before, when he failed (the front wheel goes off the track, and then they cut to his point of view). (00:46, 00:47)
3. A truck carrying cows drives off of a freeway overpass and plummets down. Strangely enough, the cows remain in place, and don't even move, as if they were models glued to the truck. (00:53, 00:54)
4. When Rosa flees the theater with a lot of other people, a woman dressed in pink is so agitated that she runs out of the building twice. (00:53)
5. During the first big earthquake, a woman with a blue dress and a yellow scarf turns to help a friend, gets a waterfall of glass shards, turns back, and shows her face covered with blood and glass slivers. However, just before she gets hit, she lifts

her head a little too much: pieces of glass are already sticking out of her face. (00:58)

6. On the dam, the colonel talks to the mayor of Los Angeles using a chopper radio. The sound we hear is of props spinning very fast, but the shadow of the props reveals them to be moving very slowly. (01:23)

Fun Fact
The drunk in the bar is played by the late Walter Matthau. This was the only movie where he used his real name in the credits: Walter Matuschanskayasky. (00:23)

EDGE, THE (4)
1997, color, 117 min.

Director: Lee Tamahori

Cast: Anthony Hopkins (Charles Morse), Alec Baldwin (Robert Green), Elle MacPherson (Mickey Morse), Harold Perrineau, Jr. (Stephen), L.Q. Jones (Styles), Kathleen Wilhoite (Ginny), David Lindstedt (James), Mark Kiely (Mechanic), Eli Gabay (Jet Pilot), Larry Musser (Amphibian Pilot).

A rich man and a photographer crash-land in the woods and meet Bart the Bear.

Bloopers
1. On the plane, Charles opens the *Lost in the Wild* book and flips only the cover to read the pinned note on the back of it. But as we come back to him, many pages have been turned—not just the cover. (00:03)

2. When Charles reads the engraving on the pocket watch he just got, the cover of it has the hinges to the left—but when has Charles snapped it closed, the cover shows the hinges to the right. (00:15)

3. Charles crosses a waterfall while a bear chases him by walking on a large tree over a river. Funny—Charles's hair is longer and puffier, like that of . . . a stunt double. (00:43)

4. When he's in the wood lodge, Charles opens his watch to read the inscription again. This is the only thing he's holding, but as he pockets it, a box of matches appears in his hands. (01:32)

ELIZABETH (3)
1998, color, 121 min.

Director: Shekhar Kapur

Cast: Cate Blanchett (Elizabeth I), Joseph Fiennes (Robert Dudley, Earl of Leicester), Geoffrey Rush (Sir Francis Walsingham), Richard Attenborough (William Cecil), Vincent Cassel (Duc d'Anjou), James Frain (Alvaro de la Quadra), George Yiasoumi (King Philip II of Spain), Christopher Eccleston (Duke of Norfolk), John Gielgud (Pope Paul IV), Fanny Ardant (Mary of

Guise), Kathy Burke (Queen Mary Tudor).

The Virgin Queen does a little ... well, let's just say the title doesn't fit so well anymore.

Bloopers
1. Lord Dudley is wearing a necklace as he and Elizabeth practice dancing. When they come to haul Elizabeth away, in the final two close-ups of their embrace, his necklace disappears. (00:10)
2. Right before the assassination attempt on Elizabeth, they are holding a nighttime regatta on the river. The paddles on the oars of one of the boats is shiny, black rubber. Not in the sixteenth century, my friend ... (01:02)
3. As the Duc d'Anjou wails over the dead body of Mary of Guise, he flops down his head next to hers. When he does so, Mary's eyes shut. And, unfortunately, dead people don't flinch. (01:35)

EMPIRE RECORDS (7)
1995, color, 88 min.

Director: Allan Moyle

Cast: Anthony LaPaglia (Joe), Maxwell Caulfield (Rex Manning), Debi Mazar (Jane), Rory Cochrane (Lucas), Johnny Whitworth (A.J.), Robin Tunney (Debra), Renée Zellweger (Gina), Ethan Embry (Mark), Coyote Shivers (Berko), Brendan Sexton III (Warren), Liv Tyler (Corey), James "Kimo" Wills (Eddie).

Weird record store has even weirder employees and the weirdest owner.

Bloopers
1. When Lucas is leafing through Joe's desk, having counted the money twice, he grabs an agreement form. The calculator has a total on its display, but after a second, it seems to be off. No number is on the display, and of course Lucas didn't touch it at all. (00:02)
2. A.J. tells Mark that "listening to this crap is guaranteed to make you sterile," holding an open CD case high in the air. In the over-the-shoulder shot, he's not holding the case at all, which appears to be on the player in front of him. (00:12)
3. As he takes the flame to the CD, he's holding the disk with his forefingers underneath it, while in the detail he has his fingers on the edge, with his hand turned over. (00:12)
4. Corey leaves the office disgusted and she puts her sweater back on. Her hair is caught in the collar of her sweater, but when she listens to A.J.'s love proposal, her hair alternates between being outside and inside the

collar—and it's definitely in when she moves away to crouch down. (00:50)

5. While dancing in the store to "Oh Rexy, You're So Sexy," Debra takes A.J.'s shirt off. In the shot where Mark is dancing, it's possible to see A.J. in the background: his shirt is back on, as it is in the subsequent wide shot—but as Leo stops the party, A.J. is bare-chested again. (00:57)

6. Eddie comes from his pizza job and takes off his shirt in order to put on a new uniform for the Empire Records job. His new white shirt is all buttoned up, but when Corey asks, "Why is this door locked?" the shirt appears buttoned in the long shot and open and unbuttoned in the close-up. (01:00)

7. Debra collects money in a jar just outside Empire Records. A detail reveals a jar filled halfway to the top (bills reach the symbol on one side of the container), but the following shot shows an almost completely empty jar. (01:16)

EMPIRE STRIKES BACK, THE (30)
also Special Edition (29)
1980, color, 124 min. / 127 min.
SE

Director: Irvin Kershner

Cast: Mark Hamill (Luke Skywalker), Harrison Ford (Han Solo), Carrie Fisher (Princess Leia Organa), Billy Dee

Williams (Lando Calrissian), Anthony Daniels (C-3PO), David Prowse (Darth Vader), Peter Mayhew (Chewbacca), Kenny Baker (R2-D2), Frank Oz (Yoda), Alec Guinness (Ben "Obi-Wan" Kenobi), Jeremy Bulloch (Boba Fett / Lieutenant Sheckil), John Hollis (Lobot), Michael Culver (Captain Lorth Needa), Kenneth Colley (Admiral Piett).

"Who's your daddy? Who's your daddy?"

Bloopers

1. On planet Hoth, while Luke's trying to calm down the taun taun he's riding, the boom mike can be seen reflected in his goggles. (00:03)

2. As Han enters the Hoth base's command center, Leia gives him a look from her place, close to the left wall of the room. When Han goes to talk to a general, Leia gives him a second look, this time from the right wall. But... wait a second! These two are the same shot, only flipped. (00:05)

3. Leaving the command center, Han is followed by Leia who wants to talk to him. When Han says, "Well, the bounty hunter we ran into on Ord Mandel changed my mind," in the background, a young, short rebel walks from the left to the right. In the following cut, he has become a taller, apparently

older rebel going the same direction. (00:06)

4. When Luke flees the wampa's grotto, his light saber is on. The off sound can be heard, but the saber is still on. Only when he's out will the saber be off. (00:09 SE only)

5. The badge on Han's jacket keeps jumping between right and left. It's to Han's right when he's on the taun taun, to the left when he's trying to pick up life forms, to the right again when he slices the dead taun taun, to the left when he comments, "This may smell bad, kid!" and so on. (00:11, 00:14)

6. Despite no news about Luke and Han, Leia orders them to close the shield doors. In the background of Chewbacca's close-up, one door starts to move—without making any noise. In the following master shot, the same door starts to move again, but this time it makes a helluva racket! (00:12)

7. Luke lies in the snow before being called by Ben. The first shot reveals his gun holster to his left side. But Luke is right-handed. (00:12)

8. Back at the base, Luke gets all the curing he needs; when Han enters saying, "How ya' doin', kid?" his voice *precedes* the sound of the door opening. (00:16)

9. The *Millennium Falcon* flees the Hoth base and flies by Luke, who follows its trajec-

tory with his eyes. Or does he? Apparently, he moves his head way ahead of the passage of the *Falcon*. (00:35)

10. Artoo is in Luke's X-wing while the two are flying to Dagobah. While on the ground, Artoo's dome is mainly silver and blue, in deep space, it is silver and black; but worry not! Once on Dagobah, it's blue again. Same thing will happen when the duo is flying toward Cloud City. (00:36, 01:28 / Fixed in SE)

> Ken Ralston, one of the special effects creators, explained that, due to the blue screen's . . . blue, R2's dome had to be painted black for the shots in space. "It was the only way to make the shot work." And he also added that "R2-D2 isn't *quite* R2-D2 in those shots."

11. When the destroyer and four TIE fighters are chasing the *Falcon* (in the first shot after the dissolve), one of the TIE fighters, below the one almost at screen center, appears a few frames into the shot. (00:36)

12. Because of a sudden movement of the asteroid in which they're hiding, Leia winds up in Han's arms. Her line, "Captain, being held by you isn't quite enough to get me excited," is mouthed by Han as well. (00:45)

13. Yoda wins his battle with Artoo for a flashlight, then yells at Luke, "No! No, no!" The arm holding the flashlight is bent in three places. Weird! (00:49)

14. After Han talks to Leia while she's trying to fix the *Falcon,* the two eventually kiss: in the matching wide shot, her left arm pops up around Han's neck. (00:51)

15. Han and Leia's kiss is interrupted by C-3PO: look how a spring from his right arm, already dangling, drops silently to the floor. The spring will come back right away. (00:51 / 00:52 SE)

16. Captain Needa is killed by Darth Vader and collapses to the floor. When two officers take the body away, the dead Needa practically stands up by himself to help the two poor saps. (01:12, 01:13 / 01:13 SE)

17. On the *Falcon,* Leia deactivates C-3PO. The robot's lights go off, and it stops moving. But it keeps breathing, betraying its purportedly idle state. (01:14)

18. As he's packing his stuff to leave Dagobah, Luke has a yellow ladder to reach the cockpit of his X-wing. Once inside the cockpit, the ladder is gone and nobody knows if it's still on Dagobah. (01:21, 01:23 / 01:22, 01:24 SE)

19. When the remains of C-3PO are on the conveyer belt, the crew can be seen reflected in his shiny head. (01:25 / 01:26 SE)

20. In Cloud City, Han, Leia, Lando, and Chewbacca walk to get a drink. Lando and Han switch positions in the following cut, yet they carry on the same conversation. (01:26, 01:27 / 01:27 SE)

21. Before being frozen in the graphite, Han has a final exchange with Leia: he's wearing his black vest in the close-ups ("I love you!" "I know.") but not in the wide shot. (01:34 / 01:34, 01:35 SE)

22. Han is lowered into the graphite well with his hands handcuffed in front. But once in the block of graphite, Han has his hands close to his face. Discuss amongst yourselves. (01:34, 01:35 / 01:35, 01:36 SE)

Han Houdini

When Han is frozen in the graphite, he has two black restrainers on his biceps. (01:34) When he's defrosted in *Return of the Jedi,* the restrainers are gone. (00:18 / 00:19 SE)

23. Right before turning on his light saber, Darth Vader is already holding the gray "stunt double" of the saber. You can briefly see it, aligned with the camera, in front of Vader. (01:39 / 01:40 SE)

24. During their duel, Vader blocks Luke's light saber,

coming from Luke's upper left. Vader says, "Now release your anger . . . only your hatred can destroy me!" And now Luke's saber is *above* Vader's, even though the two have crossed weapons and not moved until that moment. (01:43 / 01:44 SE)

25. Luke makes Vader fall off of a platform. Then, Luke jumps off of the platform himself— a loud *plap!* marks his landing as if it were dozens of feet down—but then his head pops up into the shot as if he only jumped several feet. (01:44)

26. After Artoo gets electrocuted on Cloud City, the group of heroes run away from the camera. You can see Chewbacca's shoes' soles (and not his "paws"). (01:46 / 01:47 SE)

27. When Luke is trapped by Vader, who's inviting him to rule the universe hand in hand, Vader's saber is on. Then, suddenly, with a suspicious hiss (and *not* the usual off sound) his saber is off. (01:49 / 01:50 SE)

28. Lando opens the top hatch of the *Falcon* to let Luke enter the ship. When he does, he's flooded by white light. Not only is it sunset, but underneath Cloud City there aren't lights capable of generating that much illumination. (01:53 / fixed in the SE: the "white light" has been replaced by another porthole.)

29. Darth Vader inquires of Admiral Piett whether the *Millennium Falcon*'s hyperdrive has been deactivated. During that scene, the admiral's insignia are on the right side of his uniform. Piett (and the entire Imperial army) always has them on the left side. (01:55 / 01:56 SE)

30. Piett asks his men, "Ready for the tractor beam?" The shot of the other soldiers is, again, flipped: the standing one has the insignia on the right side of his uniform. (01:57 / 01:58 SE)

31. When Artoo abandons an almost completed C-3PO to go fix the *Falcon*'s hyperdrive, C-3PO stands on his only functional leg, holding the other one by the knee. After one cut, he's holding it by the foot. (01:57 / 01:58 SE)

Question

When Luke and Han are bidding good-bye to each other, Han tells a tiny robot that is walking on the Falcon, "Wait a second!" The robot stops, but in the following close-up of Han, can be seen walking by. Does it have a short-circuited short-term memory? (00:22)

Fun Fact

After being tortured, Han is carried by two stormtroopers back into the cell with Chewbacca. As he drops to the floor, his arm gets stuck in the helmet of one of the two soldiers (who leaves the room with his helmet askew, without missing a beat). (01:30 / 01:31 SE)

ENEMY OF THE STATE (8)
1998, color, 131 min.

Director: Tony Scott

Cast: Will Smith (Robert Clayton Dean), Gene Hackman (Brill / Edward Lyle), Jon Voight (Thomas Brian Reynolds), Lisa Bonet (Rachel Banks), Regina King (Carla Dean), Stuart Wilson (Congressman Albert), Laura Cayouette (Christa Hawkins), Loren Dean (Hicks), Barry Pepper (David Pratt), Ian Hart (Bingham), Jake Busey (Krug), Scott Caan (Jones), Jason Lee (Zavitz), (Pintero), Jason Robards (Congressman Phillip Hamersly).

A corrupt politician targets a lawyer . . . who should we root for?

Bloopers
1. Congressman Hamersly gets killed by Pratt, who passes the dog to its left and uses a syringe. When Zavitz checks the tape on his computer, Pratt passes the dog to its right and uses a syringe. Maybe they killed the congressman twice. (00:03, 00:18)
2. Brian passes a folder to Hicks: the spine of the folder is to Brian's right—but as Hicks grabs it, it has rotated 90°, and now the spine is facing Brian. (00:33)
3. Robert calls the police to report a break in. He holds the phone to his right ear, but just after the "smoke alarm cam" shot, he has the phone to his left ear. (00:41)
4. In order to remove every bug from his person, Robert strips in Mr. Wu's hotel room. When he's by the window, he removes his pants twice (wide shot and close-up). (01:06)
5. When in Rachel's bathroom, Robert spots his "RD" cufflinks. Before he grabs them, they change positions. (01:21)
6. The 25-second countdown to the detonation of the bomb in Brill's "coop" lasts 40 seconds. (01:33)
7. Pintero pushes Reynolds so hard that his glasses fly off. Then, Reynolds slams against a metal door. And his glasses fly off. Again. (02:00)
8. Robert is staring at himself on his TV set. But a video image doesn't work like a mirror, so why is the gigantic left-temple bandage on his right temple on the TV? (02:05)

Questions
1. In the hijacked Mercedes, Robert takes Brill's cat out of a bag. In the background, is that a manual window crank? On a modern Mercedes? (01:38)
2. It is suggested that the camera that is filming Robert is in the smoke alarm on the ceil-

ing. So why is the image practically shot at the same level as the TV and not from the ceiling level, as it was earlier? (00:41, 02:05)

EXECUTIVE DECISION (8)
1996, color, 134 min.

Director: Stuart Baird

Cast: Kurt Russell (Dr. David Grant), Steven Seagal (Lieutenant Colonel Austin Travis), Halle Berry (Jean), John Leguizamo (Rat), Oliver Platt (Dennis Cahill), Joe Morton (Cappy), David Suchet (Nagi Hassan), B. D. Wong (Louie), Len Cariou (Secretary of Defense Charles White), Whip Hubley (Baker), Andreas Katsulas (El Sayed Jaffa), Mary Ellen Trainor (Allison), David Birznieks (Firefighter), Paul Bollen (Firefighter).

Bomb on a plane, expert on a plane, and Steven Seagal squeezed somewhere in-between.

Bloopers

1. According to the map of Italy, there is a city called Bolano (top-left corner). The real city is Bolzano, with a *z*. (00:01)

2. Flight 343 departs from Athens, Greece, in the morning (usually, flights from Europe to the U.S. take off mid-morning). Supposedly, a terrorist blows up a restaurant in London simultaneously: but for some reason, the sky is *dark*, and a lot of people are having dinner. And then we see the same plane again, and it's flying in daylight. But from Athens to Washington, this plane has to pass near England, so? . . . (00:08, 00:10)

3. When they are talking via computer with Cahill, the image from Washington seems to have a series of buttons and commands on the bottom bar, but a closer shot of the computer reveals the words "Video on-line." Later on, the buttons are back. (00:24)

4. Preparing for takeoff, the Remora F117X stops right at the yellow line with the front wheel. When the engines fire (as seen from behind), the yellow line is gone. When it takes off, the line is back. (00:28)

5. Helped by Rat, David slides along a cable to check the probes placed in the plane cabin. David places his right foot on the cable, then the left on top. When he reaches the first probe, it's the left foot on the cable and the right one on top. (01:00)

6. Rat slides along the cable: he has nothing on his head. When he gets off of the cable, he's wearing headgear with light and strap. (01:15)

7. Flight 343 is cleared to land at "Dulles International Air-

port." Yet, when it arrives, ⌐☺☺ the names of everything on that map are in Arabic. Wouldn't Washington, D.C., be in Arabic too? (01:06)

there are only "Dulles MU-NICIPAL Airport" firetrucks. Except that when one fire-fighter says, "What the hell?" he is standing in front of a "Dulles International Air-port" truck. (01:46, 01:57, 02:01)

8. When David finally lands the jumbo jet, its left wing smashes through a series of smaller planes: the second to last crash causes the third engine to detach from the wing, but in the following shot it's back in place. Then it's gone for good. (02:03)

Questions

1. A 747 from Athens to Wash-ington, D.C., needs to have more than two pilots on board. According to regulations, there should have been one captain, one first officer, one second officer, and probably a co-captain (or substitute pilot). But this would have made the cockpit a little too crowded, right? (00:10)

2. Jean discovers Nagi's map:

3. In the cockpit of the 747 there is a bookshelf filled with handbooks, including the ever-popular *Pilot Operating Handbook, Flight Manual,* and in this case probably *Complete Commercial Jet Operation for Dummies.* Since when? (01:58)

EYES WIDE SHUT (13)
1999, color, 159 min.

Director: Stanley Kubrick

Cast: Tom Cruise (Bill Harford), Nicole Kidman (Alice Harford), Sydney Pollack (Victor Ziegler), Marie Richardson (Marion Nathanson), Rade Serbedzija (Milich), Todd Field (Nick Nightingale), Vinessa Shaw (Domino), Alan Cumming (Desk Clerk), Sky Dumont (Sandor Szavost), Fay Masterson (Sally), Leelee Sobieski (Milich's Daughter), Thomas Gibson (Carl).

COMPUTER CRASH

Cyber-bloopers.

The Cygnus's console in *The Black Hole*	Blooper No. 2
A computer in *Empire Records*	Blooper No. 1
A Washington screen in *Executive Decision*	Blooper No. 3
Keanu Reeves's monitor in *Johnny Mnemonic*	Blooper No. 3
Keanu Reeves's computer in *Point Break*	Blooper No. 1

Tom and Nicole find themselves in a world of sexual danger. And annoying piano players.

Bloopers

1. Nick plays "I'm in the Mood for Love" on the piano at Victor Ziegler's party. We can clearly see that his hands are not playing the high trills with the same ferocity as the underlying music would indicate. (00:04)

2. On the Harford's bed, Alice, after having heavily inhaled on a joint, exhales in the close-up . . . but no smoke comes out. (00:22, 00:23)

3. On the same bed, Bill is behind Alice as she tokes on a joint. In one shot, he has his right hand on her left thigh ("They were just a couple of models"), but in the wide shot his hand is behind her. (00:24)

4. Bill and Alice are arguing. During his "I happen to be a doctor" speech, the ashtray on the bed is not right in front of the place where the pillows overlap. But then when he later says, "I can assure you, sex is the last thing on this f***ing hypothetical woman-patient's mind" the ashtray is suddenly sitting right in front of where the pillows overlap. (00:28, 00:29)

5. In the bedroom argument, Alice crosses to the window sill, where compact discs are neatly stacked on the left and VHS tapes are neatly stacked on the right. After she sits down beneath the sill, and says, "I could hardly move," the compact discs have gone askew, and the stack of tapes has rotated. And she never touched either stack. (00:29, 00:33)

6. Bill visits his newly deceased patient. At the entrance to the bedroom, there are two tables, each with a sculpture on them. When Carl arrives six minutes later, the sculpture to the left of the door has vanished. (00:38, 00:44)

7. Bill has gone to a prostitute's apartment, and we cut to Alice sitting at home eating cookies. There are no cookies in the row of the carton that is farthest from her. When she calls Bill on his cell phone, there is now one cookie in that last row. When she says, "I'm going to go to bed now" the cookie vanishes. (00:50, 00:52, 00:53)

8. Bill visits the Sonata Jazz Club, and there are pictures of Nick's band outside. The drummer is listed as Larry McVey, and the bassist as Kip Fleming. However, at the end of his set, Nick introduces the drummer as Kip Fleming and the bassist as Larry McVey. (00:55, 00:56)

9. Bill pulls up to the costume shop for the first time; there's a blue U.S. mailbox on the left, and, as he gets out, we

see that there's also one about twenty feet to the right (a little close by, no?). When he returns to the costume shop, the second mailbox has been mysteriously removed. (01:01, 01:44)

10. As Bill is wandering through the orgy, he passes a table where two hooded figures (blatant digital inserts), one sitting and one standing, are watching a sex scene taking place on top of the table. As Bill passes and we look behind him, the two hooded figures are suddenly gone. (01:20)

11. Bill wanders through the orgy scenes at the mansion. As he finally stops, the man with the tri-cornered hat comes up from behind him with a naked woman on his arm. We cut to a shot that now includes Bill, and the woman is suddenly different. She has the same mask, just different private parts. (01:21)

12. Bill picks up a newspaper and reads about Mandy's un-

timely demise. Later, he also shows the article to Ziegler in the pool room. In this article, there are three places where lines are repeated twice—first column, second paragraph: "Hotel by security personnel after her agent asked them to check on her be-"; second column, second paragraph: ". . . her at the time she ingested the drugs."; third column, third paragraph: " 'She has many important friends in the fashion and entertainment worlds.' " (02:05, 02:20)

13. Bill has confronted Victor about Mandy's death following the incident at the orgy, and they're talking next to the pool table. The chalk near Victor is on the right, then jumps to the left ("You wanna know what kind of a charade? I'll tell you exactly what kind . . ."), and then back. The alignment of the cue ball and red solid ball on the table in front of Victor changes as well. (02:21, 02:22)

F

FAMILY MAN, THE (5)
2000, color, 126 min.

Director: Brett Ratner

Cast: Nicolas Cage (Jack Campbell), Téa Leoni (Kate Reynolds), Don Cheadle (Cash), Jeremy Piven (Arnie), Saul Rubinek (Alan Mintz), Josef Sommer (Peter Lassiter), Makenzie Vega (Annie Campbell), Jake Milkovich (Josh Campbell), Ryan Milkovich (Josh Campbell), Lisa Thornhill (Evelyn Thompson), Harve Presnell (Big Ed), Mary Beth Hurt (Adelle), Amber Valletta (Paula), Tom McGowan (Bill).

Successful single man lives a glimpse of how his married life would have been had he made different choices. And spent more time at the bowling alley.

Bloopers

1. The story takes place on Christmas Eve, 2000. The day seems to be an ordinary working day . . . but December 24, 2000 was a Sunday. (00:03, 00:06)

2. When Jack wakes up in the alternate "glimpse," the clock on the nightstand reads what seems to be a few minutes to nine. He freaks out and runs away, and when he comes back, his "new" wife tells him that he left at 7:30. (00:18, 00:31)

3. At a Christmas party, Jack finds out that his "new" wife is a nonprofit lawyer. She eats one of the two olives she has on a toothpick, in the following shot she still has two olives on the toothpick, and then only one. (00:37)

4. Jack has to change little Josh's diaper. Just before he tears it apart, we see the changing station to Jack's right. When he tosses the soiled diaper away, on the changing station now there's a large, azure, brand-new bag of diapers. (00:40)

5. At the bowling alley, Arnie gives Jack an analogy about

his wife being like the Fidelity Bank and Trust. His gloves lie on the table, neatly placed to one side. Next shot, they're crooked and closer to the beer, next shot, they're neatly to one side again. (01:04)

Non-Blooper

At the Christmas party, Bill mentions to Jack that the next day he's going to have a triple bypass, and the next time they see him, he's bowling with the boys. But there's nothing to indicate that this game of bowling occurred immediately after his operation (no Christmas or New Year's decorations, for instance). (00:35, 01:00)

FATHERS' DAY (11)

1997, color, 98 min.

Director: Ivan Reitman

Cast: Robin Williams (Dale Putley), Billy Crystal (Jack Lawrence), Julia Louis-Dreyfus (Carrie Lawrence), Nastassja Kinski (Collette Andrews), Charlie Hofheimer (Scott Andrews), Bruce Greenwood (Bob Andrews), Dennis Burkley (Calvin), Haylie Johnson (Nikki), Charles Rocket (Russ Trainor), Patti D'Arbanville (Shirley Trainor), Jared Harris (Lee), Louis Lombardi (Matt).

Let's take two GREAT comedy actors, one GREAT comedy director, two GREAT comedy writers

. . . What could possibly go wrong? Well, how about EVERYTHING?!?

Bloopers

1. Collette tells Jack about his alleged son; Jack almost gulps the whole dry martini down, but when he says, "My son?" there's more martini in the glass than before—and no waiters in sight. As she digs into her purse for a picture, the glass is again almost empty. (00:04, 00:05)

2. Dale and Jack are driving over a bridge, followed by many cars, the first of which is an ivory minivan. As we cut inside Dale's car, the van has been replaced by another car. (00:14, 00:15)

3. Dale fakes crying to impress Mrs. Trainor so that she will reveal where Scott might be. Her medallion keeps flipping front and back as she tells the Sugar Ray story. (00:19, 00:20)

4. While driving to Sacramento, Dale hits the brakes and tells Jack about a body he *might* have run over. Tall yellow grass can be seen through the window behind Jack, however, in the last shot before Dale restarts the car, the landscape is completely different and now there's a small hill. (00:24, 00:25)

5. During the Sugar Ray concert in Sacramento, Jack and Dale split. Dale fishes in his

pocket for the picture of Scott. Then, as he walks down the aisle, he fishes again and takes it out one more time. (00:26)

6. Bob Andrews lowers his car only to find out that the spare tire is flat, too. The key he used to unscrew the bolts changes position from the detail (it's heading to the right) to the wide shot (or, to the left). (00:38)

7. In order to flee, Scott pours a whole coffee pot in Dale's lap. Dale flips the table, which hits the floor and remains askew, a large coffee stain on it. When Carrie enters the room, she finds the table, no longer stained, leaning on a chair. (00:47, 00:48)

8. Scott steals Dale's clothes, so Dale, dressed as Scott, slowly walks along one of the hotel's halls and bumps into Carrie. A maid passes by, then opens a door and vanishes—but in the following shot, she's still halfway down the hall. (00:47)

9. As Scott gets hit by Jack's car, he rolls on the street: underneath his shirt it's possible to catch a quick glimpse of stunt pads. (00:51)

10. Jack gives Dale a pass to go backstage at a concert and look for Scott. Dale wears his around his neck, but after the duo splits, the pass vanishes. It returns as soon as Dale finds the guys he's looking for. (01:15, 01:19)

11. Dale tries to steal a picture of

Scott as a kid (black and blue books in the background) from a picture album, but Jack stops him. As Dale flips the very same page, now there's a red picture in place of the one Dale wanted to steal. (01:26)

Fun Fact
An almost-unrecognizable Mel Gibson appears as an extremely pierced guy. (01:19)

FEAR—HALLOWEEN NIGHT, THE (5)
1999, color, 95 min.

Director: Chris Angel

Cast: Gordon Currie (Michael "Mike" Hawthorne), Stacy Grant (Peg), Phillip Rhys (Mitch), Myc Agnew (Chris), Emmanuelle Vaugier (Jennifer), Kelly Benson (Lisa Anne), Brendan Bliser (Ned), Racher Hayward (Trish), Larry Pennell (Grandfather), Betsy Palmer (Grandmother "Mams"), Jon Fedele (Morty), Garvin Cross (Stephen Hawthorne).

Ancient ritual turns out to be a modern massacre, thanks to the wood-carved Morty.

Bloopers
1. As soon as they arrive, Mams hugs Michael, then she de-hugs twice. (00:08)

2. The only photo of Stephen shows him holding an axe to the left of the photo. Later

on, when Michael explains the Fear Circle, he gets closer to the photo: the detail shows Stephen's picture "flipped": the axe now is to the right. (00:11, 00:18)

3. When Crow says, "You will enter the dream state. It is there . . ." the statue of Morty blinks. (00:13)

4. Michael grabs Morty's talisman with his left hand, but when Crow tells him that it's raven wings, he drops it. From his right hand. (00:14)

5. Morty the wooden statue bends (for instance, when Chris pulls a prank and pretends to be attacked by the statue). (00:29)

FINDING FORRESTER (5)
2000, color, 136 min.

Director: Gus Van Sant

Cast: Sean Connery (William Forrester), Rob Brown (Jamal Wallace), F. Murray Abraham (Professor Robert Crawford), Anna Paquin (Claire Spence), Busta Rhymes (Terrell), April Grace (Ms. Joyce), Michael Pitt (Coleridge), Michael Nouri (Dr. Spence), Richard Easton (Matthews), Glenn Fitzgerald (Massie), Zane R. Copeland Jr. (Damon), Stephanie Berry (Janice), Fly Williams III (Fly).

Bond plays reclusive Salingeresque writer who encourages a ghetto kid to write.

Bloopers

1. Forrester returns Jamal's backpack, tossing it from a window. The backpack lands on a street crossing, in-between two white lines. When Jamal picks it up, it has moved on top of one of the white lines. (00:19)

2. Forrester tapes a bird he identifies as a Connecticut warbler. The footage is of a Yellow warbler (we knew you'd have to ask: the Connecticut warbler has a yellow belly and olive plumage; the Yellow warbler has mostly yellow plumage. So now you know). (00:36)

3. During Professor Crawford's lesson, Jamal's tie is flipped in the close-ups, straightened down in the wide shots. (00:46)

4. Forrester tells Jamal that Professor Crawford "wrote a book a few years after mine." He leans against the door: from the back, his fingers are extended, from the front they're a fist. (01:00)

5. Jamal opens a letter Forrester sent him, and we hear Forrester's voice reading it. However, the first two lines of the letter we can see are, "Someone I once knew . . . that all we need doing . . ." Forrester says, "Someone I once knew wrote that we walk away from our dreams." (02:09)

FIRM, THE (7)
1993, color, 154 min.

Director: Sidney Pollack

Cast: Tom Cruise (Mitchell Y. "Mitch" McDeere), Jeanne Tripplehorn (Abby McDeere), Gene Hackman (Avery Tolar), Hal Holbrook (Oliver Lambert), Terry Kinney (Lamar Quinn), Wilford Brimley (William Devasher), Ed Harris (Wayne Tarrance), Holly Hunter (Tammy Hemphill), David Strathairn (Ray McDeere), Gary Busey (Eddie Lomax), Steven Hill (F. Denton Voyles), Tobin Bell (The Nordic Man).

A thriller about a honest lawyer who exposes the illegal yet lucrative practices of his firm. No, no, wait: it's sci-fi.

Bloopers
1. Abby is given a poster by her classroom: the poster has been rolled from the left side to the right, but as she removes the ribbon, the poster appears as if it has been rolled from right to left. (00:12)
2. Mitch and Abby drive to their new house in their old car, which has a dent in the middle of the hood. But it vanishes (second shot of the car) and it's back as they park at the house. The hood is once again okay when she leaves home for her last day at school, but it's dented again later on, when she stops along a road. (00:13, 01:39, 01:43)
3. When Wayne talks for the first time to Mitch in the diner, a Tabasco bottle keeps turning on the table: now you see its label, now you don't, now you do . . . (00:26)
4. Mitch is handed a bunch of photos by Devasher: the photos have a white border around them, but only in the wide shot: when Mitch passes them one by one, they do not have borders whatsoever. (01:17)
5. Avery goes to say good-bye to Abby while she's at school. He grabs the fence that separates them, and one of the wires is between Avery's index and middle finger (from the back), and between the middle and the ring fingers (from the front). (01:39)
6. Mitch enter Avery's office to print from his computer a summary of combined accounts. The noise we hear is of a dot-matrix printer, but when he gets the stack of paper, he does it from a laser printer. (02:02, 02:03)
7. When Mitch takes the ski car and is chased by the albino killer, a shot shows the blades of the camera chopper reflected in the windows of the car. (02:11)

Questions
1. Abby gets home in bright daylight and finds that dinner has been "fixed" by

Mitch. He shows her a bottle of wine, and his wristwatch reads, 10:10. So . . . do they dine very early in the morning or does he buy cheap watches? (00:06)

2. One of the first surprises Mitch and Abby find in the new home is a food basket and a champagne bottle in ice. The ice is in a glass container and isn't melted. How did anyone know the exact time Mitch and Abby would have reached their home? Quite curious, isn't it? (00:14)

3. Tammy, Ed Lomax's secretary, is underneath Ed's desk when two hitmen enter the office and shoot the detective. Later on, at the Front Deli, Tammy gives Mitch a perfect description of the duo, adding even where Ed shot them. But from where she was, she couldn't see anything. So . . . who is the mole? (00:55, 01:14)

4. Mitch and Abby say that they're going back to Boston. Still, they drive south of Memphis, along the Mississippi River. Which means they're going toward New Orleans. Are they taking the scenic route to Boston? (02:30, 02:31)

FIRST BLOOD (6)
1982, color, 96 min.

Director: Ted Kotcheff

Cast: Sylvester Stallone (John J. Rambo), Richard Crenna (Colonel Samuel Trautman), Brian Dennehy (Sheriff Will Teasle), Bill McKinney (Kern), Jack Starrett (Gait), Michael Talbott (Balford), Chris Mulkey (Ward), John McLiam (Orval), Alf Humphreys (Lester), David Caruso (Mitch).

Ex-Green Beret fights against a sheriff, his men, his town . . . and most of the time, he wins.

Bloopers

1. Sheriff Will drops Rambo just outside of town, and salutes him with a "Hope this ride helped you out!" As the sheriff drives away, a boom mike is visible reflected in the car's rear window. (00:07)

2. Fleeing from the police station, Rambo steals a Yamaha motorcycle with four phases. But the sound it makes is that of a two-phases engine. (00:17)

3. Rambo attacks Sheriff Will and places his knife under the poor sap's neck, on the left side. In the following close-up, the knife has moved to the right side of the Sheriff's neck. (00:41)

4. Rambo hijacks an army truck, but soon he's chased by a police car. As Rambo drives on the path in the forest, the headlights of the truck are on. They're off when the truck jumps onto the road, then they're on again when Rambo bumps into the police car,

they're off one more time, and finally they're on when Rambo pushes the police car against a parked car. (01:11, 01:12)

5. The army truck has a front bumper that says "WARNG" on the left side, and something like "C6" on the right side. The "C6" part is gone when the truck is on the road, bumping into the police car, but it's back when Rambo forces a roadblock and literally flies above a police car. (01:11, 01:13)

6. When Rambo blows up a gas station, two cars (one of which is red) explode, their rear ends jolting up into the air. A Kool Light poster is in the background. Less than five seconds later, the same two cars explode again, tilting up their rear ends one more time. (01:15)

FIRST WIVES CLUB, THE (6)
1996, color, 102 min.

Director: Hugh Wilson

Cast: Bette Midler (Brenda "Bren" Morelli Cushman), Goldie Hawn (Elise "Lisey" Eliot Atchison), Diane Keaton (Narrator / Annie MacDuggan Paradis), Maggie Smith (Gunilla Garson Goldberg), Sarah Jessica Parker (Shelly "Shell" Stewart), Dan Hedaya (Morton "Morty" Cushman), Stockard Channing (Cynthia Swann Griffin), Victor Garber (Bill Atchison), Stephen Collins (Aaron Paradis), Elizabeth Berkley (Phoebe "Phoeb" LaVelle), Marcia Gay Harden (Dr. Leslie Rosen), Bronson Pinchot (Duarto Feliz).

Three middle-aged ex-wives get their revenge.

Bloopers
1. The picture the four friends took in 1969 is different from the one Cynthia has in her

---

BLOOPERS TO TOW AWAY

Call AAA, quick!

Carole Bouquet's Citroën in *For Your Eyes Only*	Blooper No. 7
Two parked cars in *First Blood*	Blooper No. 6
Christopher Lloyd's wipers in *Clue*	Blooper No. 1
Tom Cruise's car in *Days of Thunder*	Question No. 1
Dylan McDermott's seat belt in *In the Line of Fire*	Blooper No. 4
Jennifer Cooke's car in *Friday the 13th Part VI: Jason Lives*	Question No. 2

album in the present day (it was taken from a different angle). (00:03)

2. Cynthia makes a toast to a neighbor, and passes her glass to her left hand. As she walks on the terrace, the glass has zapped back to her right hand again. (00:05)

3. Elise is sitting on a couch, her champagne glass almost empty. After Annie stands up, Elise reaches her: her glass is now almost full. (00:35)

4. Annie grabs a full glass of champagne, holds it in front of her and, in turn, herself, Elise and Brenda drop their wedding rings into it. The level of champagne has decreased noticeably. When they make a toast, though, the very same glass is almost filled to the brim again. (00:36, 00:37)

5. Annie, Brenda, and Elise sing "You Don't Own Me." Elise's shoes change from having two laces (inside the building) to one-lace (outside, on the street). (01:36, 01:38)

6. When the three singers put their coats on, Elise's hand gets caught in Annie's belt, but only from behind. In front, her hands are free. (01:38)

FOR YOUR EYES ONLY (23)
1981, color, 127 min.

Director: John Glen

Cast: Roger Moore (James Bond 007), Carole Bouquet (Melina Havelock), Topol (Milos Colombo), Lynn-Holly Johnson (Bibi Dahl), Julian Glover (Aristotle Kristatos), Cassandra Harris (Countess Lisl), Jill Bennett (Jacoba Brink), Michael Gothard (Emile Locque), John Wyman (Erich Kriegler), Jack Hedley (Havelock), Lois Maxwell (Moneypenny), Desmond Llewelyn (Q).

For his twelfth mission, Bond comes back to Earth for a very funny and exciting adventure.

Bloopers

1. The bald guy who controls the flying chopper turns his device on. On two monitors there are two images: one of the inside of the chopper, one—presumably—of what appears in front of it. The image we see on the screen is of the Tower Bridge, but as we cut to the chopper, it's flying by the House of Parliament and Big Ben. They are on the Thames, too, but a few miles away from the bridge. (00:02)

2. Just as he regains control of the chopper, Bond captures the man in the wheelchair: as the chopper takes off with the man trapped outside, Bond can be seen wearing earphones. He didn't have them before, and he won't later. (00:05)

3. When flying alongside the

chopper, the bald guy on the wheelchair clearly wears a skull cap to hide his hair: it's possible to see a lot of wrinkles on his neck. (00:06)

4. Gonzales shoots Melina's parents on the bridge of their boat. When Melina runs up to her dad, his shirt is clean—and in the following shot, it's stained with a lot of blood. (00:16)

Tula, Are You Really a? . . .

Among the Bond Girls who appear in Gonzales's villa, is white-bikinied model Tula, who subsequently revealed that she was born Barry Kenneth Cossey. (00:20)

---

5. Running away from Gonzales's villa, Bond uses a white umbrella as a parachute. One of the henchmen fires four times at Bond, but there are six holes in the umbrella. (00:22)

6. 007 flips Melina's Citroën down a hill, and when the car stops, the right front wheel is almost parallel to the ground. But Melina shifts the gear, and the car leaves in reverse—without any problem. (00:26)

7. During the car chase, the Citroën loses the glass on both headlights—there's a detail showing it. However, after Bond says, "I love a drive in the country, don't you?" there's a shot of the car with both lights crooked, but with the glass intact. (00:26, 00:27)

8. 007 meets with Luigi at Tofana ski resort in Cortina; you can see the whole crew reflected in Luigi's sunglasses. (00:35)

9. After the motorcycle incident, Bond places Melina on a coach and orders the driver to go to the station. Melina is upset, and she says, "It was my parents they killed, not yours. Let me out! Driver, stop!" Half of the line is shot with a beautiful landscape behind Melina (blue screen), part of it is shot in front of a building. (00:41)

10. After seeing Erich's performance, Locque enters his car: the crew and lights can be seen reflected in the car window. (00:46)

11. When the motorcycles chase Bond, who's on his skis, it's already possible to see tire tracks in the snow (more than one take, anyone?). (00:51)

12. Bond, skiing with only one pole, places it between two trees to stop one of the two bikes, and dashes away. Right after the first image of the bobsled, Bond can be seen skiing with one pole again. (00:53)

13. Bond is skiing into the bobsled track, while Erich is after him on a motorcycle. Just before Bond decides to jump

out of the track, Erich fires his motorcycle's machine guns—but the shot of Erich shows him on the ski track, not on the bobsled track. (00:54)

14. Once he crashes into a shack, Erich throws his gun at Bond, then he lifts the motorcycle and tosses it as well. But when Erich lifts the bike, both wheels are in place. When the bike lands by Bond, it's missing the front wheel—which will be tossed a couple of seconds later. (00:55)

15. During the attack of three hockey players, Bond manages to avoid one blade of their skates: the blade hits a board in the wall and breaks it. But as they keep going with the fight, the board seems to be okay. (00:57)

16. Playing chemin de fer with Bunky, 007 deals a five of diamonds and a queen of spades. But the croupier says that 007 has won the game with nine points. Huh? (01:00)

17. The first round of the game finds 007 dealing a five of diamonds and a queen of spades. In a second round, he deals cards again—and he deals himself a five of diamonds and a queen of spades. What are the odds? (01:00, 01:01)

18. At a restaurant with Kristatos, Bond orders prawns, salad, and Bourdetto, then he closes the menu and passes it to the waiter. But the menu is open again. (01:02)

19. Locque runs over the Countess Lisl while she's running on the beach. 007 approaches to check her pulse—and she blinks. (01:10)

20. 007 and Columbo reach Kristatos's warehouse at night. Locque blows the place up (still night), flees on his Mercedes uphill (at dawn), is reached by 007, and skids and gets stuck on the edge of the hill (bright day). (01:18, 01:19)

21. During the final part of his mountain climb, 007 stabs Apostis, one of Kristatos's henchmen. As Apostis falls, you can see the roof of the soundstage where part of the mountain was built to accomplish this stunt. (01:52)

22. Columbo and Kristatos fight for the possession of the A.T.A.C. computer. Kristatos runs up a flight of stairs outside the monastery. Columbo stops him, punches him, yells "You're not as fast as you used to be!" Kristatos falls to the ground and he's not by the stairs anymore, but in the following shot he's back. (02:01)

23. The detail of Bond's wristwatch in the end reveals a perfectly still watch and a wrist that actually moves. Can we all say, bad superimposition? (02:03)

Questions

1. When in San Martin, Spain, by Hector Gonzales's villa, Bond passes by several farmers harvesting olives. At Gonzales's villa, everyone is by the pool: ladies in bikinis, men in trunks. But olives are harvested in December or January. Are all of Gonzales's friends members of the Polar Bear Club? (00:18, 00:20)

2. Bond enters his hotel room just in time to hear the shower being turned off. A couple of seconds later, Bibi steps out of the bathroom, a towel around her body, and she slips under the sheets in Bond's bed. However, she's perfectly dry. What kind of shower did she take? (00:43)

Fun Fact

At the end of the car chase, one of the chasing cars ends up on an olive tree. The harvesters are surprised and make several comments about it. They are in Spain. The comments are in Italian (perhaps loop audio from the incident in Cortina . . . ?). (00:28)

FRANKENSTEIN (12)

1931, black & white, 70 min.

Director: James Whale

Cast: Colin Clive (Dr. Henry Frankenstein), Mae Clarke (Elizabeth), John Boles (Victor Moritz), Boris Karloff (The Monster), Edward Van Sloan (Doctor Waldman), Frederick Kerr (Baron Frankenstein), Dwight Frye (Fritz), Lionel Belmore (The Burgomaster), Marilyn Harris (Little Maria), Francis Ford (Hans, the Wounded Villager).

Mary Shelley's modern Prometheus story is first brought to the screen (with sound, that is).

Bloopers

1. At the end of the lesson at the Goldstalt Medical College, two lab assistants cover a corpse's feet with a white cloth, then—in the following shot—they cover them again. (00:06)

2. During that same lesson, there are two jars with typewritten labels ("*Cerebrum—Normal Brain*" and "*Disfunctio Cerebri—*Abnormal"). But when Fritz approaches the containers to steal the brain, the labels are handwritten. (00:07, 00:08, 00:09)

3. During Fritz's theft, a lab skeleton moves up and down on the spring of its hook. But in the wide shot of the lab, the skeleton is barely moving. But when Fritz realizes he's dropped the brain, the skeleton is going up and down again. (00:08, 00:09)

4. Just before Victor enters Elizabeth's room, there's the detail of a picture of Henry Frankenstein at the same

height as a lit candle. But when Victor and Elizabeth walk by the table where the picture stands, now the candle appears to be much higher than the picture. (00:09)

5. When Baron Frankenstein asks Victor and Elizabeth what's wrong with Henry, the baron is holding his pipe by the stem in the close-up, and by the bowl in the wide shot. At the same time, his handkerchief keeps popping in and out his jacket pocket. (00:25)

6. After the experiment with the light, the Monster sits down, waving his hands as if asking for more. In the following matching shot he's still as a statue. (00:33)

7. When Fritz torments the Monster with his torch, the Monster jumps to attack him and a chair flips sideways—but in the following shot it has rotated 90 degrees without anybody touching it. (00:33)

8. When the sedative kicks in, the Monster collapses to the ground, onto his back. As Henry opens the door, the Monster is lying facedown. (00:37, 00:38)

9. Elizabeth visits Henry who, exhausted, falls flat onto the floor, on his face. But when his father reaches him, Henry is lying on his back. (00:40)

10. Little Maria sees the Monster while she's holding a few flowers and her little cat. As she stands up, the cat is no

longer in her arms: it's on the ground, and flees (by the way, doesn't it look like she was about to drop her flowers instead?). (00:48)

11. Looking for the Monster, Henry finds one of the villagers, Hans, beaten up. Henry kneels down holding his torch with his right hand, but as he stands up, the torch has moved to his left hand. (01:01)

12. The Monster knocks Henry out cold, causing some blood to drip from the left side of his mouth. Once in the windmill, the blood has become a pale stain on the side of Henry's mouth, but when he's playing cat and mouse with the Monster around the windmill's gears, the blood is fresh once again. And when Henry tries to jump off of the handrail, his mouth is as clean as a whistle. (01:03, 01:04, 01:05)

Fun Fact

After receiving an injection by Doctor Waldman, the Monster fights with Doctor Frankenstein: look at its head (makeup), it begins to smoke when hit by the torch. (00:37)

FREDDY GOT FINGERED (9)
2001, color, 87 min.

Director: Tom Green

Cast: Tom Green (Gord Brody), Rip Torn (Jim Brody), Marisa

Coughlan (Betty), Eddie Kaye Thomas (Freddy Brody), Harland Williams (Darren), Anthony Michael Hall (Mr. David Davidson), Julie Hagerty (Julie Brody), Jackson Davies (Mr. Malloy), Connor Widdows (Andy Malloy), John R. Taylor (Farmer #1), Robert Osborne (Farmer #2), Fiona Hogan (Pregnant Woman).

Beyond indescribable.

Bloopers

1. In front of his new Le Baron, Gord says his parents love him more than his brother, and Freddy says, "No, no, no," raising his right hand. But in the close-up he's raising his left, and in the next shot his right one again. (00:05)
2. Gord shows his drawings to Mr. Davidson, who holds the portfolio with his left hand in the detail, but with his right in the shot after the "bag of eyes" drawing. (00:14)
3. From his car, Mr. Davidson tosses the portfolio back to Gord: a few pages fall to the ground. Gord never picks them up, yet when Mr. Davidson leaves, there's no sign of any paper on the ground. (00:15)
4. Gord completes his skateboard halfpipe in front of his house. After his date with Betty, a shot of the house reveals the halfpipe, half hidden by two parked cars, and still unfinished. (00:19, 00:32)
5. Betty flips a small creamer onto the counter at the hospital, making it always land right side up. Yet as Gord walks in looking for his friend, the creamer, which just landed correctly, now appears upside down. (00:21)
6. When Jim gets home, he parks his yellow truck and marches to the door: the camera crew can be seen reflected in the side of the van. (00:35)
7. During his romantic dinner with Betty, Gord's drink keeps moving from his left (if he's in the shot) to in front of Betty's glass (if she's in the shot). (00:40)
8. While fighting with his dad, Gord grabs a violin and jumps onto the bar, kicking away a glass with a slice of lime in it. The glass comes back in the following shot, then it's gone again, then it's back again . . . (00:44)
9. In Pakistan, for reasons we'll choose not to discuss here, Gord crouches down while his dad's house falls on top of him. As the house lands, the front door bursts open. Yet as Gord emerges from the house, he reopens the very same door. (01:16)

FRIDAY THE 13TH PART V: A NEW BEGINNING (10)
1985, color, 92 min.

Director: Danny Steinmann

"MISS MATCH, YOU SAID?"

. . . I think I've seen you.

A half-pipe in *Freddy Got Fingered*	Blooper No. 4
Greg Kinnear's beer bottle in *The Gift*	Blooper No. 4
A truck light in *Hard Rain*	Blooper No. 1
Britt Ekland in *The Man With the Golden Gun*	Blooper No. 16
Jim Carrey's gun in *Me, Myself and Irene*	Blooper No. 2

Cast: John Shepherd (Tommy Jarvis), Melanie Kinnaman (Pam), Shavar Ross (Reggie), Vernon Washington (George), Richard Young (Matt Peters), Tiffany Helm (Violet), Juliette Cummins (Robin), Jerry Pavlon (Jake), Debisue Voorhees (Tina), John Robert Dixon (Eddie), Marco St. John (Sheriff Cal Tucker), Carol Locatell (Ethel Hubbard).

. . . and on, and on (but this was a low point) and on, and on . . .

Bloopers

1. Tommy places the alien mask he wore to scare Reggie on his bed: the mask slides along the wall and remains askew. But when Tommy takes out a second mask, the alien one is lying flat on the bed, away from the wall. (00:13)

2. The amount of chocolate on the left side of Joey's mouth gets smaller as he walks from the porch to Rob and Violet. (00:18)

3. The boom mike gets reflected in the bottom part of the rear-side window of the ambulance as it comes to a stop at Pinehurst. (00:21)

4. When Eddie gets killed, the killer's hands turn a branch behind a tree; the detail shows the killer's left hand pushing up from below, but Eddie's shot reveals the right hand of the killer pushing up, exactly where the left hand should have been. (00:46)

5. Demon braces himself the first time the potty he's in shakes. The amount of toilet paper off the roll changes, depending on if the shot is from the front or from the side. (00:53)

6. The amount of stew Ethel is cooking in a pot changes if the shot is from the side or from the front; also, when her face falls into it, the level has increased almost to the brim. (00:57, 00:59)

7. The killer whacks Ethel in the middle of the head with a meat cleaver; a small waterfall of blood appears, but when the cleaver is retracted, it appears to be spotless. (00:58)

8. Reggie discovers three bodies in one room: Violet's body is leaning against the wall in the long shot, and lying down in the detail—then against the wall again. (01:08, 01:09)

9. Pam and Reggie run in the forest, away from Jason. Pam has a salmon pink sweater that she apparently loses before they reach the ambulance, but then she has it back. And again, as she and Reggie separate when running away from the vehicle, her sweater seems to vanish and come back during her sprint. (01:10, 01:11)

10. After walking in the rain back and forth through the woods and at the camp, the soles of Jason's shoes seem quite clean when he goes up the ladder in the barn. (01:20)

FRIDAY THE 13TH PART VI: JASON LIVES (13)
1986, color, 86 min.

Director: Tom McLoughlin

Cast: Thom Mathews (Tommy Jarvis), Jennifer Cooke (Megan Garris), David Kagen (Sheriff Garris), Kerry Noonan (Paula), Renée Jones (Sissy Baker), Tom Fridley (Cort), C.J. Graham (Jason Voorhees), Darcy DeMoss (Nikki), Vincent Guastaferro (Deputy Rick Cologne), Tony Goldwyn (Darren), Nancy McLoughlin (Lizabeth), Ron Palillo (Allen Hawes), Michael Swan (Officer Pappas), Courtney Vickery (Nancy).

. . . and on, and on, and on . . .

Bloopers

1. Jason's body appears to be covered with a multitude of maggots, worms, and other creepy crawlers when Tommy opens the coffin. Yet, when a bolt of lightning hits the metal pole driven through his chest, Jason's face appears to be bug-free. Yet when he opens his eye, the maggots are back again. (00:04, 00:06)

2. Still lying down in the coffin, Jason opens one eye: from his eyebrow, one maggot falls down . . . horizontally. Shouldn't it be falling right into the eye? (00:06)

3. After Tommy has pulled the rod out of Jason, he removes his right glove. In the next shot, he removes it again. (00:07)

4. Tommy runs away from the graveyard and jumps into his truck: the engine revs before he has any time to so much as put the key in the ignition. (00:08)

5. Jason jumps in a puddle of water, his feet on either side of Lizabeth's head. But as she "sinks," it appears as if Jason has taken one step to his right—which he hasn't—because now his feet are together. (00:15)

6. As the kids enter the police station, Cort jumps onto a cabinet: his earphones are around his neck. But after a remark by Sheriff Garris, Cort removes the earphones from his ears. (00:15)

7. Cort's sunglasses are hanging by his shirt's collar; the lenses are to his right, but when Megan gets close to Tommy's cell ("Jason is out there, he's looking for me."), Cort is in the background and his glasses have rotated 180°; and when Sissy asks if Tommy is talking about "the" Jason, the glasses have rotated back. (00:15, 00:16)

8. Once at Camp Forest Green, Cort and Paula grab a box of provisions and walk to the kitchen; but their reflections on the side of the Jeep shows them simply walking off camera, placing the box down, and waiting for the other actors to end the scene. (00:18)

9. Two prisoners and a commando walk into the forest, complaining that "the game's not over till it's over." A branch to the left of the screen vibrates as if hit by something—like a steadicam walking backwards. (00:23)

10. When Cort is having fun with Nikki in the motor home, his tank top rolls itself up above his nipples in his close-up, but then appears all the way down in every other shot. (00:35)

11. Leaving the rest area, Cort fires up the engine of the motor home: he is flooded by the interior light, and so is Nikki. But when they drive on the road, as well as when the vehicle flips, the light seems to be off. (00:38, 00:39, 00:40)

12. While driving, Cort turns the radio on and Alice Cooper's "Teenage Frankenstein" blares out of the speakers. However, Cort spins the knob twice when he turns the radio on, yet the volume doesn't change at all. (00:39)

13. Little Nancy brings Jason's bloody machete to Paula, who's asleep. The machete is almost horizontal, but when Paula asks Nancy where she found it, Nancy is holding it almost vertical. (00:52)

Questions

1. Jason's eyes look greenish brown the first time we see them in the coffin; yet, underwater, when he's hit by the boat propeller, he seems to have grayish pupils. And they are back to greenish brown when he shows us that he ain't so dead after all.

So, what's his actual eye color, or has he jumped onto the tinted contacts bandwagon? (00:06, 01:21, 01:23)

2. Megan's car doesn't have a front license plate. When she and Tommy stop at the roadblock, she flees the scene, going in reverse. Officer Pappas chases her, and calls Sheriff Garris via radio, giving him the plate number. Does he have ESP, since up until that moment he has only seen the front of the car? (00:48, 00:50)

3. The chase after Megan's car happens at night, however, it seems that one shot (after Megan has straightened up the car) was taken at dawn. And, after that, it's pitch black again. What happened? (00:49, 00:51)

FRIDAY THE 13TH PART VII: THE NEW BLOOD (11)
1988, color, 90 min.

Director: John Carl Buechler

Cast: Lar Park-Lincoln (Tina Shepard), Kevin Spirtas (Nick), Susan Blu (Mrs. Shepard), Terry Kiser (Dr. Crews), Susan Jennifer Sullivan (Melissa), Elizabeth Kaitan (Robin), Jon Renfield (David), Jeff Bennett (Eddie), Heidi Kozak (Sandra), Diana Barrows (Maddy), Larry Cox (Russel), Kane Hodder (Jason Voorhees).

... and on, and on, and on ...

Bloopers

1. When Tina goes to open the door to Nick, we see that the fridge's door has magnets, a pocket-organizer, a cloth, etc. Yet later on, when Tina's mom is in the kitchen, she closes a fridge door that now has only one solitary magnet. Is Jason also a magnet collector? (00:17, 00:31)

2. Eddie asks Tina if she thinks that "Starlicon" could be a good title for one of his works. He takes his notes, but you can't see them—however, in the over-the-shoulder, he's holding them up quite visibly. (00:21)

3. The tent where Dan and Judy are planning to spend the night is large, squarish, and orange. When Jason approaches it, it has become a paler orange, and mostly round. But when he rips it to get in, the tent is back to its original shape. (00:25, 00:27)

4. Robin tells Maddy that she's gonna stick to the deal of having a good time, then she opens her arms. In the following, matching shot, she opens them again. (00:33)

5. Tina runs away, taking her mom's car: the front light to the right is not working. But when she swerves to avoid the vision of Jason on the road, the light is working fine. (00:44, 00:45)

6. After a few moments of terror, Maddy believes Jason has left the shack she's hiding in. She bends over quickly to pick up her shoes, then...she does it again. (00:49)

7. Ben and Kate are making out in the van. Their blue blanket becomes a beige blanket when Kate lurches up to a sitting position. (00:50, 00:51)

8. When David refers to himself as a Neanderthal, his right hand is caressing Robin's breast. But in the following, matching shot, the hand is gone. (00:55)

9. Looking for Maddy, Robin walks to knock on a door. Just before she reaches the door, a shadow on the wall moves out of the way. Who is that guy? Jason working overtime? (01:01)

10. Robin is thrown backwards by Jason through a window, but she exits the window face first. (01:04)

11. The hole Tina creates underneath Jason changes size and shape before Jason falls through it. (01:19)

Questions

1. Tina's mom, Amanda, gets out of the car and walks to the house by the lake while Dr. Crews carries a large briefcase. She has only a bag. As they enter the house, she is carrying her bag *and* the large briefcase, while Dr. Crews has another briefcase, a small bag, and a tripod. Quick in picking it up (since it was all lined up on the house porch near him), ain't he? (00:08)

2. After the lake begins to bubble, in the shot from water level, is that a cloth that's covering what's underneath the dock? (01:23)

The Miraculous Underwater Slasher Makeover

In *Part VII*, Jason's wardrobe is in bad shape: there are holes everywhere, and you can see Jason's spinal cord. (00:15) Yet in *Part VIII*, Jason's wardrobe is in much better shape: at least his overalls have been fixed and you can't see his spine anymore. (00:09, 00:30) And all of this mending was done while he was chained underwater?

FRIDAY THE 13TH PART VIII: JASON TAKES MANHATTAN (11)
  1989, color, 100 min.

Director: Rob Hedden

Cast: Jensen Daggett (Rennie), Scott Reeves (Sean Robertson), Barbara Bingham (Colleen Van Deusen), Peter Mark Richman (Charles McCulloch), Vincent Craig Dupree (Julius), Martin Cummins (Wayne), Saffron Henderson (J.J.), Sharlene Martin (Tamra Mason), Kelly Hu (Eva Watanabe), Gordon Currie (Miles Wolfe), Todd Shaffer (Jim Miller), Kane Hodder (Jason Voorhees).

. . . and on, and on, and on . . .

Bloopers

1. On Jim's boat, by the radio, is a boat in a bottle. The cork of the bottle is to the left. When Jim gets up to check the noise Suzy heard, the bottle has turned 180° and now points to the right. (00:03, 00:07, 00:09)

2. Jason emerges from Crystal Lake and grabs the handrail of Jim's boat. For a rotten corpse, Jason's pinkie and thumb—peeking out of his left glove—look quite pink and human. (00:07, 00:11)

3. During their trip on the *Lazarus*, Sean stuffs his hand into his jacket pocket to grab a present for Rennie. He never hands it to her, yet in the following shot she's holding it already. (00:17)

4. Wayne is videotaping J.J. while she's playing her guitar. In the over-the-shoulder shot he's holding his left hand by the focus of his camera, but from the front he isn't. (00:19)

5. In the power room, Jason slowly walks down a flight of stairs to reach J.J. The first shot ends with Jason putting down his left foot—but in the matching shot, he's putting down his right. (00:21)

6. The extra-fast Jason smashes J.J. right in the face with her own guitar. But the blood splatters *before* the guitar actually hits her. (00:22)

7. Performing the old hot-rock-through-the-stomach gag, Jason kills a kid in the sauna. But Jason only *seems* to have run a rock through the kid's stomach, for when he leaves, the kid's blood is on his chest. (00:29, 00:30)

8. Rennie is pushed overboard by Tamra while the *Lazarus* is cruising. Nobody yells "woman overboard!" yet Rennie always maintains the same position by the ship—kinda as though the ship was solidly anchored when they did this stunt. (00:30)

9. Once in New York, Rennie, Colleen Van Deusen, Charles McCulloch, and Sean Robertson all climb into the backseat of a police car. Rennie manages to jump into the front seat, and subsequently the car crashes against a wall. At that point, Sean gets out of the car from the passenger door. How did he manage to do that, since he was still in the backseat when the car hit? (01:14, 01:15)

10. After fleeing from the subway, Sean and Rennie walk in Times Square. Sean comments, "It's over," while they're walking on the grates to the subway and then on the following sidewalk. But when Jason looks at them from the subway exit, Sean and Rennie have moved back, and are still walking by the grates. (01:26)

11. Just before seeing young

Jason in the sewer, Ronnie's position on the ladder keeps changing—from very close to Sean, to a few steps lower, then close again. (01:34)

Questions
1. Four punk kids are loitering in Times Square. When two days later Jason chases Rennie and Sean, he walks by the same group of punk kinds. Fine. They are in the same place they were originally. Fine. But with the exact same clothes? (00:00, 01:26)
2. As J.J. spots Jason, she panics and drops her guitar to run away. But is she so conscious about the energy crunch that she manages to turn off the tape player? (00:22)
3. When Jason shoves Tamra against the mirror, doesn't her hair look darker? (00:38)

FRIDAY THE 13TH PART IX: JASON GOES TO HELL
see **JASON GOES TO HELL—THE FINAL FRIDAY**

FROM DUSK TILL DAWN (3)
1996, color, 108 min.

Director: Robert Rodriguez

Cast: Harvey Keitel (Jacob Fuller), George Clooney (Seth Gecko), Quentin Tarantino (Richard Gecko), Juliette Lewis (Kate Fuller), Ernest Liu (Scott Fuller), Salma Hayek (Santanico Pandemonium), Cheech Marin (Border Guard / Chet Pussy / Carlos), Danny Trejo (Razor Charlie), Tom Savini (Sex Machine), Fred Williamson (Frost), Michael Parks (Texas Ranger Earl McGraw), John Hawkes (Pete Bottoms).

It's Outlaws vs. Vampires in an all-night cage match.

Bloopers
1. While talking with the Texas Ranger, Pete the gas station clerk is reading a magazine. When the Ranger asks Pete for a bottle of Jack, Pete's magazine pages turn without anyone touching them. (00:01)
2. While they leave the exploding gas station, Richard and Seth are arguing. Rubble falls all over the road—which appears clean as the two criminals fishtail away in their car. (00:09)
3. In the hotel, while Seth is talking to him, Richie eats a burger—or drinks a beer, depending on the camera angle. (00:22)

FUGITIVE, THE (22)
1993, color, 127 min.

Director: Andrew Davis

Cast: Harrison Ford (Dr. Richard David Kimble), Tommy Lee Jones (Deputy U.S. Marshal Samuel Gerard), Sela Ward

(Helen Kimble), Julianne Moore (Dr. Anne Eastman), Joe Pantoliano (Cosmo Renfro), Andreas Katsulas (Frederick Sykes), Jeroen Krabbé (Dr. Charles Nichols), Daniel Roebuck (Robert Biggs), L. Scott Caldwell (Poole), Tom Wood (Noah Newman), Ron Dean (Detective Kelly), Joseph F. Kosala (Detective Rosetti), Richard Riehle (Old Guard), Eddie Bo Smith, Jr. (Copeland), Peter J. Caria IV (Billy).

Doctor is wrongfully accused, and not because he screwed up in the operating room.

Bloopers

1. To go on the bus to Menard, Dr. Kimble is belted and handcuffed. After one of the guards says, "Copeland, you be nice now!" Kimble lifts his arms, which for some reason aren't handcuffed anymore, and another guard places the belt around his waist one more time. (00:13)
2. During the accident, the bus rolls downhill, and Kimble slams against one side, his hands loose and free. But when the bus stops, he asks a guard to uncuff him, and he shows that the chains are still around his wrists. (00:16)
3. The bus ends its journey against a large tree, and rests parallel to the hill. Needless to say, there's not a railroad track in sight—even

if later on the bus is shown to be lying precisely on top of one). (00:16, 00:17)
4. While the survivors scramble off the bus, Copeland's right leg is against the bus window through which Kimble sees the approaching train. A few moments later, both feet are by the window, then they change positions. Finally, as Kimble works his way out, the feet are neatly placed by the window. (00:16, 00:17)
5. After the train wreck, when Kimble looks up from his hideaway, it's possible to see the head of a man wearing a hat looking down toward the camera. [NOTE: This blooper was "doctored" and erased for the Special Edition DVD (2001)—it would have been at the beginning of Chapter 7.] (00:18)
6. Illinois police badges are six-point stars, not seven as seen on the officers at the train-wreck site. (00:21)
7. Kimble calls his friend Walter on the phone, while a bell rings five times before, and once while Kimble says, "Walter, this is Richard." Played back, the tape of this conversation has six dings after "Walter, this is Richard." (00:50, 00:51)
8. While listing towns with an elevated train, Cosmo says that "Milwaukee has got an El." Well, in fact, no. (00:52)
9. As he walks out of the tennis club, Dr. Nichols gets his

BMW. The driver's window is halfway rolled down, but as he sits down, the window is completely down (he hands a tip to Billy, the valet). Yet, when Nichols drives away, the window is once again halfway rolled down. (00:53)

10. Kimble steals the ID of a maintenance engineer, and takes his pictures wearing a green uniform that he won't buy until the following scene. (00:59, 01:00)

11. In the ER, a black, male nurse in red scrubs says, "I need a doctor, over here!" The boom mike can be seen reflected in the cabinet behind him. (01:07)

12. The male nurse on roller skates passes by Kimble when he pushes the kid on the stretcher. But as Dr. Eastman sees Kimble checking the boy's X-ray, the roller-skating nurse is once again in the background—but coming from where he was coming from right before. (01:09)

A "Man's Actor"

When Dr. Eastman confronts Kimble, he limps, like when he walks away from the stairs in the Federal Prison Cook County Jail. (01:11, 01:20) Apparently, Harrison hurt himself in the stairs scene, yet insisted on not halting production.

---

13. When he runs out of the Cook County Prison, Kimble passes by a couple of pedestrians: the woman has a fuchsia scarf around her head; as he's running to the Picasso statue, she's in front of him. But when Sam Gerard causes a flock of pigeons to take off, the fuchsia-headed lady is in the background, walking away from him. (01:21, 01:22)

14. Chasing Kimble in the St. Patrick's parade, Sam Gerard looks behind a barricade in front of a Florsheim Shoe store. Kimble is ahead of him and in front of a Citibank (which is on the corner of the next block), but when Kimble loses his coat, he is in front of Florsheim's. (01:22, 01:23)

15. As the parade marches on, the Citibank clock reads 1:03 (a bagpipe player is in the shot), definitely a different time (but too hard to tell exactly what) when Gerard walks by, and then 1:01 when Kimble loses his coat. (01:22, 01:23)

16. When Kimble calls Sykes, the address on the printout reads (freeze-frame), "247 Shenstone Drive, Chicago, IL." But when Cosmo says that they've got the address Kimble is calling from (which is Sykes's apartment), he says that it's "256 South St. Lawrence." So why does the door close to Sykes's build-

ing read "11219"? (01:25, 01:30, 01:31)

17. In the *Chicago Sun-Times,* an article reads, "Master of Ceremonies Ed O'Flannery said he did not recall a more lively parade . . ." When Deputy Biggs reads the article aloud, he says, "Parade Master of Ceremonies Ed O'Flannery said he did not recall one more lively parade . . ." (01:29)

18. In Sykes's apartment, Kimble picks up a prescription and a picture, the picture on top. When he stands up, the picture appears under the prescription. (01:30, 01:31)

19. Kimble goes to visit Dr. Kathy Wahlund in her lab, and the two hug. She places both arms on his back—but in the over-the-shoulder shot, her left arm is on his shoulders. (01:41)

20. Kimble handcuffs Sykes to one of the subway poles, then grabs his coat with both hands. But when he says, "You missed your stop," one of Kimble's hands is on the handrail next to his head. In the following shot, Kimble is holding Sykes by the hair with his right hand. (01:48)

21. Sam steers violently to go to the Hilton Tower Hall. However, he spins the wheel to the right, and the car veers left. (01:50)

22. At the Hilton, Kimble enters an elevator and pushes button 24—yet button 25 lights up. (01:51)

GET CARTER (5)
1971, color, 111 min.

Director: Mike Hodges

Cast: Michael Caine (Jack Carter), Ian Hendry (Eric Paice), Britt Ekland (Anna Fletcher), John Osborne (Cyril Kinnear), Tony Beckley (Peter), George Sewell (Con McCarty), Geraldine Moffat (Glenda), Dorothy White (Margaret), Rosemarie Dunham (Edna), Petra Markham (Doreen), Alun Armstrong (Keith), Bryan Mosley (Cliff Brumby).

Bad guy fights bad guys to find out who killed his bad brother.

Bloopers
1. Carter walks into a pub at 9:35 and orders a pint of beer; 15 seconds later, the phone rings: it's for Carter, who walks to the counter. Now the clock reads 9:40. (00:07)
2. After he slaps Margaret, Carter walks away: you can see the shadow of the camera on the bridge pillars to Carter's right. (01:03)
3. As Carter leaves Mr. Brumby's future restaurant building, the shadow is diagonal to the wall he's walking by; but as Glenda stops her car and (cut) he jumps on, the shadow is exactly perpendicular to the same wall. (01:09)
4. After seeing the exhaust pipe of Glenda's white Sunbeam, camera pans up to a building: it's possible to see a reflection of a crew member in the rear bumper of the car. (01:10)
5. After Brumby dies, landing on a parked car, his tie zaps from being on his chest, onto his head side, leaning down the car, and back onto the chest but all crumpled. (01:30)

GET CARTER (7)
2000, color, 102 min.

Director: Stephen T. Kay

Cast: Sylvester Stallone (Jack Carter), Miranda Richardson

(Gloria Carter), Rachael Leigh Cook (Doreen Carter), Rhona Mitra (Geraldine), Johnny Strong (Eddie), John C. McGinley (Con McCarty), Alan Cumming (Jeremy Kinnear), Michael Caine (Cliff Brumby), John Cassini (Thorpey), Mickey Rourke (Cyrus Paice), Mark Boone Junior (Jim Davis), Garwin Sanford (Les Fletcher).

Pretty much the same as before.

Bloopers
1. Carter stops and shushes Mr. Davis by raising his left hand, but in the following cut he lowers the right one. (00:01)
2. During a call between Carter and Connie, who's in Vegas, two men behind him walk in the same direction and pass him by. After returning to Carter, we go back to Connie: the two man have moved farther back and approach again. (00:14)
3. Sneaking underneath the "crime scene" tapes, Carter enters Doralee's house, which is deserted. If you don't count the arm of a man who moves in the backyard, which can be seen through the window when Carter walks to a desk (bottom-left corner of the window). (01:03)
4. After Eddie's "suicide," Carter gets into his car under a massive downpour; but the chase that follows happens in drier weather (there's even a whole tai chi class practicing outside). (01:18)
5. During the chase, Carter fishtails his car in a larger avenue (when a men with a yellow slick darts away so as not to be run over); only during the fishtailing does Carter's car have the windshield wipers on. (01:19)
6. Carter's front-left headlight gets damaged and is off; but during a 180-degree spin, both lights are on and seem fine; when Carter plays chicken with Connie's car, the light is off but seems undamaged; and finally, both lights work fine when Carter reaches the party. (01:20, 01:21)
7. After being pushed through a glass door by Cyrus, Carter stands up: it's possible to see a protective pad underneath his shirt. (01:25)

Question
Carter hangs up his cell phone while talking to Connie. Connie receives a dial tone. Since when do cell phones give a dial tone? (00:15)

GIFT, THE (12)
2000, color, 111 min.

Director: Sam Raimi

Cast: Cate Blanchett (Annie Wilson), Giovanni Ribisi (Buddy Cole), Keanu Reeves (Donnie Barksdale), Katie Holmes (Jessica King), Greg

WATCH YOUR WATCH

Bloopers fly when you're having fun.

Anthony Hopkins in *The Edge*	Blooper No. 2
Cate Blanchett in *The Gift*	Blooper No. 2
A kid in *Glory*	Blooper No. 5
Jason Gedrick in *Iron Eagle*	Blooper No. 3
Cheech Marin in *Spy Kids*	Question No. 2

Kinnear (Wayne Collins), Hilary Swank (Valerie Barksdale), Gary Cole (David Duncan), Rosemary Harris (Annie's Granny), Michael Jeter (Harold Weems), Kim Dickens (Linda), J.K. Simmons (Sheriff Johnson), Chelcie Ross (Kenneth King), Erik Cord (Buddy's Father), Lynnsee Provence (Mike Wilson).

Bayou psychic gets caught up in some good ol' crimes of passion.

Bloopers

1. Annie makes Valerie take off her glasses to reveal one heck of a gigantic black eye. The same day, Mike gets in a fight at school, and also gets a black eye. Donnie comes one night to warn Annie to leave his wife alone, and we see that Mike's eye is indeed black, albeit not as bad as Valerie's was. So it's either the same night, or one of the next few nights. On what seems to be the next day, Mike is painting the wall—

and his eye is no longer black. Valerie comes in and says, "Sorry about the other night," and her eye is also no longer black. SOOOO... it seems that both Valerie and Mike have very rapidly healing eyes. If you happen to be from the camp that says "the other night" can mean "weeks ago" then we'll parry with this: in court, Donnie's attorney mentions that Annie's run-in with Donnie was "just a few weeks ago." From finding the body to the start of the trial would have to be at least a couple weeks just by itself, and a black eye like Valerie's would take at least a couple of weeks to heal. 'Nuff said. (00:06, 00:19, 01:09)

2. During this post-trial reading for Valerie, Annie's watch is on the table to her left as she's examining the cards. After Valerie asks, "Are you seein' sumpin' bad?" Annie clears the cards... with her watch suddenly back on her left wrist. (00:16, 00:18)

3. Kenneth comes up to Annie,

Linda, Wayne, and Jessica at the country club; Jessica's right dress strap is on her shoulder. Her dad asks her to dance, and the strap is suddenly off her shoulder. But it's back in the next shot when she kisses him. (00:24)

4. Annie and Wayne talk outside the country club while leaning on a fence. Wayne rests his arm on the fence, and his bottle of Dos Equis beer jumps from one side of his arm to the other a few times during the scene. Most notably after Annie says, "So many thoughts, I couldn't count 'em," and also right when Jessica arrives. (00:26, 00:27, 00:28)

5. Outside of church, Linda tells Annie about Jessica's disappearance. Annie is carrying her sweater, then puts it on when Linda says, "... her bed hadn't even been slept in." As she starts to get into her car, Annie's holding the sweater, not wearing it. Then when she's in the car, she's wearing it again. (00:37, 00:38)

6. Annie is about to start dealing cards for Kenneth King's reading, when she removes her wristwatch and places it to her left on the table with the watch face up. As she shuffles the cards, the watch face is now on its side. After Kenneth tells the sheriff to shut up, the watch is facing up again. As she starts to lay down the cards, it's back on

its side, and much better lit. As she starts to describe what she sees, the watch has jumped back onto her wrist. Then when she says, "... and some pillars," it's back on the table—face up. (00:43, 00:44, 00:45)

7. Buddy pours gasoline all over the upper part of his father's body. But when his father is lit on fire, for some reason only his legs are burning. (01:03, 01:04)

8. Weems cross-examines Annie, and places a dollar bill on the witness stand. When he says, "A distinction worthy of a lawyer," the bill has moved closer to Annie. When Weems says, "I mean if I had psychic powers..." it's back in its original position. (01:07, 01:08)

9. Annie reads for Valerie after the trial ends; from behind her, we can see that the bottom card on the deck is the "wavy lines" card. But from the front, the bottom card has become a "star." (01:16, 01:17)

10. Right after Annie says to Prosecutor David Duncan, "I know you had an affair with Jessica," we catch a glimpse of a crew member moving in the reflection of the first upper window pane to the right. (01:27)

11. The killer hits Annie in the head with a flashlight, and she falls to the ground. A river of blood trickles down the right side of her face. In

all subsequent shots, the blood is gone. (01:38)

12. After the sheriff tells her that Buddy hanged himself, she goes home. When she opens the door to check on her kids, she's wearing a blue horizontally striped shirt or dress under a white sweater. When she walks to her kid's bed, it has changed into a floral dress. (01:45)

Non-Blooper

Many think that when Donnie arrives to give Annie his warning, he has no baseball cap—and then later it suddenly appears on his head when he shows Annie the voodoo doll. You can actually see him take it off in the window's reflection while he's still outside, after Annie says, "Can I help you?" and then he's holding it in his left hand until he decides to be rude and put it back on while he's still in the house. (00:16, 00:17)

Question

Donnie comes to Annie's house twice in his truck (to warn Annie to stay away from his wife, and to fetch his wife later on). We don't hear his truck either time, but both times that he leaves, the truck's engine roars like a chopper without a muffler. Is he coasting into Annie's front yard with the engine off, or does he use some sort of advanced stealth technology for surprise entrances? (00:15, 00:18, 00:20)

GLORY (8)

1989, color, 122 min.

Director: Edward Zwick

Cast: Matthew Broderick (Colonel Robert Gould Shaw), Denzel Washington (Trip), Cary Elwes (Major Cabot Forbes), Morgan Freeman (Sergeant Major John Rawlins), Jihmi Kennedy (Jupiter Sharts), André Braugher (Thomas Searles), John Finn (Sergeant Major Mulcahy), Donovan Leitch (Charles Fessenden Morse), John David Cullum (Henry Sturgis Russell), Alan North (Governor John Albion Andrew), Bob Gunton (General Harker), Cliff De Young (Colonel James M. Montgomery).

A tale of the first black, fighting regiment in the American Civil War.

Bloopers

1. In the opening montage of Shaw's early days as a Union soldier, the rank insignia on his epaulets goes from captain (two horizontal bars inside the epaulets) to second lieutenant (no bars)—a demotion—and then back to captain. (00:01, 00:02, 00:03)

2. Shaw is passed out unconscious after the movie's first battle. He is awakened by the future Sergeant Rawlins, and he can hardly see him because the sun's behind Rawlins's head. On the cut back to Shaw, the shadows

indicate that the sun is now clearly coming from behind Shaw instead. (00:06, 00:07)

3. Rawlins reads the serial numbers of the Enfield rifles as he takes them out of the crate. Enfield rifles didn't have serial numbers. (00:30)

4. After the black soldiers protest their reduced pay, Shaw agrees: "If you men will take no pay, then none of us will," and tears up his own check. This is the only shot in the whole scene in which there isn't a stark shadow on the left side of his face. (00:55)

5. The platoon marches past some black children in the South, and Rawlins tells some little boys it's the "year of the jubilee." The boys wave to the soldiers, and the one whose hand is in the lower-right corner of the screen wears a translucent digital watch. (01:01)

6. Shaw and Cabot are talking to Harter and Montgomery about sending their unit into combat when Harter asks Montgomery to bring an ashtray. From the front, Cabot has his hands on his lap, but from behind he leans his head on his right hand. (01:16)

7. In his first battle, Trip grapples with a Confederate soldier who loses his hat. But just before Trip finally clobbers him with a piece of wood, his hat's back on. (01:21)

8. The weather on the beach,

particularly the amount of sunlight, changes almost shot-to-shot from the preparation through the charge on Fort Wagner. (01:38)

GO (6)
1999, color, 103 min.

Director: Doug Liman

Cast: Sarah Polley (Ronna Martin), Desmond Askew (Simon Baines), Scott Wolf (Adam), Jay Mohr (Zack), Katie Holmes (Claire Montgomery), Nathan Bexton (Mannie), Timothy Olyphant (Todd Gaines), William Fichtner (Burke), Breckin Meyer (Tiny), Taye Diggs (Marcus), James Duval (Singh).

One wild ride of a night.

Bloopers

1. Simon offers his shift to Ronna. She accepts because he gives her "cash up front," and he lifts a wad of money, folded toward Ronna. When we see the same shot from Simon's point of view, he lifts the money folded toward him. (00:03, 00:35)

2. When Ronna accepts Simon's money, he says, "I'll throw an extra twenty for a blowjob." Later on, when we see the scene for the second time, he says, "I'll give you an extra twenty for a blow-job." (00:04, 00:35)

3. Talking to Ronna in the mar-

ket, Adam states that he "took Music Appreciation twice." But when he says that again, in his segment, he says that he "took Music Appreciation. Twice." (00:05, 01:08)

4. When a departing lady places a Santa's hat on Todd's head, the pompom is to his right— then, in the following shot, it's on the left. (00:09)

5. Todd tells Ronna, "I take it this is not a social call," as he lifts his arm to bring the cigarette to his mouth. In the over-the-shoulder shot, he lifts the arm again. (00:09)

6. Todd wants to do some sexual business with Ronna. She removes her shirt, and, invited by Todd, turns for him. But in the following shot, Ronna has yet to begin turning. (00:10)

GODZILLA (7)

1998, color, 140 min.

Director: Roland Emmerich

Cast: Matthew Broderick (Dr. Niko Tatopoulos), Jean Reno (Philippe Roaché), Maria Pitillo (Audrey Timmonds), Hank Azaria (Victor "Animal" Palotti), Kevin Dunn (Col. Hicks), Michael Lerner (Mayor Ebert), Harry Shearer (Charles Caiman, WIDF Anchor), Arabella Field (Lucy Palotti), Vicki Lewis (Dr. Elsie Chapman), Doug Savant (Sgt. O'Neal), Masaya Kato

(Japanese Tanker Crew Member).

Take a little bit of King Kong *and a little bit of* Jurassic Park, *add a pinch of* Love Story *and you have . . . well,* Godzilla.

Bloopers

1. In the beginning, Philippe asks everybody to leave him alone with the old Japanese sailor and the interpreter. Later on, both on TV and in Dr. Nick's tent, there is a tape of the same conversation that Philippe had with the sailor. Except at the time of the interview, no videocamera was in the room. (00:08, 00:12, 00:59)

2. Citizens of New York are physically thrown up in the air as Godzilla's approaching footsteps create gigantic tremors. As the movie progresses, these tremors subside—for instance, when the lizard leaves Victor after their first face-to-foot meeting. Evidently, Godzilla has learned to tiptoe. (00:26, 00:30, 01:00)

3. In front of a pile of fish, Dr. Nick takes a few snapshots with a disposable Kodak camera. However, its flash bulb makes the sound of professional flash equipment. (00:48)

4. Manhattan has been evacuated, and three choppers

chase Godzilla along the avenues. But there is still a tremendous number of lights on in the buildings (which were evacuated during daylight). (00:49)

5. Crossing a dense crowd under heavy rain, Dr. Nick decides to go into a pharmacy and buy a pregnancy test. Here he also meets with his former girlfriend Audrey. When they step out of the pharmacy, the crowd has dispersed, the rain has stopped (it'll be heavy again a few moments later, when they're having a cup of tea) and the sidewalk looks barely wet. (00:54, 00:56)

6. An infant Godzilla chews on a bag of popcorn while peering at Nick, who is standing in an otherwise empty elevator. Nick quickly closes the door. Later, when Nick peeks out of the elevator, more than one bag of popcorn lies on the floor of the car. (01:42)

7. The taxi that outruns Godzilla has a sign on its roof that every now and then dangles (as if off the hooks that hold it), then sometimes is firmly back in place. The very same sign is alternately lit and unlit. (01:57)

Questions

1. How did they manage to evacuate all of Manhattan, which has an estimated 3 million people, in so few hours? A clock on a wall says it's about 12:40 A.M., and they are talking about the ten o'clock news . . . but the island is empty way before 9:00 P.M. In real life, it actually took two hours just to empty the World Trade Center at the time of the first bombing in 1993. (00:31, 00:32, 00:38)

2. If an army helicopter can't outrun Godzilla ("He's right on my tail, sir. I don't think I can shake him!"), why doesn't the helicopter try ascending? (00:52)

3. If an army helicopter can't outrun Godzilla, how come a New York taxicab can? (00:52, 01:55)

4. How does a 200-foot tall lizard hide in a subway tunnel and get inside Madison Square Garden? (01:28)

5. While chasing the cab, Godzilla gets entangled in the Brooklyn Bridge's cables, ripping them off the base. Yet, the bridge stands. So, are the cables just for show, or do they support the bridge? (02:01)

Fun Fact

Pregnancy tests made for human beings can't be used on blood samples of other living creatures. (00:57)

GOLDEN CHILD, THE (8)
1986, color, 94 min.

Director: Michael Ritchie

Cast: J.L. Reate (The Golden Child), Eddie Murphy (Chandler Jarrell), Charles Dance (Sardo Numspa), Charlotte Lewis (Kee Nang), Victor Wong (Gunpa, the Old Man), Randall "Tex" Cobb (Til), James Hong (Doctor Hong), Shakti (Kala), Tau Logo (Yu), Tiger Chung Lee (Khan).

Goofy detective is hired to find a mystical, living legend.

Bloopers

1. In the house where Sharon Moses is found, Chandler snaps a photo with his Polaroid camera. The first bulb of the line of flashbulbs flashes. Without taking any other picture, Chandler walks into another room: now two bulbs are spent. (00:13, 00:14)

2. After the first meeting with the mysterious Kala, Chandler and Kee leave the store. As they walk, an extra in the background to the right can be seen punching numbers at random into a payphone. As soon as he's done dialing, he immediately hangs up, grabs his briefcase, and walks away from the booth. (00:20)

3. To get the Adjante dagger, Chandler has to enter the bottomless room, while holding a glass of water in his left hand. But when he turns before entering, the glass is in his right. (00:58)

4. A wooden bridge on the path blows up and plummets into the abyss. When Chandler looks at the bridge's flaming remains still attached to a chain, a few drops of water drip from the glass. The same glass he was supposed to not lose one single drop from. And yet, it doesn't seem to matter. (01:01)

5. Still in the bottomless room, Chandler has to walk over several pillars holding the glass of water. When one pillar suddenly goes down, Chandler finds himself dangling in the air. He places the glass down on the pillar he's holding on to, he lifts himself up, and then grabs the glass back... from another pillar. Who moved it? (01:01, 01:02)

6. When Chandler finally grabs the Adjante dagger, the weapon turns 180° in his hands as he retracts it from the altar. (01:03)

7. Chandler asks the help of the Old Man, who raises his little finger to his nose—but the little finger turns into an index finger. (01:04)

8. A parrot flies onto the Golden Child's right shoulder. The parrot faces forward, but in the following shot, the parrot faces backwards, and then forward again. (01:28)

GONE WITH THE WIND (25)
1939, color, 222 min.

Director: Victor Fleming

Cast: Clark Gable (Rhett Butler), Vivien Leigh (Scarlett O'Hara),

Leslie Howard (Ashley Wilkes), Olivia de Havilland (Melanie Hamilton Wilkes), Hattie McDaniel (Mammy), Thomas Mitchell (Gerald O'Hara), Barbara O'Neil (Ellen O'Hara), Evelyn Keyes (Suellen O'Hara), Ann Rutherford (Carreen O'Hara), Fred Crane (Brent Tarleton), George Reeves (Stuart Tarleton), Oscar Polk (Pork), Harry Davenport (Dr. Meade), Eddie "Rochester" Anderson (Uncle Peter), Everett Brown (Big Sam).

Frankly, my dear, it's a long movie. Damn!

NOTE: Timing taken with the *whole* movie length — 3:53:04. BUT, if you want: Overture — 2:32 min.; Intermission — 4:03 min.; Entr'acte — 1:37 min.; Exit Music — 4:19 min.

Bloopers

1. Talking on the patio about the barbecue at Wilkes's, Scarlett says that she will waltz with both Brent and Stuart Tarleton. As Brent dances happily, in the next Scarlett close-up, a few dogs appear behind her. (00:07)

2. Scarlett meets with Pa as he dismounts from the horse. He has his riding whip in his right hand, but as she fixes his ascot, the whip has jumped into his left hand. (00:10)

3. When Scarlett is forced by Mammy to eat before going to the barbecue, she lifts the cover of one tray and holds it by its longer side. In the following close-up, she's holding it by its handle, and then she holds it again by its longer side. (00:17)

4. After giving "glorious news" at the bazaar, Dr. Meade (seen from behind) raises his arms to hush the crowd; when we see him in front, he raises them again. (00:39)

5. Upon his return from Paris, Rhett brings Scarlett a green hat, then he produces a cigar out of his carrying case, pockets the case, and brings the cigar to his mouth with his left hand. In the following cut, he's still holding the carrying case. (00:46)

6. The chicken chased by Uncle Peter because it doesn't want to be Christmas lunch wanders in front of the same pile of wood twice. (00:53)

7. Scarlett and Melanie take care of the wounded in the military hospital. Their shadows on the walls don't make the same movements they do. (00:58)

8. Horrified, Scarlett leaves the nursery. When she walks underneath an archway decorated with "Peace be with thy walls," the shadow of the boom mike can be seen on the door to the right — twice. (01:04)

9. When Scarlett exits the hospital, she slams the main door shut behind her; someone opens it completely (and leaves it open), but in the fol-

lowing shot the door is closed again. (01:04)

10. During the Atlanta battle, Scarlett looks for Dr. Meade. As she walks by the railroad, now turned into a huge infirmary, try to spot all of those lousy mannequins among the extras. It's not hard, and it's fun for the whole family! (01:15)

11. When Scarlett finally spots Dr. Meade, she walks by what looks suspiciously like an electric lamppost. At the time of the Civil War? (01:16)

12. Melanie finally gives birth to her baby, after a pregnancy during the Civil War that has lasted twenty-one months. (01:18)

13. After fleeing a burning Atlanta, Rhett's carriage is in a procession of wounded, tired soldiers. One of them, an old man smoking a pipe, is carrying a fellow fighter. A few moments later, after Scarlett has taken a good look at "the old South disappearing," a young soldier faints. The man behind him, an old man smoking a pipe, passes his rifle to another soldier and picks up the one who fell down. Good God! The second old man bears a striking resemblance to the one we saw earlier!! (01:26)

14. Scarlett reaches Tara, which has burnt down to the ground. As she goes to talk with Mammy, her father in the background brings his left hand to his mouth. In Scarlett's close-up, her father's hand is lowered, and in the following shot is up to his mouth again. (01:36)

15. Melanie removes her nightgown to help Scarlett hide a dead Yankee. Melanie should be nude underneath the gown, but as she removes it, a flesh-colored bra makes its appearance. (01:56)

16. As Scarlett begins to run toward a returning Ashley, the shadow of the boom mike can be seen on the doorframe to the right. (02:02)

17. After Ashley tells Scarlett, "Nothing. Nothing except honor," she leans against a pole. Right before he enters the frame, there is a match cut (look at Scarlett's head position. It "jumps" briefly). (02:07)

18. While talking about Rhett's hanging, Scarlett opens the door gate: on the doorframe it's possible to see the shadow of the boom mike. (02:18)

19. Big Sam rescues Scarlett from the Yankees, then jumps onto her coach and rides with her. But the following shot shows a coach driven by Scarlett—Big Sam is nowhere to be seen. (02:31, 02:32)

20. After it is revealed that Ashley is wounded, Rhett wants to bring him to his room. Melanie grabs a lamp ... with an electric cord? (02:40)

21. The flower Rhett picks up from a wreath on the floor is smaller than the one that he actually brings up to his lapel. (02:47)

22. When Rhett tells Mammy that "boys aren't any use to anybody," he has a cigar in his mouth while pouring a glass of sherry. In the following, matching cut, the cigar has "flown" to the hand that's holding the glass. (02:57)

23. By the desk where he keeps the store books, Ashley comments to Scarlett, "Oh, the lazy days . . ." and he places his right hand on the book. In the following matching close-up, the right hand is by the side of his face. (03:09)

24. When Melanie greets Scarlett at Ashley's birthday party, the boom mike shadow can be seen on a column to the right. (03:13)

25. After Bonnie wakes up from a nightmare, the Nanny enters and lights a lamp on the wall by the door. While Rhett bawls her out, their shadows can't possibly be generated by that single lamp because they are projected on the door. (03:23)

GORGO (3)
    1961, color, 76 min.

Director: Eugene Lourie

Cast: Bill Travers (Joe Ryan), William Sylvester (Sam Slade), Vincent Winter (Sean), Bruce Senton (Prof. Flaherty), Joseph O'Conor (Prof. Hendricks), Martin Benson (Dorkin), Barry Keegan (Mate), Christopher Rodes (McCartin).

Do you remember Godzilla? Well, pretty much the same thing, only this time in Ireland, lasse.

Bloopers

1. Joe is about to go scuba diving: he wears his mask, and the blue air filter in the front becomes transparent: you can see the sea and the island *through* Joe's head (Blue Screen glitch)! (00:12)

2. The navy is looking for Gorgo's mom, on a bright day. When one of the sailors spots the monster emerging from the water, Gorgo's mom appears . . . at night. The navy then begins to bomb it in broad daylight. (00:51)

3. Joe and Sam jump into their car and follow an army truck. When they leave, Joe is driving a left-steering wheel car. When they reach the truck, the car has become a right–steering wheel car. (01:02, 01:03)

Question
The news that a monster has been captured off the coast of Nara Island is broadcast in London, where a bunch of pedestrians (particularly a man with a red tie and another one with a black hat) crowd a sidewalk to

CAP FEAR

A disease known also as "hatlosephobia."

John Cusack's hat in *Grosse Point Blank*	Blooper No. 4
Rachel Ticotin's uniform hat in *Con Air*	Blooper No. 3
Chris Isaak's clown hat in *Married to the Mob*	Blooper No. 5
A policeman in *The Man With the Golden Gun*	Blooper No. 12
Will Smith's cowboy hat in *Wild Wild West*	Blooper No. 10

watch a TV screen in a store window. The following day, Gorgo's arrival is televised. The same bunch of pedestrians stand in front of the same TV screen in the window store. Are they regulars? (00:26, 00:32)

GROSSE POINT BLANK (5)
1997, color, 107 min.

Director: George Armitage

Cast: John Cusack (Martin Q. "Marty" Blank), Minnie Driver (Debi Newberry), Alan Arkin (Dr. Oatman), Dan Aykroyd (Mr. Grocer), Joan Cusack (Marcella), Hank Azaria (Steven "Steve" Lardner), K. Todd Freeman (Kevin McCullers), Jeremy Piven (Paul Spericki), Mitch Ryan (Mr. Bert Newberry), Michael Cudlitz (Bob Destepello), Benny Urquidez (Felix La PuBelle).

Professional killer goes to his high school reunion.

Bloopers

1. Debi's radio station, 75.9 WGPM is waaaaaaay below the standard FM broadcast frequencies. (00:19)

2. Debi and Martin have a drink at the Hippo Club. The lemon slice on Martin's glass keeps moving to the left and the right of the glass. (00:46)

3. During the same evening, all of a sudden a martini glass appears in front of Debi, before Amy arrives and drops her martini glass in front of Debi. (00:47, 00:48)

4. Martin places his hat on one of the bed stands, gives Debi an "airplane," then leaves without retrieving his hat. But as he walks to the door, the hat is in his hand. (00:56, 00:57)

5. In the Cuppa Joe place, Martin shows Mr. Grocer his nutrients pills. The pills are aligned on the table, then grouped, then aligned, then grouped . . . (00:59, 01:01)

H

HALLOWEEN II (7)
1981, color, 93 min.

Director: Rick Rosenthal

Cast: Jamie Lee Curtis (Laurie Strode), Donald Pleasence (Doctor Sam Loomis), Charles Cyphers (Leigh Brackett), Jeffrey Kramer (Graham), Lance Guest (Jim), Pamela Susan Shoop (Karen), Dick Warlock (The Shape / Patrolman #3), Hunter Von Leer (Gary Hunt), Leo Rossi (Budd), Gloria Gifford (Mrs. Alves), Tawny Moyer (Jill), Jack Verbois (Bennett Tramer), Nancy Loomis (Annie Brackett), Tony Moran (Michael Myers, age 23).

The Shape is back for a little more.

Bloopers
1. The movie takes place entirely on October 31, 1978. In front of the burnt corpse of Bennett Tramer, Doctor Loomis says that "Michael Myers is twenty-one." In the closing credits, Tony Moran is credited as "Michael Myers (age twenty-three)." Huh? (00:00, 00:40, 01:28)
2. The porch lights of the Strode's house are on, then off as Loomis approaches it, and on again when the Shape (a.k.a. Michael Myers) falls from the balcony. (00:00, 00:01, 00:02)

Nice Same Ol' House. So . . . Different!

The balcony Michael Myers plummets from looks different from the "same" balcony in *Halloween*. The rail seems to have developed small columns that weren't there.

3. Loomis bursts into Laurie's house and fires seven shots at the Shape. Subsequently, when he meets a patrolman, Loomis states "I shot him six times!"—three times in a row. The fact that he shot him "six times" is also men-

tioned twice later on in the movie. (00:02, 00:08, 00:18, 00:24)

4. Loomis and Sheriff Brackett chase a suspect who resembles the Shape (later on, it turns out to be Bennett Tramer). The suspect is hit by a police car, which pins him against a van. After a big explosion, the flaming torso of the victim falls onto the trunk of the police car, but in a following close-up, the flaming body is standing up straight. (00:19)

5. When they're taking out Annie's dead body, Sheriff Brackett closes Annie's eyes. They twitch. (00:22)

6. A mob of angry people literally attacks the Myers's house (which displays the number "709" above the main entrance). Yet, when agent Hunt calls for backup, he says on the radio to send it to "The old Myers house: 45 Lampkin Lane." (00:41)

7. The Shape appears behind nurse Jill and stabs her with a scalpel, lifting her dying body up. Her clogs fall to the floor, one on its right side. In the following shot, the same clog lies on its left side. (01:08)

Questions

1. When Michael Myers is on the balcony and flinches before falling down, doesn't it look like the balcony floor is at the *same level* as the handrail? Who is the architect? (00:02)

2. Nurse Karen wears her uniform at the hospital, and as a final touch she puts on a fuchsia belt. Yet later, when she's startled by a buzzer, she's wearing a white belt. Is the hospital dress code that strict that she had to change for her night shift, or . . . ? (00:31, 00:44)

HARD RAIN (3)
1998, color, 95 min.

Director: Mikael Salomon

Cast: Morgan Freeman (Jim), Christian Slater (Tom), Randy Quaid (Sheriff), Minnie Driver (Karen), Edward Asner (Uncle Charlie), Michael A. Goorjian (Kenny), Dann Florek (Mr. Mehlor), Ricky Harris (Ray), Mark Rolston (Wayne Bryce), Peter Murnik (Phil), Wayne Duvall (Hank), Richard A. Dysart (Henry Sears), Betty White (Mrs. Sears).

"I wanna know . . . have you ever seen the rain?"

Bloopers

1. Responding to the fire at the armored-car attack, Tom shoots the second light to the left of Jim's truck. However, when Jim takes it out on Kenny, the light is fine again. (00:14)

2. When the electric pole smashes Tom's jail door, Tom has one hand on the wall, the

other on the bars. In the wide shot, the hand that was on the bars is in front of his face. (00:37)

3. When old Henry turns the boat to bring his wife back to the thieves, in the distance Jim and Tom are standing side by side. As Henry says, "Or me!" Jim and Tom switch positions. (00:54)

HELP! (10)
1965, color, 90 min.

Director: Richard Lester

Cast: John Lennon (John), Paul McCartney (Paul), George Harrison (George), Ringo Starr (Ringo), Leo McKern (Clang), Eleanor Bron (Ahme), Victor Spinetti (Professor Foot), Roy Kinnear (Algernon), John Bluthal (Bhuta), Patrick Cargill (Superintendent).

The Fab Four have a ring problem and a lot of fun.

Bloopers
1. While the Beatles sing "Help!" in a black-and-white movie, the first three darts Clang throws at the screen change positions. (00:02)
2. Ringo is pulled out of bed by a mechanical arm and falls onto the floor with sheets and all. As he wakes up and looks around, the sheets are back on the bed. (00:07)
3. The Fab Four tape "You're Gonna Lose That Girl." Ringo smokes a cigarette and plays the drums. Later on, during the same take, he plays two small congas (but the drums keep going without pause) then he's back on drums. Paul does the same: first he's on guitar and vocals, then on the piano, then back—and the song runs along smooth as velvet. (00:12, 00:14)
4. When Paul is shrunk by mistake, he stands close to a crystal ashtray on the floor. But when he's tiny and hides in it, the ashtray has turned white. (00:32)
5. While taping "I Need You" surrounded by tanks, Ringo fixes his hat twice, using his hands, and again the drums don't miss a single beat. (00:49, 00:50)
6. Inside Buckingham Palace, Professor Foot and Algernon set a device called the "Relativity Cadenza." From behind, the device is parallel to the rug on the floor, from the front it's quite askew. (01:03)
7. Ringo is trapped in a room underneath a pub. The door can't be used, and a ladder is leaning against it. As Ringo moves, he knocks the ladder to the ground: it doesn't make a sound. (01:05)
8. In the Bahamas, the Beatles flee from a temple via a water tunnel that brings them into a pool. They enter the tunnel wearing shoes, as they swim underwater they're barefoot, then when they're

on a bicycle, they have their shoes again. (01:14)

9. Ringo jumps off Professor Foot's boat without wearing any shoes, he's immediately captured and tied up on the beach. When he sets himself free, he's wearing shoes again. (01:25, 01:26)

10. The red paint on Ringo's jacket during the final ritual diminishes between the time he's lying down and when he gets up. (01:26)

HERBIE GOES TO MONTE CARLO (9)

1977, color, 91 min.

Director: Vincent McEveety

Cast: Dean Jones (Jim Douglas), Don Knotts (Wheely Applegate), Julie Sommars (Diane Darcy), Jacques Marin (Inspector Bouchet), Roy Kinnear (Quincey), Bernard Fox (Max), Eric Braeden (Bruno Von Stickle), Xavier Saint-Macary (Detective Fontenoy), Alan Caillou (Emile), Laurie Main (Duval), Mike Kylcsar (Claude), François Lalande (Monsieur Ribeaux).

The car with a heart goes to France.

Bloopers

1. As the Lancia slows down and stops during the first qualification race, Herbie keeps going, but hits the brakes and comes back at once. Well, *almost* at once: keep your eyes on the Lancia driver, it's possible to see a "jump" as if a few frames have been dropped to speed up Herbie's comeback. (00:21)

2. Seeking a way to clean the dirt from his trunk, Herbie passes by a fountain. In the background, the sidewalk is very crowded. In the following cut, the sidewalk is almost deserted. (00:30)

3. Right after seeing Herbie and his Lancia friend on the boat in Paris, Jim places his right hand close to his jacket—"Maybe I can explain this over dinner, tonight." As Diane leaves, and he says, "Maybe not," the jacket has moved behind Jim's hand. (00:36)

4. As Herbie has lost interest in the race, he drives slowly on the circuit. The background behind Jim and Wheely is a full-speed race background that has been slowed down very clumsily. In other words, it sucks. (00:40)

5. As Herbie wanders on the sidewalk looking for the Lancia, the background shows people who, if they really were where they appear to be, would have been run over by the car. (01:04)

6. When Wheely tells Herbie "She took off in that race like you never existed," it's possible to see a red-jacketed man with sunglasses and moustache in the background walk-

ing toward Herbie, while a woman with long hair and a green-strapped dress walks away from the car. A few seconds later, Wheely says "Might as well face it. You've been deserted. Jilted. Abandoned." In the background, the same red-jacketed man is walking toward Herbie—again—and the green-strapped woman's walking away—again. (01:06)

7. After Herbie comes back from the lake and back into the race, Bruno spots the car in his rearview mirror. But the reflection is not a reflection: the 53 on Herbie's trunk is clearly not flipped like it should be. (01:12)

8. Herbie gets covered with brown rocks and debris after the yodeling moment. He backs up, and then all of a sudden he's clean as a whistle. (01:19)

9. To prove that the tank has no problems whatsoever, Wheely sticks his hand into it and comes out with a diamond ... and with a hand as dry as a bone. (01:22)

Questions

1. Don't you think there are an awful lot of people in Paris who speak English? Cops, extras, the museum curator ("The most magnificent diamond in the world, monsieur!"), etc. (00:03, 00:04, 00:14)

2. The first time Herbie spots

the Lancia, he stops and turns to the left by himself. So then why is Jim Douglas turning the steering wheel when the shot is from outside of Herbie? (00:18)

HIDDEN, THE (4)
1987, color, 97 min.

Director: Jack Sholder

Cast: Kyle MacLachlan (Lloyd Gallagher / Alhague), Michael Nouri (Thomas Beck), Claudia Christian (Brenda Lee Van Buren), Clarence Felder (Lieutenant John Masterson), Clu Gulager (Lieutenant Ed Flynn), Ed Ross (Cliff Willis), William Boyet (Jonathan P. Miller), Richard Brooks (Sanchez), Larry Cedar (Bren), Katherine Cannon (Barbara Beck), John McCann (Senator Holt), Chris Mulkey (Jack DeVries).

*Alien loves fast cars, beautiful women, and money.
Wait! Is he an alien after all?*

Bloopers

1. Jack DeVries flees from a bank in a black Ferrari that has a white California license plate (something like 23T0638). After Jack rams his car into another one, the plate appears to be tilted to one side. When the Ferrari barely misses a roadblock made with two police cars parked in a V, a shot reveals the

Ferrari's plate: not only is it not tilted anymore, but it's now blue and reads 555 XIR. It'll become white and tilted again right after a man in a wheelchair is run over. (00:02, 00:03, 00:04)

2. Beck steps out of a car at a roadblock: he removes his jacket and places it distractedly on the car door, with the sleeves inside out. In the following shot, the jacket is neatly hanging from the door. (00:06)

3. When Beck and Lloyd are pursuing Brenda in the car, Beck sticks his head out of the window and fires a couple of shots at the green car in front of them. The same car that passes very close to an orange cone used by New Line to control traffic during the Hollywood chase. (00:53)

4. While walking in a hotel hallway, Detective Willis is stopped by a police officer: the detective raises his hands and stops, but in the over-the-shoulder shot, he's reaching for his pocket. (01:22)

Question

DeVries is shot and almost blown up by police. Once in the hospital, he's attached to all sorts of tubes and machinery. Did nobody think to x-ray the poor guy? They would have found a two-foot-long alien parasite inside of him and saved themselves a lot of chasing. (00:07, 00:08)

HOOPER (5)
1978, color, 97 min.

Director: Hal Needham

Cast: Burt Reynolds (Sonny Hooper), Jan-Michael Vincent (Ski Chinski), Sally Field (Gwen Doyle), Brian Keith (Jocko Doyle), John Marley (Max Berns), Robert Klein (Roger Deal), James Best (Cully), Adam West (Himself), Alfie Wise (Tony), Terry Bradshaw (SWAT Commander), Norman Grabowski (Hammerhead), George Furth (George Budwell, Humane Society Representative).

Amusing movie that shows you how stunt movies are NOT done.

Bloopers

1. Hooper is about to perform a stunt for Adam West involving a dog. "No dog is gonna fall from that," George Budwell, Humane Society Representative, declares. Nonetheless, Hooper is given a real dog to do the stunt: but when he falls from the cable, the "real" dog is a dummy. It'll turn into a real dog again on the landing airbag. (00:11, 00:12)

2. The SWAT Commander tears Hooper's shirt open, revealing a gray undershirt. When Hooper turns to his group, the undershirt is gone. (00:31, 00:32)

3. Sitting in the front yard,

Hooper and Jocko talk about stunts. When Jocko ribs Hooper that he always tried to "top every gag I did," the cigar Hooper is holding in his mouth vanishes. (00:40)

4. During a discussion under a gazebo, temperamental director Roger asks Max, the producer, if Hooper still has a job in this picture. When he does so, Roger places his right hand on a column. Max answers, and for the entire time Roger has his hands along his sides. When he turns back to Max and Hooper, his right hand is again against the column. (01:15)

5. Ski stops the car a few yards from the collapsed bridge and tells Hooper that his life's worth more than a piece of film. Hooper's window is almost completely rolled down, but in the shot from inside the car it's almost completely rolled up. (01:31, 01:32)

SO, WHAT'S WRONG WITH YOUR CAR?

Just check the fluids, and see if I have any bloopers, please.

Sylvester Stallone's trunk in *Cobra*	Blooper No. 3
Arnold Schwarzenegger's truck in *Commando*	Blooper No. 5
A Mercedes in *Die Hard With a Vengeance*	Blooper No. 8
Burt Reynolds's window in *Hooper*	Blooper No. 5
George Clooney's Mercedes in *The Peacemaker*	Blooper No. 4
Tom Cruise and Jeanne Tripplehorn's car in *The Firm*	Blooper No. 2

I KNOW WHAT YOU DID LAST SUMMER (6)
1997, color, 100 min.

Director: Jim Gillespie

Cast: Jennifer Love Hewitt (Julie James), Sarah Michelle Gellar (Helen Shivers), Ryan Phillippe (Barry Cox), Freddie Prinze, Jr. (Ray Bronson), Muse Watson (Benjamin Willis / Fisherman), Bridgette Wilson (Elsa Shives), Anne Heche (Melissa "Missy" Egan), Johnny Galecki (Max), Stuart Green (Officer), J. Don Ferguson (Emcee), Deborah Hobart (Mrs. James), Mary McMillan (Mrs. Cox).

Four kids run over this guy. One year later, the guy tries to run over the kids—to return the favor.

Bloopers

1. After the four friends run over the guy, Barry's face and shirt collar are stained with blood. A few minutes later, when he emerges from the water holding Helen's crown, his collar looks pretty clean. But when he's walking to the car, yapping that their misadventure is "Merely a future therapy bill," the blood on the collar has returned. "Out, out, damned spot!" (00:14, 00:22, 00:23)

2. When underwater struggling for the possession of the crown, Barry seems to not be wearing an undershirt. But when he emerges on the dock, something has appeared and is visible through his sweater's collar. (00:22)

3. After staring at a diploma on a wall, Julie is handed some mail from her mom. The boom mike is reflected in the picture in the middle of the wall. (00:27)

4. Barry's shirt collar is alternatively up and down while he's standing in front of his stolen car. (00:40, 00:41)

5. When Barry gets run over with his car, he lands in a pile of wood, one board on his

arm and shoulder. Yet in the following shot, the board is gone. (00:41)

6. Ben Willis revs the engine of his boat, then speeds up. Julie's gun falls overboard ... in the opposite direction it should have: if a boat speeds up, and you are on the foredeck, you fall toward the stern of the boat, not toward the bow. (01:26)

Questions

1. Six "Croaker Queen Finalists" walk onstage, and the emcee asks Helen (finalist number 3): "In the spirit of Mother Teresa, blah blah blah." Helen answers, then the emcee opens the envelope and announces she's the winner. Why did the emcee only ask Helen a question? Who are the other five, production rejects or something? (00:04, 00:05)

2. Max the fisherman gets killed when the Fisherman hooks him straight in the throat, and drags him over the counter he's working on. Yet, when Max's body appears in Julie's trunk, covered with crabs, it doesn't seem to have any holes under its chin. Is the Fisherman a plastic surgeon as well? (00:38, 00:59)

3. When Julie enters Benjamin Willis's boat, she realizes he's a very disturbed man: the walls of the boat are wallpapered with articles and pictures of the four kids—including a photo of Helen as Croaker Queen. But that parade took place only a few hours earlier. Is Benjamin employed at one of those "1 Hour Photo" labs, too? (01:25)

IDLE HANDS (6)
  1999, color, 90 min.

Director: Rodman Flender

Cast: Devon Sawa (Anton Tobias), Seth Green (Mick),

BLOODY BLOOPERS!

If bloopers happen, don't despair, keep your chin up, and think positive. RH positive, possibly.

Jack Hadley's shirt in *For Your Eyes Only*	Blooper No. 4
Ryan Phillippe's shirt in *I Know What You Did Last Summer*	Blooper No. 1
Jim Carrey's arm in *Me, Myself & Irene*	Blooper No. 7
Tarzan's chest in *Tarzan*	Blooper No. 1
Bruce Willis in *Twelve Monkeys*	Blooper No. 6

Elden Ratliff (Pnub), Jessica Alba (Molly), Christopher Hart (The Hand), Vivica A. Fox (Debi), Jack Noseworthy (Randy), Katie Wright (Tanya), Sean Whalen (McMacy), Nicholas Sadler (Ruck), Fred Willard (Mr. Tobias), Connie Ray (Mrs. Tobias), Donna W. Scott (Nurse).

Murderous possessed hand finds itself on wastoid teen.

Bloopers

1. Mrs. Tobias, investigating things downstairs, trips on a flashlight and falls down. She discovers blood on the floor, and quickly gets up: she's wearing knee pads to brace her for her recent fall. (00:06)

2. Anton brings Molly her lost book of lyrics. In one over-the-shoulder shot of Anton on her porch, we can see the street in the background is soaked, and rain drips from the roof. However, it's dry outside before and after this scene. (00:15)

3. The undead Mick is throwing cheese puffs at the detached head of the undead Pnub. The number of puffs changes between long shots and close-ups. Also, when Mick asks, "What's with the hand?" the puffs near his mouth have moved to his forehead. They'll be back at his mouth in the following shot. (00:42, 00:44)

4. The guys arrive at the dance to find a couple murdered in their car. Anton tells Mick and Pnub: "Go in the dance, protect Molly. I'm goin' after that f***ing hand!" and moves Mick aside by grabbing his shoulder ... *with his infamous right hand*, which he already had cut off in a previous scene (00:53) and now seeks! (01:08)

5. At the Halloween dance, the first time we see Molly there are two extras dancing behind her: a "harem girl" and what might be called "Little Red Riding Ghoul." A few moments later, there's a shot near the entrance to the dance, and there they are again, and again, and again ... always together, in almost every shot, no matter what the angle. (01:09)

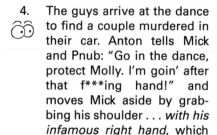

Flender Waxes Poetic About Pesky Extra

In the DVD audio commentary, director Rodman Flender recites his poem, *Ode to Harem Girl*: "An extra once put a director to the test / To cut her out of the film like the rest / Though extra's work's tough / She worked hard enough / To appear in all shots east and west."

6. When Molly is visiting Anton in the hospital at the end, a nurse comes in and says, "It's time for your meds." Anton is then visited by his

now angelic pals Mick and Pnub. The nurse says visiting hours are over. Anton's pals leave shortly thereafter and turn out the light, but the nurse never gave Anton his meds and never left the room. (01:27, 01:28)

Question
Anton finishes burying his parents and friends in his backyard. When both Mick and Pnub's headless body dig themselves out of the ground, they back Anton up toward his house, where he almost steps on Pnub's severed head. Did it dig itself out of the ground, or did Anton just not deem it worthy of a proper burial? (00:41)

IN THE LINE OF FIRE (8)
1993, color, 128 min.

Director: Wolfgang Petersen

Cast: Clint Eastwood (Frank Horrigan), John Malkovich (Mitch Leary / John Booth / James Carney), Rene Russo (Lilly Raines), Dylan McDermott (Al D'Andrea), Gary Cole (Bill Watts, Secret Service Presidential Detail Agent-In-Charge), Fred Dalton Thompson (Harry Sargent, White House Chief of Staff), John Mahoney (Sam Campagna, Secret Service Director), Gregory Alan Williams (Matt Wilder), Jim Curley (President / Traveler), Sally Hughes (First Lady), Clyde Kusatsu (Jack Okura), Patrika Darbo (Pam Magnus).

Presidential body guard chases a killer who is becoming really annoying.

Bloopers
1. When Watts leaves the White House meeting room, Sam crosses his legs. When he turns to Frank, he crosses his legs again. (00:17)
2. In the bank, Mitch talks about Minnesota with Pam. When he says, "Wow. There was when I was there," he lowers his left arm, which his head was resting on. In the following shot, his head is resting on his left arm. (00:33)
3. To enter the alleged Mitch's house, Frank shatters the upper pane of a window . . . yet he enters through the lower pane of the window. And—strangely enough—there's no glass on the carpet. (01:10)
4. Al tells Frank he wants to resign. His seat belt is fastened. Then he yells, "I can't do it!" The seat belt isn't there anymore. A few seconds later, he discusses the word "cockamamie." The seat belt is back on. (01:15, 01:16)
5. Mitch places two bullets, head first, inside his keychain. Later on, at the hotel, he extracts them: one of the bullets has turned 180 degrees inside that tiny, little, narrow keychain. (01:35, 01:50)

6. Frank gets out of his car at LAX—and as he opens the door, a few crew members (particularly Mr. Red Sweater) are seen reflected in it. (01:43)

7. Mitch shatters the lamps in the Bonaventura Hotel's elevator: the bulbs go off one instant before he actually hits them. (01:55)

8. From the elevator, Frank has a great view of Mitch's cadaver: but maybe he should've noticed the arms changing positions in-between takes. (01:59)

INDIANA JONES AND THE TEMPLE OF DOOM (18)
1984, color, 118 min.

Director: Steven Spielberg

Cast: Harrison Ford (Indiana Jones), Kate Capshaw (Willie Scott), Amrish Puri (Mola Ram), Roshan Seth (Chattar Lal), Philip Stone (Captain Blumburtt), Roy Chiao (Lao Che), Jonathan Ke Quan "Ke Huy Quan" (Short Round), David Yip (Wu Han), Ric Young (Kao Kan), Chua Kah Joo (Chen), Dan Aykroyd (Weber).

Indy helps some Indians get back a magic stone, and, as usual, lands himself in some hairy situations.

Bloopers

1. The bag of coins on the revolving tray changes position without anybody touching it. (00:05)

2. Short "fender-benders" a carriage with a sailor and a woman on board. As Short pushes the carriage, the sailor and the woman switch positions more than once. (00:11)

3. As the trio is about to jump from the plane into the rubber dinghy, Short yells "Indy, I can't breathe!" but his mouth is clearly closed. (00:17)

4. As Indy, Willie, and Short are jumping up and down cruising the river in the yellow dinghy, they switch positions in almost every shot. (00:18)

5. Indy walks toward an Indian village (a matte shot), and the tip of his hat is "sliced" by the painting. (00:20)

6. In the jungle, a boa snake tossed away by Willie makes a rattling sound. Boas don't rattle; rattlers do. (00:34)

7. When Indy pushes in a statue to open a passage to the secret temple beneath the palace, he lights a match and his hand casts a shadow on the wall. It's impossible for a hand holding a match to cast a shadow on a wall. (00:53)

8. Short has a knife in his right hand. Despite the fact that he's watching a fight between Indy and one thug, Short finds the time to hide the knife. (00:55)

9. At the beginning of the Thugee ceremony, the skull

in the center is alternately lit and unlit. (01:00)

10. Willie is placed in the cage for the sacrifice; she wears a very elaborate necklace and a flower garland, but when Mola Ram gets close to her, she brings her hand up to her chest: the necklace is now gone, but the garland is still in place. During her descent toward the molten lava, her cage stops for the first time: when it resumes the descent, the necklace is back; it vanishes when the flowers begin to drop from her hair, but it's back again a few moments later. (01:18, 01:24)

11. As Willie descends into the red pit, the flowers around her neck appear both burned and still fresh in many shots. (01:22)

12. Mola Ram sees that Indy has snapped out of his hypnotic state and is now after him. Mola Ram removes his helmet with the horns, but when Indy charges him, he's still wearing it. When Mola smiles and escapes via a trapdoor by the altar, he's not wearing the helmet anymore. (01:24)

13. Indy comes back to his senses and fights back against the thugs. During the whole scene he has a strap around his chest that goes from his left shoulder to his right side. But when Short gives Indy his hat back, the strap has switched sides. (01:26)

14. As Indy swings to the train car on a rope: from the front, his arms are stretched; from the back, he's pulling his torso up. (01:34)

15. When Willie is hanging on to the muddy cliff, she is barefoot. When she gets on the bridge, she's wearing sandals. (01:41, 01:47)

16. Indy fights two thugs with machetes. Indy uses his whip, and the first machete flies off a cliff. However, as the second thug charges, Indy has the machete in his hand and there's a man knocked down to the ground. The new thug has no more machete. (01:42)

17. Short jumps onto the bridge and falls through a hole—a hole that later on vanishes. (01:42)

18. Mola Ram forces Willie and Short onto the bridge. Willie is in front, and Short follows. When they reach Indy, they've switched positions. (01:44)

INSPECTOR GADGET (3)
1999, color, 78 min.

Director: David Kellogg

Cast: Matthew Broderick (John Brown / Inspector Gadget / Robo Gadget), Rupert Everett (Sanford Scolex / Dr. Claw), Joely Fisher (Brenda Bradford / RoboBrenda), Michelle Trachtenberg (Penny), Andy

Dick (Kramer), Cheri Oteri (Mayor Wilson), Michael G. Hagerty (Sikes), Dabney Coleman (Chief Quimby), D.L. Hughley (Gadgetmobile), Rene Auberjonois (Artemus Bradford), Frances Bay (Thelma).

"Du nuh nuh nuh nunt, Inspector Gadget, dunt duh duh duh dunt, dunt daaaaah!"

Bloopers

1. After the accident, John wakes up in the lab. He leans to the left, falls flat, and then tries to stand up . . . from the right side of the bed. (00:16, 00:17)
2. John runs away from the lab and he has thousands of colored cables on his back. They keep changing positions and colors during the cuts. (00:18)
3. Sikes wears the stolen helmet with a strap under his chin. When he screams "Mamma!" the strap is undone, but when Claw gets closer, the strap is done up again. (00:20, 00:21)

IRON EAGLE (3)

1986, color, 116 min.

Director: Sidney J. Furie

Cast: Louis Gossett, Jr. (Col. Charles "Chappy" Sinclair), Jason Gedrick (Doug Masters), David Suchet (Minister of Defense), Tim Thomerson (Col. Ted Masters), Larry B. Scott (Reggie), Caroline Lagerfelt (Elizabeth), Jerry Levine (Tony), Robbie Rist (Milo), Michael Bowen (Knotcher), Bobby Jacoby (Matthew), Melora Hardin (Katie), David Greenlee (Kingsley).

Or, The Karate Kid *on a plane.*

Bloopers

1. The two planes in the exercise at the beginning have missiles under their wings and a pretty visible fuel tank under their bellies. Yet after they're attacked, the missiles vanish and then come back (Col. Masters fires two of them and destroys two MIGs), then vanish again. (00:00, 00:02, 00:03, 00:04)
2. Col. Masters blows up one of the enemy planes by firing the missile at the end of his right wing. He then proceeds to blow up a second plane by firing the exact same missile. (00:03)
3. Doug enters the flight simulator and pops Queen's "One Vision" into his Walkman (showing his black wristwatch). When he pushes a lever during the "Skill Level 7" simulation, the wristwatch is gone. The watch is back after the first explosion, then it's gone one more time ("I don't believe it!") up to when he removes his headset. But as he steps out of the simula-

tor, dingdong the watch is back. (00:30, 00:31, 00:32)

Questions

1. During the valedictorian's speech, Doug remembers the conversation he had with his dad regarding the last time they would have flown together. Doug says, "Oh, come on, Dad!" and his dad replies, "Don't 'Come on' me, Dad!"—shouldn't that have been "Don't 'Come on, Dad' me!"? (00:39)

Sweeping an Incestuous Slip of the Tongue Under the Rug

NOTE: neither DVD subtitles nor Close Captioning list that line; they skip from the previous line to the following line.

---

2. Why are Arab military personnel talking amongst themselves in English? For practice? (00:42)

JACKAL, THE (11)
1997, color, 124 min.

Director: Michael Caton-Jones

Cast: Bruce Willis (The Jackal), Richard Gere (Declan Mulqueen), Sidney Poitier (Carter Preston), Diane Venora (Valentina Koslova), Mathilda May (Isabella), J.K. Simmons (Timothy Witherspoon), Richard Lineback (McMurphy), John Cunningham (Donald Brown), Jack Black (Lamont), Tess Harper (The First Lady), Leslie Phillips (Woolburton), Stephen Spinella (Douglas), Philip Le Maistre (Bored Teenage Clerk).

Mysterious killer is hired to perform the Mother of All Assassinations. But someone is after him.

Bloopers:

1. While using a voice-activated computer, the Jackal gives an address for the delivery of a weapon: "Letterham Shipping, Montreal, Quebec, Canada, GIH 876." Addresses in Canada have postal codes that alternate letters and numbers (i.e., 8G7 I6H). (00:18)

2. When Declan visits Isabella in her new home in Phoebus, Virginia, it appears that the tide is high. But when he leaves a few minutes later, the tide has suddenly become low. (00:32, 00:34, 00:35)

3. The Jackal enters the Cyberia Café and goes to a computer. The bored clerk leans his head against his left arm—but in the next shot, both his arms are on the counter. (00:47)

4. Just before turning the weapon toward Lamont, the Jackal places a belt of ammo onto the side of the gun. The belt falls down as the Jackal moves the gun clockwise, and comes back in place a few seconds later, without the Jackal moving or doing anything. (00:58)

5. Smoke comes out from the nozzle of the gun when he points it at the poor guy, but

only if Lamont is in the shot. Otherwise, no smoke. (00:58)

6. While everyone is checking a map on the hood of a car at the Marina, Major Koslova has a lit cigarette, and in the following shot she's lighting one. Also, the same cigarette appears to be slightly bent from one side, and perfectly straight from the other. (01:08)

7. Carter Preston brings out a tape recorder in the middle of a meeting. As he places it on the table, his FBI ID flips, and then is straightened again without him touching it. (01:16)

8. Agent Whiterspoon gets shot and killed, and his blood splatters on a wall by the stairs. When the Jackal leaves Major Koslova on the floor, he stands up, revealing the wall behind Whiterspoon's corpse: it's spotless (the wall, that is). (01:24, 01:26)

9. The marina helicopter used by Carter and his crew to reach Washington is number 28 (painted both on one side and on the front). When Carter and the crew get out of the chopper, it has become number 29. (01:36, 01:39)

10. Fleeing the scene of the non-crime and heading for the subway station, the Jackal swipes the ticket with the magnetic strip up, not down as it should have been, to go through the turnstile to the tracks. No matter, it still worked . . . after all, he's the Jackal. (01:45)

11. Declan follows the Jackal at the train station: he passes by a woman with glasses and a ring in her hair—twice. The first time, she's to the right of a bearded man, the second time (Declan's shot is from the back) she's to the left of a kid with dyed hair. (01:47)

Non-Blooper
Carter is in line to slide down from the chopper to the roof of one of the Washington buildings.

BLOODY BLOOPERS (AGAIN)!!

Be a blooper donor.

Tom Hanks's hand in *Cast Away*	Blooper No. 5
Arnold Schwarzenegger in *Commando*	Blooper No. 3
J.K. Simmons in *The Jackal*	Blooper No. 8
Steven Culp in *Jason Goes to Hell: The Final Friday*	Blooper No. 11
Henry Thomas in *Legends of the Fall*	Blooper No. 9

His legs do not suddenly become white due to a miscast stuntperson, but simply because Carter is NOT the second person in line to slide along the ropes. The second person is a white man who has, as it should be, a white stuntperson. (01:40)

JASON GOES TO HELL: THE FINAL FRIDAY — The Unrated Director's Original Cut **(15)** 1993, color, 91 min.

Director: Adam Marcus

Cast: Kane Hodder (Jason Voorhees / Security Guard #2 / Razorblade-fingered Hand), John D. LeMay (Steven Freeman), Kari Keegan (Jessica Kimble), Steven Williams (Creighton Duke), Steven Culp (Robert Campbell), Erin Gray (Diana Kimble), Rusty Schwimmer (Joey B), Richard Gant (Coroner), Leslie Jordan (Shelby), Billy Green Bush (Sheriff Ed Landis), Kipp Marcus (Officer Randy Parker), Andrew Bloch (Josh), Dean Lorey (Assistant Coroner), Michelle Clunie (Deborah, The Dark-Haired Camper), Michael B. Silver (Luke, The Boy Camper).

... (yeah, right!) and on, and on, and on ...

Bloopers
1. Agent Marcus enters the log cabin, removes the lightbulb from the lamp, places it on the ladder, replaces it with a new one, then folds the ladder ... and the old bulb doesn't fall! What a great trick! (00:02, 00:03)
2. Attracted by a noise, Marcus goes barefoot from the bathroom to the living room, then outside the house while chased by Jason. But in the woods she's wearing some sort of black sneakers (in the shot where she's running toward the camera) and a pair of clear shoes (the detail of her running feet, as well as when she stands up after the lights have been turned on around Jason). (00:03, 00:05, 00:06)
3. Marcus falls from the second floor onto a table, smashing it. The right leg pops away, but in the following shot, that very leg is tucked underneath the table. (00:05)
4. Jason raises his head when he hears an approaching bomb. He has no machete in his hand. When the bomb hits behind him, Jason is holding the machete. (00:06)
5. The assistant coroner places a pizza box with a few drinks on top of it on the guards' table. When he picks the pizza up, the drinks have moved from one corner of the box to the opposite corner. (00:15)
6. In the kitchen, Joey B shows how to make a Jason patty: she cuts two eyeholes with her finger, but the patty

moves all around the counter in-between shots. (00:21)

7. While in Steven's car, Deborah (the dark-haired camper) says that she's not worried about being slaughtered. Luke, her boyfriend, kisses her on the neck—but when we see Steven, and Deborah is in the background, Luke is nowhere to be seen. (00:25)

8. Deborah goes inside the tent to make out with Luke; the silhouette reveals that he is removing Deborah's vest— but inside the tent, she still has it on. (00:28, 00:29)

9. The mailbox on the Voorhees's house reads, "Vorhees." (00:36)

10. When he's about to shave Josh, who's tied to a table, the coroner applies some shaving cream to the man's neck and mustache. The amount of cream changes in the following cut. (00:37)

11. During Jason's passage from Josh to Robert, a trail of blood drips from the right side of Robert's mouth. But when he stands up, the blood has moved to the left side. (00:59, 01:00)

12. Steven "kidnaps" Jessica and takes her away from Robert. As they get to Steven's car, the cameraman can be seen reflected in the passenger's window. (01:03)

13. When Steven backs his car over Robert, Robert's shirt gets pretty dirty, and his right arm winds up on his chest. In the following, matching cut, Robert's arm is along his side and his shirt is much, much cleaner. (01:03)

14. Brought to the police station, Steven sees Jessica in jeopardy. He brings his handcuffed hands from behind his back to the front by jumping up and slyly sliding them underneath his feet. . . . But the cuffs stretch a little too much for being regular "metal" cuffs. Prop department, anyone? (01:08)

15. Jessica finds a note in her daughter's improvised crib. The note, by Duke, reads: "I have what you want. Come to the Voorhees house *alone!* Duke." When Steven finds the same note by Vic's body, it reads: "I have your baby. Come to the Voorhees house *alone*. Duke." (01:11, 01:14)

Questions

1. Whoever is possessed by Jason casts a reflection of Jason: the coroner does when he walks out of the morgue, Josh does when he's trying to kill Diane. . . . So then why does Robert NOT when he's reaching for Steven in the car (check the reflection on the hood)? (00:06, 00:39, 01:03)

2. Deborah tosses a condom away, then begins a love match with Luke. When the coroner (Jason) approaches, he sees what seems to be a

136 The Jewel of the Nile

tent with a zipped-up door, yet he steps on the condom, that now is on the outside. Huh? (00:31, 00:32)

Jason Goes to Hell—The Final Cameos

At the Federal Morgue, the standing security guard, the one who frisks, is Kane Hodder—who plays Jason in the movie. (00:08) He also plays the Kruegerlike gloved hand that in the end drags Jason's mask down to hell. (01:27)

The police badges read, "Cunningham County." Is this a coincidence, or is it an homage to Sean S. Cunningham, the director / producer of the first *Friday the 13th*? (00:22)

The book Steven finds in the Voorhees's house is the same Necronomicon from the *Evil Dead* series. (00:56)

Officer Bish, one of the three cops who finds the "dead" Robert at the station, is *Jason*'s director Adam Marcus. (01:08)

The chained box in the Voorhees's basement, labeled "Arctic Expedition—Julia Carpenter, Horlicks University" is the crate that caused a lot of commotion in *Creepshow*. (01:20)

---

3. Jessica calls her mom while holding her baby daughter,

Stephanie, who is as bald as Mr. Clean. But when Jessica enters her mom's house (presumably very soon, due to the emergency of her visit), Stephanie now sports a great 'do. Does she have very active hormones, or is her real father Marv Albert? (00:38, 00:41)

JEWEL OF THE NILE, THE (7)
1985, color, 115 min.

Director: Lewis Teague

Cast: Michael Douglas (Jack T. Colton), Kathleen Turner (Joan Wilder), Danny DeVito (Ralph), Spiros Focás (Omar Khalifa), Avner Eisenberg (Jewel), Paul David Magid (Tarak), Howard Jay Patterson (Barak), Randall Edwin Nelson (Karak), Samuel Ross Williams (Arak), Timothy Daniel Furst (Sarak), Hamid Fillali (Rachid), Holland Taylor (Gloria Horne), Hyacinthe N'iaye (Nubian Wrestler).

How to romance two birds with one stone.

Bloopers

1. Joan sits down to talk with Jack: she's wearing two pearl earrings. When she declares, "Jack, this is just becoming a blur ..." the left earring is gone. It'll be back as she receives a bunch of flowers. (00:04, 00:07)

2. While surfboarding, Jack passes very close to the boat

Joan is writing on. He sprays her, and she brings her right hand to her hat. But in the following close-up, the hand is gone. (00:05)

3. During a small conversation at a party, Gloria, Joan's publisher, takes a long sip from a drink. When Omar says, "Then permit me to tell you," the glass is gone. (00:10)

4. Fleeing in the desert on a jet plane, Jack activates the afterburner, entering a sandstorm. The afterburner flame is gone in the third shot. (00:52)

5. Jack has to fight with a huge Nubian wrestler. He unbuttons his shirt almost completely, but after the first punch, as he rolls on the ground, he has an almost completely buttoned shirt. (01:05)

6. Ralph finds himself on a bed of hot coals. He starts turning to his left—but a detail of his feet shows him turning right. (01:10)

7. From the time she's in Africa, Joan wears soft, cord shoes. Those are the very same shoes she has when she jumps onto the train to Kadir, but when she dangles from the side of a car, she's wearing sandals. (01:18)

JOE DIRT (3)
2001, color, 90 min.

Director: Dennie Gordon

Cast: David Spade (Joe Dirt),

Brittany Daniel (Brandy), Dennis Miller (Zander Kelly), Adam Beach (Kicking Wing), Christopher Walken (Clem), Jaime Pressly (Jill), Kid Rock (Robby), Erik Per Sullivan (Little Joe Dirt), Megan Taylor Harvey (Joe's Little Sister), Caroline Aaron (Joe's Mom), Fred Ward (Joe's Dad), Hamilton Camp (Meteor Bert), John Farley (Security Guard).

David Spade plays a likable guy with the same virtuosity that Joe Pesci would play Miss America.

Bloopers

1. Joe forces the gate at the radio station, smashing both the wing of his car and the black-and-white security bar. But as the guard goes to *comfort* the bar, it is now in mint condition. (00:01, 00:02)

2. Still during his entrance, Joe clenches his teeth and steers the car to what appears to be the right. Yet the car goes to the left. (00:01)

3. After the blast of the atom bomb and the literal dissolution of Kicking Wing, Joe screams. The shot has been flipped (check the "I choked" written on his T-shirt). (00:33)

Question
During his forced tooth balloon, Joe Dirt is shown to be landing on a South Dakota map, but his voiceover says, "I'd floated all the way to North Dakota." Huh? (00:25)

JOHNNY MNEMONIC (5)
1995, color, 103 min.

Director: Robert Longo

Cast: Keanu Reeves (Johnny), Dina Meyer (Jane), Ice-T (J-Bone), Takeshi Kitano (Takahashi), Dennis Akayama (Shinji), Dolph Lundgren (Street Preacher), Henry Rollins (Spider), Barbara Sukowa (Anna Kalmann), Udo Kier (Ralfi), Tracy Tweed (Pretty).

The movie that proves once and for all that Keanu has a hole in his head.

Bloopers
1. The reflection of the wake-up call in Johnny's eye is not a reflection at all. (00:01)
2. The wake-up call is for "Thursday, 17 January 2021." A-hem. In the year 2021, January 17 will be a Sunday. (00:01)
3. Johnny calls Ralfi: the number appears in a black box, bottom-screen left, and the symbol "DataFlow" appears bottom-screen right ("And hello to you, too.") But the number and symbol vanish in closer shots of the video-phone ("I'm sorry, Johnny."), then they are back, then they are gone again. (00:03)
4. Johnny puts his goggles on to load the data. Then he plugs in the jack, but the detail shows no goggles at all on his hair. (00:10)
5. The Street Preacher crucifies Spiter using scalpels: he grabs one from an operating tray, uses it, then grabs a second one from the same tray . . . wait a second! There was no second scalpel on the operating tray!! (01:00)

Questions
1. Johnny lives in a future where the currency is a mysterious K ("800 K should cover it"). But during one rant, Johnny yells that he wants, among other things, "a ten-thousand-dollar-a-night whore." What would that be in K? (Also, he bribes Jane with the promise of 20 grand, and a parking sign states that the fare is $25.00 each 1/2 hour or less. Hmmm . . .) (00:03, 01:05)
2. Why do the Central Beijing police have "Police" written on their shields, when all of the other signs are in Chinese? (00:04)
3. Takahashi is shot while standing in front of Johnny: the bullets go in (his back), come out (his chest) . . . but neither Johnny, nor the aquarium with Jones inside, get hit. Huh? (01:17)

JUDGE DREDD (3)
1995, color, 96 min.

Director: Danny Cannon

Cast: Sylvester Stallone (Judge Joseph Dredd), Armand Assante (Rico), Rob Schneider (Herman "Fergie" Ferguson), Jürgen Prochnow (Judge

Griffin), Max von Sydow (Chief Justice Fargo), Diane Lane (Judge Hershey), Joanna Miles (McGruder), Joan Chen (Ilsa), Balthazar Getty (Olmeyer), Maurice Roëves (Warden Miller), Ian Dury (Geiger), Christopher Adamson (Mean Machine), Mitchell Ryan (Vardas Hammond).

Futuristic street judge is a hero, is condemned, is a felon, and is a hero again.

Bloopers

1. TV reporter Hammond says, taping his piece, ". . . fifty-three hospitalized, five of them children; nineteen dead." Later, when Dredd sees the same news bulletin, Hammond says, ". . . fifty-three hospitalized, nineteen dead." (00:12, 00:15)
2. Because of a hit, Dredd has a bloody wound on the left side of his face. The amount of blood decreases and increases all through the picture: it's almost gone when Dredd confronts Rico, there's much much more when he's falling and then riding a defective flying motorbike, then the wound is almost clean, then the blood is again almost all over the left side of his face as he reaches the Janus building. (00:50, 01:09, 01:11, 01:14, 01:18)
3. Dredd wants to run through a vent in the city's incinerator. But there's a burst of fire every 30 seconds. Well, almost. While Dredd is arguing with Fergie, between the first two flames there's a pause of 37 seconds, the next one comes after 22 seconds, and the last one we see after 23. (01:05, 01:06)

K

KARATE KID, THE (6)
1984, color, 126 min.

Director: John G. Avildsen

Cast: Ralph Macchio (Daniel Larusso), Noriyuki "Pat" Morita (Miyagi), Elisabeth Shue (Ali Mills), Martin Kove (John Kreese), Randee Heller (Lucille Larusso), William Zabka (Johnny Lawrence), Ron Thomas (Bobby), Rob Garrison (Tommy), Chad McQueen (Dutch), Tony O'Dell (Jimmy), Israel Juarbe (Freddy Fernandez), William Bassett (Mr. Mills).

Remember Rocky*? Same thing, only with a kid. And karate.*

Bloopers
1. When mother and son Larusso leave New Jersey, they have a bicycle on the roof of the car—the handle toward the back of the car. As they're driving (and Mom is singing, "California, here we come!"), the bicycle has rotated 180 degrees on the roof of the car. (00:00, 00:01)

2. During the beach party, Johnny pushes a stereo against Daniel. When he shoves it, the speakers are pointed toward Daniel. When Daniel falls, the speakers are pointed toward Johnny. (00:12)

3. In the restaurant in front of the karate school, Daniel places his hand against his head, but when we cut to the inside, his hands are both on the table. (00:23)

4. Ali spots Daniel at the costume party because he's dressed as a shower. She inserts a flower through the curtain, holding it with her left hand. In the inside, Daniel is offered a flower held by a right hand. (00:35)

5. Daniel shows Mr. Miyagi "paint the house," moving his right arm from side to side. But then he lowers his *left* arm. (01:16)

6. During a fancy dinner at the Encino Oaks Country Club, Johnny sits at a table while

Ali dances with her dad. As he tells her what time it is, Johnny pops up behind them, dancing with Ali's mother. He is one fast mother. And she is, too. (01:24)

KING COBRA (2)
1998, color, 92 min.

Directors: David Hillebrand and Scott Hillebrand

Cast: Pat Morita (Nick "Hash" Hashimoto), Scott Brandon (Doctor Brad Kegan), Kasey Fallo (Jo Biddle), Hoyt Axton (Mayor Ed Biddle), Joseph Ruskin (Doctor Irwin Burns), Courtney Gains (Doctor Joseph McConnell), Eric Lawson (Sheriff Ben Lowry), Cedric Duplechain (Deputy Bud Fuller), Eric Estrada (Bernie Alvarez), Scott Bolan (Simpson), Efren Ramirez (Teen Boy), Iyari Limon (Teen Girl).

You guys! Let's splice the genes of two of the most lethal snakes in the world. What could possibly go wrong?

Bloopers
1. Brad pulls a fang from Mr. Simpson's leg with forceps. The curved fang keeps changing position in the forceps: first it points to the right, then to the left, to the right, and then to the left again. (00:24)

2. The teen girl freezes because she hears a rattling sound. Her right hand is on her boyfriend's chest—but in the following shot, her right hand is on the boy's shoulder. And supposedly she's totally frozen. (00:36)

Question
Doctor Hashimoto tells Jo and Irwin that "snakes pick up on vibrations in the ground," so to be careful while they're moving a large box. However, Hash jumps not once, but twice, off of his Caravan. Do those vibrations not count? (00:54, 00:55)

KRAKATOA, EAST OF JAVA (1)
1969, color, 113 min.

Director: Bernard Kowalski

Cast: Maximilian Schell (Hanson), Diane Baker (Laura), Brian Keith (Connerly), Barbara Werle (Charley), John Leyton (Rigby), Rossano Brazzi (Giovanni), Sal Mineo (Leoncavallo), Jacqui Chan (Toshi).

Late nineteenth-century volcano disaster movie.

Blooper
The volcano of Krakatoa is actually *west* of Java.

KRAMER VS. KRAMER (3)
1979, color, 105 min.

Director: Robert Benton

Cast: Dustin Hoffman (Ted Kramer), Meryl Streep (Joanna Kramer), Jane Alexander (Margaret Phelps), Justin Henry (Billy Kramer), Howard Duff (John Shaunessy), George Coe (Jim O'Connor), JoBeth Williams (Phyllis Bernard), Bill Moor (Gressen), Howland Chamberlain (Judge Atkins), Jack Ramage (Spencer), Jess Osuna (Ackerman), Nicholas Hormann (Interviewer).

Hoffman and Streep in a custody battle over an Oscar . . . oops, we mean a kid.

Bloopers

1. Ted warns Billy about "no ice cream before the Salisbury steak," but Billy goes ahead. Furious, Ted takes him to his room. During this short trip, Billy kicks in the air and loses one slipper. When Ted walks into his room, Billy has both slippers on, he then is barefoot when he lands on the bed, then he has his slippers on again, then he doesn't. (00:37)

2. Ted is in the kitchen, talking to Margaret while they're doing the dishes. When at the end he says, "You're all right," a microphone pops up from the bottom of the screen, close to Ted's right leg. (00:51/fixed on DVD)

3. Ted brings Billy to check out his new workplace. As they walk in a corridor, they can see New York on a gray but sharp day. A few seconds later, Billy enters Ted's office and darts to the window: the day has turned into a gray, foggy, and cloudy day. (01:07, 01:08)

L

LAST OF THE MOHICANS, THE (9)
1992, color, 124 min.

Director: Michael Mann

Cast: Daniel Day-Lewis
(Nathaniel "Hawkeye"),
Madeleine Stowe (Cora
Munro), Russell Means
(Chingachgook), Eric Schweig
(Uncas), Jodhi May (Alice
Munro), Steven Waddington
(Major Duncan Heyward), Wes
Studi (Magua), Maurice Roëves
(Colonel Edmund Munro),
Patrice Chéreau (General
Montcalm), Edward Blatchford
(Jack Winthrop), Terry Kinney
(John Cameron), Mac Andrews
(General Webb), Clark
Heathcliffe (Regimental
Sergeant Major).

*White guy raised by Indians
finds himself surrounded by
mean white guys and
Indians.*

Bloopers

1. The Mohicans are hunting a
   deer. When the deer first
   bounds into view, if you look
   very, very carefully, you can
   see someone wearing a red
   baseball cap just beyond the
   deer, running along with the
   animal in the woods. (00:03)

2. Major Heyward is speaking
   to the natives in one of the
   villages. As he says "His Maj-
   esty, King George II, is very
   grateful for your support,"
   the sky behind him is partly
   cloudy. Then it changes as he
   announces the plans to go
   "up to Fort William Henry." And
   when he says "for king, for
   country!" the sky is now completely white with clouds. It
   returns to partly cloudy when
   he asks, "You call yourself a
   patriot?" (00:07, 00:08)

3. When General Webb talks to
   his men in his office, he finishes by making them laugh.
   His left hand, which was on
   the table, jumps onto the
   headrest of his chair. (00:12)

4. At the beginning of the
   march to Fort Henry, Alice is
   about to climb up next to a
   waterfall. Uncas stares at her,

his earring in his right ear. The earring is in Uncas's left ear before (00:04) and later (00:25) all the way through the end of the movie. (00:23)

5. During the meeting between Colonel Munro and Monsieur Le Marquis (and respective troops), Le Marquis talks holding his right hand in front of him. When Munro answers, "I am a soldier, not a diplomat," Le Marquis lowers his hand. But it is up again in the following, matching shot. (01:05)

6. After the French have taken Fort Henry, the British are marching away through a clearing. After two Huron warriors attack, there is a shot of Hawkeye, immediately followed by a shot from behind the march. If you look at the bottom of the screen in the middle there is someone wearing a blue baseball cap, lifting a modern megaphone up. (01:14)

7. The second canoe that the fugitives push down the waterfall gains an oar (stuck between the last two seats) as it goes over the edge. (01:23)

8. Hawkeye is running up the cliff after the Hurons, who have Uncas and Alice. Just before Hawkeye yells, "Uncas!" he's running through a rock underpass and accidentally hits a fake boulder on the left of the screen that "bounces" in reaction. (01:44)

9. Chasing the Huron warriors up the cliff area, Hawkeye shoots two warriors with two rifles; the one who falls on a boulder drops his rifle, which slides off the boulder. Hawkeye runs by, grabbing the rifle, which has somehow jumped back up onto the boulder. (01:47)

Questions

1. On the march from Fort Henry, the Hurons are walking through the woods on both sides of the clearing, preparing to ambush the British. Just before the full-on attack, we see a group on the left all holding their rifles right-handed, then a group on the right, all holding their rifles left-handed. Was left-handedness or ambidextrousness that common among the Huron, or did the filmmakers just flip the negative to indicate that Huron warriors were on both sides of the clearing? (01:15)

2. Major Heyward falls and rolls down a hill. As he stops, is that the shadow of a camera and a boom mike visible on his red jacket? (01:18)

Fun Fact

After Duncan's death, Uncas runs after the Hurons. As he passes by a tree going uphill, he slides and loses his balance, regains it and keeps running. The following shot shows him passing by the same tree, sliding again, losing his balance again . . . (01:41)

LAST STARFIGHTER, THE (2)
1984, color, 101 min.

Director: Nick Castle

Cast: Lance Guest (Alex Rogan / Beta), Dan O'Herlihy (Grig), Kay E. Kuter (Enduran), Dan Mason (Lord Kril), Catherine Mary Stewart (Maggie Gordon), Barbara Bosson (Jane Rogan), Norman Snow (Xur), Robert Preston (Centauri), Chris Hebert (Louis Rogan), Maggie Cooper (Female Rylan Sergeant), John O'Leary (Rylan Bursar), George McDaniel (Kodan Officer).

Video-game record breaker is recruited to save the universe.

Bloopers
1. Centauri dies (even if later on he will admit that he was "merely dormant"): his eyes twitch. (00:55)
2. While Grig steps out of a sort of elevator and talks to Alex, Alex puts his left glove on twice. (00:57)

Questions
1. Alex is given a translator device thanks to which he will hear English, even if the aliens are speaking a different language. So how come he sees a perfect *lip-sync* of English by the aliens? (00:30)
2. The people who live at the Starlite, Starbrite trailer park finally meet Grig, the alien. They understand what he says without the translator device. Huh? (01:32)

LEGENDS OF THE FALL (11)
1995, color, 133 min.

Director: Edward Zwick

Cast: Brad Pitt (Tristan Ludlow), Anthony Hopkins (Colonel William Ludlow), Aidan Quinn (Alfred Ludlow), Julia Ormond (Susannah Fincannon Ludlow), Henry Thomas (Samuel Ludlow), Karina Lombard (Isabel Decker Ludlow–a.k.a. Isabel Two), Gordon Tootoosis (One Stab), Christina Pickles (Isabel Ludlow), Paul Desmond (Decker), Tantoo Cardinal (Pet), Robert Wisden (John T. O'Banion), John Novak (James O'Banion).

Boy loves girl, boy's brother loves girl, boy loses life, boy's brother marries girl. Then there's another brother, a bear . . .

Bloopers
1. The horses used during the war scenes are all Americans, and not crossbreeds like they should have been (at that time, at least). (00:01, 00:09, 00:38)
2. When young Samuel gets wounded by a bear, his dad runs up to him. He kneels down and orders, "Take your hand away!" Samuel obeys, and his dad orders, "Now take it away!" Hey: it is away! (00:05)

3. While Samuel and Tristan chat about sex, and Samuel states that "We're gonna wait," Tristan's hands are crossed on his lap—but in the next shot his arms are crossed over his chest. (00:21)

4. Samuel tells his dad that he's going to Canada to enlist. His brother, Alfred, is standing behind him (you can see part of his shoulder on the left side of the screen). Samuel then follows his fiancée, who's walking upstairs. As he stops, after some ten steps, a close-up reveals . . . Alfred's shoulder, who naturally didn't move at all. (00:24, 00:25)

5. Tristan opens the report book his father wrote. He flips one page and unfolds the Dakota map, but as Susannah approaches, the map appears to be smaller and only partially unfolded, and there are more than a dozen flipped pages. (00:25)

6. During one battle, the voice-over says, ". . . yet so barely." In that moment, an explosion hurls one soldier through the air. Well, that is, if you ignore the air ramps used by the stuntman. (00:35)

7. Samuel and Tristan hug in a foxhole. Samuel's face is buried in Tristan's chest, and Tristan's chin lies on Samuel's hat. In the following shot, their heads are side by side. (00:37)

8. Tristan holds his hand on his dying brother, then it's on his shoulder, subsequently he brings it to his mouth, and then it's on Samuel's chest again—after every cut. (00:37)

9. Fatally wounded, Samuel gasps blood out of his mouth. The blood runs along his left cheek . . . twice. And a few seconds later, his face is clean. (00:43)

10. On their patio, Alfred talks with Tristan about him marrying Susannah. When Alfred yells, "Yeeees!! Goddam you to hell!" the shot has been flipped (check his shirt collar). (00:57, 00:58)

11. Colonel Ludlow writes on his blackboard "Am Happy," when Tristan is by him. The writing changes shape and position between the detail and the master shot. (01:24, 01:25)

LEPRECHAUN IN THE HOOD (2)
2000, color, 90 min.

Director: Rob Spera

Cast: Warwick Davis (Leprechaun), Ice-T (Mack Daddy), A.T. Montgomery (Postmaster P), Rashaan Nall (Stray Bullet), Red Grant (Butch), Dan Martin (Jackie Dee), Lobo Sebastian (Fontaine Rivera), Ivory Ocean (Reverend Hanson), Jack Ong (Chow Yung Pi), Bleu Daving (Slug), Bebe Drake (Post's Mother).

Fifth adventure for the Leprechaun, this time really hip-n-hoppin'.

Bloopers

1. To comfort Post, Stray says that "Things will be different now, I swear," then he crosses himself—with the left hand, instead of the right. (00:33)
2. While performing "Stray Bullet to the Heart," Postmaster P removes his jacket. Twice. (01:04)

Question

Reverend Hanson is worried that the three friends are going to Vegas, leaving the Leprechaun inside a safe in his office. Stray tells him just to "keep that lock safed." The subtitle says, "keep that safe locked." Who's right? (00:59)

LIAR LIAR (5)

1997, color, 86 min.

Director: Tom Shadyac

Cast: Jim Carrey (Fletcher Reede), Maura Tierney (Audrey Reede), Justin Cooper (Max Reede), Cary Elwes (Jerry), Anne Haney (Greta), Jennifer Tilly (Samantha Cole), Amanda Donohoe (Miranda), Jason Bernard (Judge Marshall Stevens), Swoosie Kurtz (Dana Appleton), Brandi Burkett (Flight Attendant).

A lawyer is forced to tell nothing but the truth, and his world falls apart.

Bloopers

1. Jerry only appears in four scenes; in two of them his hair is parted on the right; in the other two it is parted on the left. (00:04 & 00:16, 00:09 & 01:10)
2. While fixing the cake for her son's birthday, Audrey's talking to her boyfriend in the kitchen. She takes out the box of candles and holds them in her right hand. After one shot (and without any indication of movement from her) all of the candles are beautifully arranged. (00:18)
3. The elevator door opens and Fletcher's boss comes out. Fletcher sees her and runs away, down the emergency exit stairway. He bumps into the wall (with "21st Floor Roof Access" written on it): the wall shakes as if made of cardboard. (00:32)
4. In the courtroom, Fletcher pours himself a glass of water; then, in the background, he grabs the glass with his left hand. In the close-up, he's holding it with his right. (00:50)
5. When he's being pulled out of the courtroom, Fletcher yells that he's Jose Canseco. Technically, that's a lie. (01:08)

Question

Fletcher's secretary Greta stops on her way out and asks him a question. He replies with the truth and she begins to walk away again. He yells after her that he didn't understand the question and that she should ask him again. But he DID understand the question; he simply didn't say the answer she wanted to hear. So did he lie in saying he didn't understand her question? (00:45)

LIVE AND LET DIE (22)
1973, color, 121 min.

Director: Guy Hamilton

Cast: Roger Moore (James Bond 007), Yaphet Kotto (Kananga / Mr. Big), Jane Seymour (Solitaire), Clifton James (Sheriff J.W. Pepper), Julius Harris (Tee Hee), Geoffrey Holder (Baron Samedi), David Hedison (Felix Leiter), Gloria Hendry (Rosie Carver), Bernard Lee (M), Lois Maxwell (Miss Moneypenny), Tommy Lane (Adam), Earl Jolly Brown (Whisper), Joie Chitwood (Charlie), Dennis Edwards (Baines), Arnold Williams (Cab Driver No. 1).

*A*dventure #8, and Bond #3.

Bloopers
1. Hamilton, the agent in front of the Fillet of Soul restaurant in New Orleans, assists a funeral procession, and so do two lady pedestrians: one is dressed in black, the other in blue with an apricot jacket. When Strutter is sent to keep an eye on the same restaurant, he, too, assists a funeral procession. And so too do two lady pedestrians, who, uncannily, are wearing the same outfits they did a few days before. (00:02, 01:07)

2. During the ceremony in San Monique, a voodoo dancer brings a yellow-and-green snake close to Agent Baines. The dancer holds the snake by its body when he's in the shot, but by its head when Baines is in the shot. (00:04)

3. When Bond arrives at the NY airport, his tie knot features one stripe in the middle of it. As he walks from the cab to the Oh Cult Voodoo Shop, the knot is different and now has two stripes. He sports one stripe again when he comes out of the store. (00:13, 00:17, 00:19)

4. Charlie, the driver of the taxi Bond takes from the airport, is killed while driving. The taxi moves from the center lane to the left, but when Bond says, "Easy, Charlie," he's still in the center lane. (00:14)

5. Bond tries to regain control of the taxi, and rams a red car (shot from inside the taxi). What seems to be the rearview mirror dangles in front of the camera; but in the following shots, the mirror is intact. (00:15)

6. Eventually the taxi hits the steps of a building and ends up slammed into a parked vehicle. The "dead" Charlie, wearing a gray jacket, seems to be quite alive, working on the steering wheel. (00:15)

7. Bond exits the back of the voodoo shop, and from a deserted sidewalk, hails a taxi.

But as he opens the door, a few bystanders can be seen reflected in the window. (00:20)

8. Bond is in a cab, heading toward Harlem. When the driver tells Bond that for $20 extra he would drive him to the KKK, there's a park on his left side. But to the left side of Bond there's a small hill. (00:21)

9. And now, let's play a game: can you tell where the real gun ends and the "bendable" barrel begins, when Tee Hee uses his claw on Bond's Walter PPK? (If you can't, go see an eye doctor!) (00:24)

10. Also, did you notice that the gun turns 180° in Tee Hee's claw? (00:24)

11. Tee Hee's claw bends at the wrist on more than one occasion (e.g., when he bends 007's gun and when he grabs the meat to give to the crocodiles). Yet in the end, when Bond rips his sleeve, the forearm appears to be one solid piece, with no bending parts. (00:24, 01:21, 01:58)

12. In the alley, just before reaching a fire-escape ladder, Bond pushes a few hanging wires out of his way. But in a wider shot, there are no wires to be seen. Must have been a helluva push. (00:26)

13. After frolicking in the meadows, Bond shows Rosie the queen of cups, holding it between his thumb and his index finger. But in the close-up, he holds it between his

index and middle fingers. (00:44)

14. Baron Samedi greets Bond and Solitaire, then grabs his flute with his left hand. In the over-the-shoulder shot, he grabs the flute again. (00:55)

15. Bond sneaks into Mr. Bleeker's plane and offers a "lesson" to Mrs. Bell. The plane is parked in such a way that behind Mrs. Bell there's only the sky and other parked planes, yet her close-up reveals a wall. After defeating the pursuers, the plane stops by a wall, and Bond asks Mrs. Bell if she wants another lesson. She stares at him—and it's the same close-up from the beginning. (01:04, 01:06)

16. As Sheriff Pepper drives away from behind the Louisiana sign, the camera is reflected in the rear window of his car. (01:27)

17. Just before the second thug boat jumps the road, Adam's car backs up, leaving Sheriff Pepper by himself. The shadow of the crew is visible on the ground. (01:29)

18. A chubby cop at Miller's Bridge tosses a rope to a colleague, then ... he does it again. (01:32)

19. When the police cars pile up, a few cops are wearing helmets (particularly the last one). (01:36)

20. During the final voodoo ceremony, Bond shoots and kills Goat-Head boy, who was

holding a snake. When the real Baron Samedi emerges from the grave, Goat-Head boy (with his pet snake) is standing in the middle of the crowd. (01:45, 01:46)

21. During the fight on the train between Bond and Tee Hee, you can briefly see a crew-member reflected in the mirror of the cabin—just before Bond lifts Tee Hee by his legs. (01:59)

22. When Tee Hee jumps out of the window, you can catch a glimpse of his real right arm, holding onto the rail in order to perform the stunt. (01:59)

The Original Crocodile Hunter

Ross Kananga, a Seminole Indian, was the owner of a real Louisiana crocodile farm, which featured about 1,500 animals. Not only did screenwriter Tom Mankiewicz name Yaphet Kotto's character after him, but Kananga was also 007's stunt double for the ever-popular running-over-the-crocodiles escape that is featured in the movie. They shot five takes, the last of which is the one in the movie.

LORD OF THE RINGS: THE FELLOW-SHIP OF THE RING, THE (25)

2001, color, 178 min.

Director: Peter Jackson

Cast: Elijah Wood (Frodo Baggins), Sean Astin (Samwise "Sam" Gamgee), Dominic Monaghan (Meriadoc "Merry" Brandybuck), Billy Boyd (Peregrin "Pippin" Took), Ian McKellen (Gandalf the Grey), Ian Holm (Bilbo Baggins), Viggo Mortensen (Aragorn / Strider), Orlando Bloom (Legolas Greenleaf), Liv Tyler (Arwen Evenstar), Christopher Lee (Saruman the White), Cate Blanchett (Galadriel), Sean Bean (Boromir), John Rhys-Davies (Gimli), Hugo Weaving (Lord Elrond), Harry Sinclair (Isildur).

One ring to control them all. Two rings, it's gotta be the postman.

Bloopers

1. During a battle, Sauron throws Isildur's father, the king, against some rocks. The king dies with the helmet askew on his head, but when Isildur reaches his father, the helmet is no longer on his head. (00:03)

2. On his buggy with Frodo, Gandalf the Grey is smoking his trademark long pipe. But the pipe seems to vanish (after "Half the Shire's been invited," for instance) and comes back all through the trip. And, when Frodo jumps off the buggy, Gandalf's pipe is nowhere in sight. But in the following close-up, he's bringing it to his mouth. (00:09, 00:10)

3. During his arrival in town,

Gandalf amuses a few hobbit kids with fireworks. The sun comes and goes throughout the whole sequence. (00:10)

4. When the hobbit kids cheer for the fireworks, they all jump up and down—but in the shot from the front, the second girl from the left (the one with a long golden dress) is not jumping at all. (00:10)

5. Bilbo is asked to make a speech at his 111th birthday party. While he's talking, he sports a nice green foulard around his neck. He then puts the ring on, vanishes, and reappears in his house. The foulard is still there, but after he pockets the ring, the foulard is gone. (00:18, 00:20)

6. Departing for his holiday, Bilbo opens the door of his house and stops in front of it. Gandalf catches up with him, leaving the door open. But when Bilbo leaves and Gandalf comes back into the house, he has to open the door. (00:23, 00:24)

7. After giving the ring to Frodo in a sealed envelope, Gandalf has to leave the house. He walks to the door and clears the chandelier, but when he stops at the threshold, the chandelier bobs up and down as if Gandalf hit it on his way out. But he didn't. (00:26)

8. Gandalf pulls Sam into Frodo's house through a window. As Sam lands on a desk, books and papers fall on the carpet. But they seem to keep moving on the carpet because every one of Sam's close-ups shows the objects in noticeably different positions. (00:35)

9. On their journey, Sam stops by a scarecrow because that's as far as he has ever been from home up to that moment. The position of the scarecrow changes between close-ups and long shots. (00:37)

10. In the Orthanc castle, Gandalf is standing and holding his staff as he listens to Saruman about the recovering strength of Sauron: the leather lace of the staff keeps changing position in his hand, sometimes it's around his hand, or around only his middle finger, or else his wrist. Needless to say, Gandalf doesn't seem to move a muscle during the whole conversation. (00:39)

Director Cameo

The first, plump and burping villager the four hobbits run into in Bree is *LOTR*'s director/writer/producer/mastermind Peter Jackson. (00:50)

---

11. Inside the Prancing Pony, Merry reaches his friends' table carrying a pint. Pippin wants one, too, so he leaves. But when Frodo asks the host of the tavern about

Strider, Pippin is back at the table—and Merry is missing. (00:51, 00:52, 00:53)

12. When the group decides to stop at the Watchtower of Amunan, Frodo plops down, and Pippin does the same, moaning. But a close-up of Aragorn reveals that Pippin is still standing and then proceeds to sit down. (01:00)

13. After Arwen has defeated the Ringwraiths, Frodo is lowered down from Arwen's horse and placed on the river's shore. Frodo has a pimple under the right corner of his mouth. The pimple wasn't there earlier, and will not be there later. (01:12)

14. Frodo wakes up in Rivendell with Gandalf at the foot of his bed. Frodo's shirt is open enough to show a chain around his neck. But when Frodo pulls himself to sit up in bed, the chain is gone. It will be back when Frodo and Bilbo meet again. (00:13, 00:14, 00:17)

15. Lord Elrond brings Isildur to the heart of the mountain to destroy the ring. Isildur takes a good look at the ring while holding it in his left hand, but the detail shows the ring being in his right hand. (01:21)

16. When the fellowship is en route, Sam is with a horse. On the top of the snowy mountains, though, the horse can't be seen. Yet Sam and Aragorn set the animal free when they reach the wall of Moria. Did the horse know a different path to follow and fool them all? (01:35, 01:38, 01:43)

17. Frodo falls on the mountain and rolls in the snow, and is stopped by Aragorn. Frodo's cape moves up a little too much, revealing where the "hobbit feet" makeup ends, and where the real actor's leg begins. (01:38)

18. Inside Balin's tomb, Boromir runs to the door to check on the orcs. Behind him, Aragorn puts down his torch. But after two arrows hit the door, Aragorn puts his torch down one more time. (01:55)

19. Legolas jumps on top of the cave troll and shoots an arrow right into his skull. But when Legolas jumps off of the big troll, and also when the troll is looking for Frodo, the arrow is gone. And when Legolas shoots the final, lethal arrow at the cave troll's throat, surprise! The arrow in the head has come back. (01:58, 02:00)

20. Aragorn crawls on all fours to help Frodo, who's been wounded by the cave troll. While rushing toward the hobbit, Aragorn brushes three large rocks, which move as if made of—uh—prop materials. (02:00)

21. Aragorn tells the fellowship that they will cross the lake at nightfall, and a discussion

with Gimli ensues. In the background, Sam appears to be fast asleep, then working on his sword, then asleep again—but then very alert and ready to step into action when Merry asks where Frodo is. (02:28, 02:29)

22. After disappearing from underneath Boromir by putting the ring in his right hand, Frodo gets scared of what he sees and removes the ring with his left hand, falling backward. But when he lands, his right hand is clenched into a fist with the ring in it. (02:33)

23. As Aragorn runs to a lethally wounded Boromir, one of the "dead" orcs raises his head and twirls his body. (02:41)

24. Boromir speaks his final words to Aragorn, and places his hand over Aragorn's left shoulder. But in the opposite shots, the hand isn't there. (02:41)

25. In front of the lake, Frodo can't help but cry. The tear from his right eye runs only halfway down his right cheek, the left one passes his mouth. But after one moment, it's the left tear that's only halfway down the left cheek, while the right one is by the chin. (02:44, 02:45)

Questions

1. All the hobbits are always barefoot. But, after Frodo and Sam walk by a small waterfall, doesn't it seem like they are wearing some kind of shoes when they're crossing the field? (00:07, 00:37)

2. The fellowship of the ring, on its way to Radlas, crosses mountains covered with snow. Where is their steamy breath? Sure, you can see it when they're in front of the wall of Noria, but where's their breath on the mountain? (01:38, 01:40, 01:43)

LOSER (8)
2000, color, 95 min.

Director: Amy Heckerling

Cast: Jason Biggs (Paul Tannek), Mena Suvari (Dora Diamond), Zak Orth (Adam), Thomas Sadoski (Chris), Jimmi Simpson (Noah), Greg Kinnear (Professor Edward Alcott), Dan Aykroyd (Mr. Tanneck), Twink Caplan (Gena), Robert "Bobby" Miano (Victor), Mollie Israel (Annie), Martin Roach (Veterinarian), David Spade (Video Store Man).

Honest kid tries hard to make it there, so he can make it anywhere.

Bloopers

1. After trying a new handshake, Paul raises his right hand ("See you later!"), and as he enters the elevator, he lowers . . . his left hand. (00:06)

2. When Chris tells Paul "No one likes you," his hands are holding the chair, and in the following cut they are crossed in front of him. (00:11)

3. Chris, Adam, and Noah walk near Greenwich Village. Noah says, "I try to get along with everybody," then his mouth stops moving. Yet he keeps on talking, "but that guy's got no personality." (00:22)

4. The Veterinarian tells Paul that he'll get used to the smell, she then gives him the keys: he starts getting them with his right hand—but in the following cut, he grabs them with his left. (00:25)

5. When the kids enter the school, and they find out there's an inspection for drugs and alcohol, Chris hands over his bag twice. (00:27)

6. Professor Alcott says, "If she were alive, Betty Friedan would applaud your little epiphany." Uhm—er . . . Betty Friedan was alive as of the release date of this movie. (00:34)

7. Dora and Paul sneak into a theater, presumably at the beginning of the second act of *Cabaret* (Paul asks if they ever check the tickets, and she says that they only have to pretend that they went out smoking, like everyone else). The musical number that they see is "Wilkommen,"

which actually is in the first act of *Cabaret*. (01:05)

8. Paul goes out to buy a pizza and rent a movie: when he's at the pizza place, he has a greenish bag. Then he's at the video store: no pizza, no bag. The Video Store Man gives him *Simon Birch* in a greenish bag. Later on, Paul stops at a florist, and he has pizza and greenish bag. Hmmm . . . (01:07, 01:08, 01:09)

Question
When she regains consciousness, Dora asks Paul what did they say "when you took me to the hospital." How does she know that she's been to the hospital? She fainted in the vet bathroom, and she wakes up in the same building. So? . . . (00:51)

Fun Fact
When the movie opened, during the closing credits they spelled financial aid "financial aide." It's been corrected for the home video. (01:31)

LOST WORLD: JURASSIC PARK, THE (9)
   1997, color, 129 min.

Director: Steven Spielberg

Cast: Jeff Goldblum (Dr. Ian Malcolm), Julianne Moore (Dr. Sarah Harding), Pete Postlethwaite (Roland Tembo), Arliss Howard (Peter Ludlow), Richard Attenborough (John

Hammond), Vince Vaughn (Nick Van Owen), Vanessa Lee Chester (Kelly Malcolm), Peter Stormare (Dieter Stark), Harvey Jason (Ajay Sidhu), Richard Schiff (Eddie Carr), Thomas F. Duffy (Dr. Robert Burke), David Koepp (Unlucky Bastard).

They're back.

Bloopers

1. Hammond passes to Ian, one by one, three out of the four files of the men he wants to send to the island. But as Ian walks away from the desk, he's carrying only two files. (00:11)

2. When Ian, Nick, and Eddie keep an eye on Sarah (who's petting a Stegosaurus), Nick grabs a Sony videocamera, then he holds a camera, then the videocamera again. (00:25, 00:26)

3. When the second Ingram team reaches the island, Ian grabs Eddie's binoculars—but he looks in them backward. (00:33)

4. The team captures a specimen of the Pachycephalosaurus (the one with the "helmet"), the sun comes from the right—but when the car's large pliers move into position, the sun has moved to directly in front of the camera. (00:37)

5. The young T-rex is captured and tied up. When Nick reaches it, a bottle seems to have appeared in front of the beast. (00:41, 00:46)

6. Peter broadcasts from his station to a group of investors, who appear on a small monitor. When the image vanishes for one split second ("In a moment"), the crew that is reflected in the monitor looks like the real crew for the movie—and *not* the people who surround Peter's camp. (00:43)

7. Sarah and Kelly run into a shack, close the door, and stare at it while two raptors charge it. After a few hits, two objects (one looks like a large spring) fall in front of the door. But they are gone when there's a detail of the raptors digging their way in. The objects come back, but they are gone when Malcolm enters the shack. (01:33, 01:34, 01:35)

8. Ian and Sarah reach the little T-rex in the San Diego park. As the car stops, it rams into a yellow lamp (which falls to the ground). As the car backs up from the militaries, the lamp is standing again. (01:51, 01:52)

9. One of the San Diego people (played by *Lost World* screenwriter, David Koepp) runs away from the T-rex and tries to enter a store, but he doesn't make it. However, it's

possible to see the reflection of the steadicam operator in the glass door of the store. (01:53)

Question

How did the T-rex kill all the crew on the boat and then hide inside the cargo area—all by herself? (01:45, 01:46)

Fun Fact

Kelly, Sarah, and Ian watch CNN. The reflection on the TV screen also shows . . . Mr. Spielberg??!! (01:59)

M

MAN FOR ALL SEASONS, A (4)
1966, color, 120 min.

Director: Fred Zinnemann

Cast: Paul Scofield (Thomas More), Wendy Hiller (Alice More), Leo McKern (Cromwell), Robert Shaw (King Henry VIII), Orson Welles (Cardinal Wolsey), Susannah York (Margaret), Nigel Davenport (Howard, Duke of Norfolk), John Hurt (Richard Rich), Corin Redgrave (Roper), Colin Blakely (Matthew), Cyril Luckham (Archbishop Cranmer), Jack Gwillim (Chief Justice).

Thomas More goes head-to-head against King Henry VIII. And only one head will roll.

Bloopers

1. After an explosion of anger in front of Thomas, King Henry VIII asks what time it is. The church bell has just rung eight, so the King walks away, but the shadow on the ground shows the sun's somewhere between 11 A.M. and 1 P.M. (00:42)

2. Cromwell makes a speech in front of parliament, presenting "Matters pleasing to a loyal subject." He ends the speech with both hands along his body—but in the matching close-up, his left hand is holding a booklet to his chest. (01:23)

3. Thomas sits in front of Cromwell, the Archbishop Cranmer and the Duke of Norfolk, a.k.a. the seventh commission of inquiry. A cane is on the table between them, and so are the duke's arms. When Thomas tells him that he won't take the oath, the cane is on one side or under the duke's right arm if the shot is in front or from behind him. (01:30)

4. The Duke of Norfolk shows Thomas the oath written on paper, holding it with his left hand, and simultaneously he holds the cane with the right hand. But in the over-the-

shoulder shot, he's only holding the paper—the cane is free to go anytime it wants. (01:31)

Question

The movie is set in England, 1500. While jailed in the Tower, Thomas receives several books, which look dusty and crumpled. Shouldn't they be pretty new, though? After all, the "alleged" Gutenberg Bible was printed in 1455. (01:25)

MAN WITH THE GOLDEN GUN, THE (17)

1974, color, 125 min.

Director: Guy Hamilton

Cast: Roger Moore (James Bond 007), Christopher Lee (Francisco Scaramanga), Britt Ekland (Mary Goodnight), Maud Adams (Andrea Anders), Hervé Villechaize (Nick Nack), Clifton James (J.W. Pepper), Richard Loo (Hai Fat), Soon-Tek Oh (Hip), Marc Lawrence (Rodney), Lois Maxwell (Miss Moneypenny), Bernard Lee (M), Desmond Llewelyn (Q), Marc Lawrence (Rodney), Carmen Sautoy (Saida).

Bond vs. Dracula in the ninth installment of the most famous secret agent.

Bloopers

1. Rodney, the syndicate hit man hired to kill Scaramanga on his own island, puts the silencer on his gun, then fires: *BANG!!* Really bad silencer. (00:03)

2. While on the island, Rodney steps into Scaramanga's funhouse and faces an Al Capone wax statue that blinks (twice—when he fires the machine gun, and when the arms fall to the ground)! (00:05)

3. After Nick Nack gets the money back from Rodney's pocket, check out 007's statue: it moves (Roger Moore, anyone?). (00:07)

4. Scaramanga fires at Bond's fingers: the ring goes, then the middle—but in the following, (mis)matching shot, the index finger is gone, too. (00:08)

5. In Saida the belly dancer's dressing room, Bond is attacked by three men: when he pushes one of them away, the guy hits a mirror with lights on the frame. As the mirror moves, you can see the whole camera crew. (00:18)

6. When Bond hands a towel to Andrea, he walks across the bathroom—and the head of a crewmember can briefly be seen reflected in one of the mirrors. (00:29)

7. Nick Nack checks himself out in a TV monitor in a store, side by side with Bond. Then, still in the monitor, Nick Nack turns his head and looks up to Bond. Or does he? The TV does not work as a mirror, therefore Nick Nack is look-

ing to his left—but Bond is to his right. (00:34)

8. Bond walks to the entrance of the Bottoms Up club, and Scaramanga points his golden gun at him: the barrel stops almost immediately. Crappy gun. (00:35)

9. The nieces of Lieutenant Hip talk in the back of the car: their audio is looped and they pretty much repeat the same lines. (00:48)

10. During a sword fight, two fighters begin with two swords each. They both lose one, yet when one of them gets wounded, the winner has two swords again. (00:53)

11. When Bond finally opens the closet and lets Goodnight out, she asks what time it is. He says, "Two-ish," and she repeats, "Two?!" Yet they both mouth, "Twelve." (01:13)

12. Three police cars skid and stop in the middle of the road. The driver of the car closer to the camera is not wearing a hat, but in the following shot he has one. (01:24)

13. Bond backs up the car to jump over the bridge. On the car side, it's possible to see the reflection of a crew light. (01:26)

14. The car lands after the spiral jump, and the sheriff falls back onto a gray area of the car—but one second later he is sitting in the rear seat. Where did the gray background go? (01:26)

"If My Calculations Are Correct . . ."

The "AMC Astro Spiral Jump" (01:26) is the first stunt ever conceived with the help of the computer, which calculated the correct speed of the car, the gradient of the ramps, and so on. Bumps Willard, a stunt driver on Jay Milligan's team, used a car that was perfectly balanced (the steering wheel was in the middle, the car was widened . . .) and did the jump once. Cut and print the first! Only one question: was that stupid kazoo sound *really* necessary?

15. Bond flies low toward Scaramanga's island using a seaplane that has two pontoons on its wings. As the plane lands and surfs to the shore, the left pontoon is missing. (01:32, 01:34)

16. On a control board, Goodnight spots a row of buttons marked "Computers Controlled Lock In." Referring to these, she asks Bond if she has to push the "Computer Interlock." (01:55)

17. Bond and Goodnight escape on Scaramanga's junk, and the secret agent receives a phone call from M. How did M know (a) where 007 would have been and (b) Scaramanga's junk's phone number, since it is established (00:11) that his "present domi-

cile [is] unknown." (01:57, 02:02)

The Woman Who Was There . . . and There . . . and There!

Maud Adams is the only woman who has returned to the Bond set in different roles in different movies: she appears in *The Man With the Golden Gun* as Andrea Anders (00:00), she also appears as Octopussy (01:08) in the movie of the same title and, as a personal "favour" to friend and colleague Roger Moore, Maud can be spotted in *A View to a Kill* in the Fisherman's Wharf scene in San Francisco, by the cable car. (00:58)

MARRIED TO THE MOB (5)
1988, color, 103 min.

Director: Jonathan Demme

Cast: Michelle Pfeiffer (Angela de Marco), Matthew Modine (Mike Downey), Dean Stockwell (Tony "The Tiger" Russo), Mercedes Ruehl (Connie Russo), Alec Baldwin (Frank "Cucumber" de Marco), Joan Cusack (Rose), Trey Wilson (Regional Director Franklin), Charles Napier (Angela's Hairdresser), Tracey Walter (Mr. Chicken Lickin'), Al Lewis (Uncle Joe Russo), Paul Lazar (Tommy), Chris Isaak ("The Clown").

Mafia hit man's widow tries to move on with her life.

Bloopers

1. Downey answers the phone while in bed: the hand that holds the phone shifts position substantially from the close-up to the wide shot. (00:18)

2. At Connie's birthday party, the cake has a few flower-shaped orange decorations. When Connie blows the candles, the cake has moved and the decorations appear on one side of it. After everyone claps, the cake is back in its original position. (00:31)

3. The stain caused by a milkshake on Mr. Chicken Lickin's jacket and face changes shape and even "moves" to his left shoulder. (00:36)

4. Tony and Tommy visit Angela's new abode: Tony carries a rich, large bunch of flowers. As they enter the apartment, the rich, large bunch of flowers becomes a lousy, small bunch of flowers. (00:37, 00:40)

5. Outside Burger World, Tony shoots "The Clown," who falls onto the hood of a car, losing his hat. Yet, when he stands up again, the hat is once again on his head. (00:54)

ME, MYSELF & IRENE (8)
2000, color, 116 min.

Directors: Bobby Farrelly and Peter Farrelly

Cast: Jim Carrey (Charlie Baileygates / Hank), Renée Zellweger (Irene P. Waters), Anthony Anderson (Jamaal Baileygates), Mongo Brownlee (Lee Harvey Baileygates), Jerod Mixon (Shonte Baileygates, Jr.), Chris Cooper (Lieutenant Gerke), Michael Bowman (Whitey / Casper), Richard Jenkins (Agent Boshane), Robert Forster (Colonel Partington), Mike Cerrone (Officer Stubie), Rob Moran (Trooper Finneran), Daniel Greene (Dickie Thurman).

An extreme case of split personality undermines the life of a well-mannered cop . . . Carrey-style.

Bloopers

1. Early in the story, when we "meet Charlie" on his motor-bike, we also meet the crew, reflected on the right side of the bike. (00:01)

2. When shooting at the cow doesn't seem to be the right solution, Charlie tosses his gun away and begins wrestling the cow. A few in-stants later, however, the gun is close to the cow's head. (00:32)

3 In Charlie's Chuckie Cheese Lodge and Miniature Golf Resort room, Irene catches him in bed with one of her pictures: he bolts from the bed and uses a hand lotion on his lips. The lotion squirted on the wall changes shape in-between cuts. (00:39)

4. When called to go on a chop-per, Agent Boshane turns his head to his left: the bandage he has on his left cheek has moved to the right cheek. It'll come back to the left cheek—and stay there. (00:49, 01:04, 01:05)

5. The train Charlie and Irene travel on changes engines, apparently without stopping. The engine is substantially different from the first time we see the train to the time the train stops at the station. (01:27, 01:31)

6. Dickie gets knocked out by a rubber dildo, and he falls over Charlie/Hank. Dickie's head is roughly in the middle of Charlie's back, but in the following close-up ("Warden . . . I want my own cell!"), Dickie's head has moved up, almost side by side with Charlie's. (01:29)

7. Charlie/Hank gets shot in the left arm. But during the final confrontation on the bridge, the wound has moved up on his shoulder. (01:33, 01:39)

8. When Charlie, his sons, Irene, and Whitey look for Charlie's thumb, Whitey dives with a mask and a snorkel. When he says, "I think I found it!" of course he has no snorkel in his mouth, so he puts his head underwater again—this time with the snorkel in his mouth. (01:56)

Non-Blooper

While staying at a motel, Charlie shows Irene two pictures of him and his sons. He took the pictures from his wallet—but earlier, Hank stated that he left the wallet on the dash of the car they threw off of a cliff. (00:53) In the DVD version, you'll see the scene (cut from the theatrical release) where Hank and Irene actually retrieve the wallet. (01:11)

Question

Charlie fires nine bullets at a prize cow's head (that is 1 + 2 + 6). Yet, later on, Agent Boshane states that Charlie shot "six bullets" at the poor animal. Can anybody count? (00:31, 00:50)

Fun Fact

In the same room, while Charlie gets dressed, it's possible to see, on the floor, a large watermelon with a hole in it, which seems absolutely out of context. (00:39) Well, the watermelon scene was cut (you don't need Einstein's IQ to figure out what that "device" was for) after *American Pie* came along, but the shot was left in the picture. You can find the extra scene in the DVD version of the movie.

MEET JOE BLACK (12)

1998, color, 174 min.

Director: Martin Brest

Cast: Brad Pitt (Joe Black /Young Man in Coffee Shop), Anthony Hopkins (William "Bill" Parrish), Claire Forlani (Susan Parrish), Jake Weber (Drew), Marcia Gay Harden (Allison), Jeffrey Tambor (Quince), David S. Howard (Eddie Sloane), Lois Kelly-Miller (Jamaican Woman), Jahnni St. John (Jamaican Woman's Daughter), Richard Clarke (Butler).

Death takes a holiday, Brad Pitt's body, and three hours of our lives to tell us about it.

Bloopers

1. Allison is walking down the steps of the patio, while Bill sips his coffee close to Susan. As he mumbles, "Isn't it enough to be on the Earth for sixty-five years without having to be reminded of it?" he raises the cup to his mouth—but in the shot from behind him, he's still holding the cup down, at his waist. (00:05)

2. Susan enters the Corinth Coffee Shop and approaches the counter. As the counterman places a cup of coffee, a napkin, and a spoon in front of her, she opens her briefcase. At that moment, a man who's talking on the phone causes some objects to fall. Susan is startled and turns her head—and now a notepad and a pen have appeared in front of her. But she never produced them from her case. (00:11)

3. At the counter, the young

man's having breakfast with Susan: he picks up the salt shaker, uses it, and then begins to slice his food. As the shot cuts to Susan, the young man ("Yeah, what was fascinating about it?") is still using the salt shaker. (00:12)

4. Susan pours some cream into her coffee, puts the cream down, but as the shot cuts to the young man (when she says, "Um—you and, uh, 'honey'?") Susan is pouring cream again. (00:12)

5. After breakfast, the young man and Susan separate. Still, he turns back but doesn't say a thing, so he resumes his walk. She turns back, and in the distance, a red-haired woman with a blue-gray dress and a white lab coat passes by, walking left to right. The very same woman will do this, walking in the same direction, three more times. (00:20)

6. After Joe first arrives at Bill's house, and sits down to his first dinner, the maids set his place with utensils. After a brief cut to Bill, we see Joe pick up his plate of food to smell it. The only problem is that the maids didn't bring his food yet. (00:37)

7. While they're all having dinner, Drew comments, "Joe sounds like a ringer, Bill." From that moment, the candle closest to Bill has the flame tilted to the left when Bill is in the frame, and straight up when Drew is in it. (00:38)

8. Quince approaches Bill to agree with him that Drew's proposed merger sounded bad, and to propose some ideas of his own. Bill's right arm rests on the arm of a sofa, holding a drink in a tumbler with a few large ice cubes. When Quince says, "... or the week after," we see that the ice cubes have all but melted. In the next shot they're back, but when Quince says, "... I'm in his corner," they're almost gone again. They're then back again when Quince leaves. (01:11, 01:12)

9. Bill makes a speech during the second "family" dinner. Joe has a small pendulum behind him, moving slowly. When Bill says, "Uh ... wait a minute, uh ..." the pendulum is motionless. At the moment of the toast, it's back to swinging. (01:13, 01:14, 01:15)

10. In the library, Susan asks Joe if she can kiss him, which she does. Her hair is covering the top of her right ear. After Joe says, "... the taste of your lips and the touch of your tongue—that was wonderful," we cut back to Susan, whose hair is now noticeably pushed over her ear, even though she didn't touch it. (01:35)

11. Talking with Joe about whether his wife loves him back, Quince stifles a sudden burst of tears. He then grabs a glass with his left hand and brings it to his mouth—but in the following cut, he's holding it with his right hand. (02:07)

12. Right after Quince has come clean in Bill's office, Bill and Joe are left alone. Bill removes his glasses, stands up ... removes his glasses again, and finally pockets them. (02:17)

MIDNIGHT RUN (8)
1988, color, 122 min.

Director: Martin Brest

Cast: Robert De Niro (Jack Walsh), Charles Grodin (Jonathan Mardukas), Yaphet Kotto (Alonzo Mosely), John Ashton (Marvin Dorfler), Dennis Farina (Jimmy Serrano), Joe Pantoliano (Eddie Moscone), Richard Foronjy (Tony Darvo), Robert Miranda (Joey), Jack Kehoe (Jerry Geisler), Wendy Phillips (Gail), Danielle DuClos (Denise Walsh), Philip Baker Hall (Sidney).

Wise guy escorts annoying guy across the country.

Bloopers

1. Jack Walsh is pushed to the rear seats of an FBI car, Mosley sitting in front. Mosley stretches his arm between the headrests, but when we see Walsh again, the arm ain't there. (00:09)

2. Jack checks Mosley's ID, which he just pickpocketed: Jack holds it with his right hand, against his left. After a (correct) detail, Jack is holding the ID with his left hand, against his right. (00:11)

3. At the airport car rental, Tony Darvo writes his phone number on a matchbox using a yellow pencil. When Jack checks out the same matchbox at FBI headquarters, he finds Tony's number written in blue ink. (00:13, 01:41)

4. Once in the train car, Jack finally gives in and stands up to open the toilet door: he passes his cigarette from his right hand to the left, then opens the door with his right hand. Which is holding the cigarette. (00:27)

5. Another cigarette jump happens at a diner, when Jonathan tells Jack, "Why didn't you just leave your heroin dealer alone?" Jack's cigarette pops from his right hand to his left. (01:03)

6. Jonathan falls into a river. He has handcuffs on his right wrist, but in one shot, following Jack's dive, the cuffs jump onto his left wrist. (01:08, 01:10)

7. Talking about his watch in a boxcar, Jack smokes the

umpteenth cigarette. Then the cigarette is gone as he says, "I don't think she's coming back," but only for one shot. After that, the cigarette is back. (01:26, 01:27)

8. Jack's left-and-right trick occurs another time at the diner that's "always open." Jack has a cigarette in his right hand, the lighter in his left. As Mosley slides the sunglasses on the counter, Jack's cigarette is in his left hand, and a sugar dispenser in his right. (01:38)

MISSION: IMPOSSIBLE 2 (4)
2000, color, 123 min.

Director: John Woo

Cast: Tom Cruise (Ethan Hunt), Dougray Scott (Sean Ambrose), Thandie Newton (Nyah Nordoff-Hall), Ving Rhames (Luther Stickell), Richard Roxburgh (Hugh Stamp), John Polson (Billy Baird), Brendan Gleeson (John McCloy), Rade Serbedzija (Dr. Nekhorvich), William Mapother (Wallis), Dominic Purcell (Ulrich), Matt Wilkinson (Michael).

Still incomprehensible, but this time with many more slow-motion shots.

Bloopers
1. During a car chase on a mountain road, Ethan passes to the right of a car, while Nyah swerves to the left. The shot "from up above" shows the shadow of what is probably a boom mike visible on the road. (00:19)

2. Nyah hits the left side of Ethan's car, causing at least $2,000 in damage. A few seconds later, when it's Ethan's turn to hit Nyah's car, just before they skid together toward the cliff, the damage on Ethan's car has moved to the right side. Also, both cars appear to have a right-side steering wheel. (00:19, 00:20)

3. Nyah steps out of the Palacio de Justicia with her purse strap on her right shoulder. The same image, reflected in Ethan's glasses, shows the strap... still on her right shoulder. What kind of reflection is that? (00:34)

4. A few seconds before Ethan's performance of the "balancing-on-the-motorcyle's-front-wheel-thingie," the chasing white car loses one hubcap. Yet when it skids sideways, all four hubcaps are firmly in place. (01:43)

Question
Using the radio to call the Denver Center, the plane captain states, "This is Trans-Pac 2207." When we see the plane flying low, its side says "Pan Pacific Airlines." Who's that? (00:03, 00:04)

MOONRAKER (19)

1979, color, 126 min.

Director: Lewis Gilbert

Cast: Roger Moore (James Bond 007), Lois Chiles (Dr. Holly Goodhead), Michael Lonsdale (Hugo Drax), Richard Kiel (Jaws), Corinne Clery (Corinne Dufour), Bernard Lee (M), Geoffrey Keen (Sir Frederick Gray, Minister of Defense), Desmond Llewelyn (Q), Lois Maxwell (Miss Moneypenny), Toshirô Suga (Chang), Emily Bolton (Manuela), Blanche Ravalec (Dolly), Jean-Pierre Castaldi (Pilot Private Jet).

Mission number eleven: Bond . . . in . . . space . . . ace . . . ace . . . ace! . . .

Bloopers

1. During the fight on the plane, Bond pushes the pilot against the door: the pilot's sunglasses appear crooked, then okay, then crooked again, then okay again. (00:03)
2. When Bond is pushed off the plane, he free-falls until he reaches the pilot and takes off his parachute. When Bond holds onto the chute and the pilot is grabbing his legs, Bond is wearing protective goggles. He didn't have them before, and won't have them after. (00:03, 00:04)
3. Drax plays the piano like a virtuoso, yet his fingers' movements do not match with the music we hear. (00:14)
4. Corinne Dufour is fired by Drax, then turned into a target for the man's two dogs. As Corinne runs toward the woods, she's wearing high heels, but when she's dashing into the woods, she's wearing black boots with white soles. (00:32)
5. Bond meets Dr. Goodhead in a Venetian *calle*: their shadows stretch back, perfectly aligned with their bodies. As they resume walking, the shadows on the ground are skewed to the side. (00:36)
6. On his gondola, 007 can be seen lifting his left leg to cross it over his right. However, in the following shot, it's his right leg on top of the left. (00:37)
7. Just before the funeral boat comes by, 007's gondola passes under a bridge. As we cut to the hearse boat and back, the bridge is gone. It'll come back to knock the coffin down into the water. (00:38)
8. When the coffin on the hearse boat opens, the "corpse" has its right hand on top of its left. In the next shot, it's the left on top of the right. (00:38)
9. Bond uses his special gondola on Piazza San Marco, and we hear the "Trish-Trash Polka" by Strauss, presumably played by one of the orchestras in the bars. Well, that polka has no accordion part (still, the accordion player is giving it his best). (00:40)
10. During the fight in the Venini

Glass display, Bond throws Chang into a shelf, which falls but whose frame remains in almost one piece. As Chang stands up, the whole shelf is pulverized, except for the base. (00:46)

11. When Bond gets the sword and tries to hit Chang, from Chang's point of view, Bond aims to the left, but in the wide shot, Bond's blade was to the right of Chang. (00:46)

12. Before meeting 007 in her hotel room, Dr. Goodhead shuts her balcony doors. As we pan from the bed to the window a few moments later, the doors are wide open. (00:49, 00:52)

13. Bond hands M a vial of lethal liquid; he holds it with his left hand, but in the following shot holds it with his right. (00:54)

14. Facing Jaws in the Brazilian Alley, Manuela produces a knife with the blade in. In the following shot, the blade is completely out. (01:00)

15. After spotting Dr. Goodhead with a telescope, Bond approaches her and places his hand on top of both of hers, which are on the telescope. In the following shot, only her right hand is on the telescope. (01:04)

16. On the cable car in Rio, Dr. Goodhead wears high-heeled shoes. When she and Bond jump off the cable and roll on the ground, she's wearing flat, ballerina-style

shoes. And as they recover from the fall, she's wearing high heels again. (01:05, 01:09, 01:10)

17. To escape from underneath one of the shuttles, Bond checks his wristwatch: the time reads 10:08:10, 20 ... But when he flips it open, after one second, the time reads 10:08:42 — and doesn't move. The same time is displayed when Bond uses the watch as a detonator a few seconds later. (01:28, 01:29)

18. *Moonraker 6*'s tank detaches and falls almost vertically from the ship. But in space, shouldn't it float freely? (01:33)

19. Again, when the space city explodes, a few pieces fall straight down and there's also a lot of noise and smoke. In space? (01:55, 01:57, 01:58)

Questions

1. Q gives Bond the "standard equipment" wrist weapon; Bond wears it (00:10), has it, and uses it on the simulator in Drax's laboratory (00:22), but doesn't have it when he drives the boat on the river (01:16), when he hang glides over the waterfall (01:19), when he fights with the python (01:22), or any other time ... except when he really needs it, on Drax's space station (01:57). Is it just us, or is this a little suspicious?

2. How was Drax's space station ever built if the radar-

jamming device wasn't operative at the time of its construction? (01:35)

MULAN (6)
1998, color, 88 min.

Directors: Barry Cook and Tony Bancroft

Cast: Ming-Na Wen (Fa Mulan / Fa Ping), Lea Salonga (Fa Mulan / Fa Ping—singing voice), Eddie Murphy (Mushu), BD Wong (Captain Li Shang), Donny Osmond (Captain Li Shang—singing voice), Harvey Fierstein (Yao), Jerry Tondo (Chien-Po), Gedde Watanabe (Ling), Matthew Wilder (Ling—singing voice), James Hong (Chi Fu), Frank Welker (Cri-Kee), Miriam Margolyes (The Matchmaker).

Young woman pretends to be a man and goes to battle. The war version of Victor/Victoria, *if you will.*

Bloopers
1. While the matchmaker is examining Mulan, she grabs our hero by one arm (the one Mulan wrote notes on). The matchmaker's hand is covered with ink, yet as she grabs the teapot she doesn't leave any marks on it—but as she touches her face, she draws a mustache on herself. (00:10)

2. As Mulan stares in disbelief at the matchmaker's mustache, she pours some tea on the table instead of in a cup. The tea puddle is to the left of the cup; however, in the detail that shows the lucky Cri-Kee using the cup like a hot tub, the tea pool has moved to the right of the cup. (00:10)

3. The position of the three little red tents on General Li's map changes from the detail to the master shot. (00:31)

4. Captain Li Shang shoots an arrow at the tip of a pole. The arrow hits its target, and from a shot up above the pole we see that it's parallel to two lines of tents. When Mulan is about to give up, and sees the arrow up there, from a shot up above we see the arrow has become almost perpendicular to the tents. (00:36, 00:37, 00:40)

5. Trying to retrieve an arrow on the tip of a very tall pole, Yao slides down—leaving a very long mark caused by his teeth. The mark vanishes as other soldiers try to retrieve the same arrow on the same pole. (00:37)

6. Coming back to her father, Fa Zhoe, Mulan hands him the sword of Shan-Yu and the crest of the emperor (a fancy medallion). Fa Zhoe drops them to the ground and hugs Mulan. The wide shot in front of the lake shows a gorgeous reflection in the water of Fa Zhoe and Mulan hugging each other, the bench, the

tree . . . but the sword and the medallion reflections aren't there. (01:19)

Questions

1. When Mushu the dragon appears for the first time in front of Mulan, he makes a theatrical entrance, projecting his silhouette onto a rock. However, the silhouette has two eyes. Does that mean that Mushu's eyes are translucent all the way through his skull . . . ? (00:27)
2. Before passing out after a fight, a soldier makes the "hand by the forehead" military salute to General Li. Was that in use in the Chinese Army, too? (00:32)

MUMMY RETURNS, THE (14)
2001, color, 129 min.

Director: Stephen Sommers

Cast: Brendan Fraser (Richard "Rick" O'Connell), Rachel Weisz (Evelyn Carnahan-O'Connell / Princess Nefertiti), John Hannah (Jonathan Carnahan), Arnold Vosloo (High Priest Imhotep), Oded Fehr (Ardeth Bay), Patricia Velazquez (Meela / Anck-Su-Namum), Freddie Boath (Alex O'Connell), Alun Armstrong (Mr. Hafez), Dwayne Johnson (The Scorpion King), Adewale Akinnuoye-Agbaje (Lock-Nah), Shaun Parkes (Izzy), Bruce Byron (Red), Joe Dixon (Jacques), Tom Fisher (Spivey).

He's back, wraps and all.

Bloopers

1. When the Scorpion King's army stops in front of their opponents, their shadows go to the left, but as they charge, the shadows go to the right (in the frontal shot), then to the left again. (00:00, 00:01)
2. In the Egyptian worksite, Rick is scared by his son Alex, who appears in front of him when Rick turns. But they meet face-to-face, although Alex is much, much, *much* shorter than Rick. (00:06)
3. Rushing to leave the site, Spivey yells "Come on!" to Jacques, then heads for the exit: he is visible in the background just before Jacques jumps off the ladder to get Alex. But when Jacques is down, Spivey is still running for the exit. (00:15)
4. 1933 London is quite unique: the Tower Bridge has been moved next to Big Ben, and they are both close to St. Paul's Cathedral. Did they remodel the whole town after the thirties? (00:21)
5. After Jonathan emerges from a bathtub that's filled to the brim, the foam vanishes from Jonathan completely as he and Rick jump through the window. (00:31)
6. The thugs who get hit by the fire coming from the formaldehyde crate in the British Museum are wearing protective masks. (00:41)

7. While saving Evelyn in the British Museum, Rick hands her a gun that jams after the first shot—yet she keeps firing. Not bad. (00:41)

8. Swerving to the left, the double-decker bus smashes a light post. Jonathan steers right halfway through the curve, yet the bus keeps going to the left. (00:45)

9. When Jonathan crosses the Tower Bridge driving the bus, Alex jumps on, hugging him. But as Jonathan stops the bus, Alex is nowhere to be seen. (00:47)

10. Rick can't reach his son's kidnapper because the Tower Bridge gets raised. But when Imhotep takes a look at London from his balcony, the Tower Bridge appears to be lowered. Yet as we move back to Rick and his friends, the bridge is still raised and lowering. (00:47, 00:48, 00:49)

11. When Ardeth meets with his pet bird, Horus (which seems to have a tiny wire around one leg as it flies to its master), he raises his right hand and speaks to the commanders of the Magii. But his hand is lowered, and then raised again. (00:58)

12. During their flashback-fight, after Anck-Su-Namum says, "Let's not scar that pretty face," Nefertiti jumps to her feet, leaving the daggers on the floor. But they jump back into her hands immediately. (01:07)

13. When Evelyn gets stabbed in front of the pyramid of the Scorpion King, the sun keeps coming and going after every shot (check the shadows on the ground). (01:35)

14. After the death of the Scorpion King, Meela / Anck-Su-Namum abandons Imhotep—who is hanging on for his life with his right arm on the floor, the left hand barely visible. After Meela leaves, Imhotep looks at Rick—and now is his left arm on the floor, the right hand barely visible. (01:56, 01:57)

A Tattoo Tall Tale?

Rick says that the "sacred mark" on his arm was slapped onto him when he was in an orphanage in Cairo. (00:06, 00:35) But in *The Mummy*, he didn't have any tattoo at all.

Questions

1. Ardeth tells Alex that he has started a chain reaction that could bring on the next apocalypse. Did we sleep through the first one, or does Ardeth know something we don't? (00:33)

2. The double-decker bus is chased by four mummies: Rick blows one to bits when it jumps from one building (00:43); one is snapped in half (00:44) and is eventually killed by Evelyn (00:45); one

is smashed against an overpass that "decapitates" the
bus (00:46). What happened
to the fourth?

3. Rick and Alex run toward the
pyramid, fleeing from the
sunlight, which is getting
closer and closer. Besides
the speed that Rick would
have had to have reached,
wouldn't the light hit the *top*
of the pyramid first, and *then*
the bottom—not vice-versa?
(01:34)

MY GIANT (4)
1998, color, 103 min.

Director: Michael Lehmann

Cast: Billy Crystal (Sam
"Sammy" Kamin), Kathleen
Quinlan (Serena Kamin),
Gheorghe Muresan (Max
Zamphirescu), Joanna Pacula
(Lilliana Rotaro), Zane Carney
(Nick "Nicky" Kanin), Jere

Burns (Weller, the Movie
Director), Harold Gould (Milt
Kaminski), Dan Castellaneta
(Portlow), Raymond O'Connor
(Eddie), Rider Strong (Justin
Allen).

*Agent discovers huge star
who is an even bigger
human being.*

Bloopers
1. Driving in Romania, Sammy's
car seems to not have a
rearview mirror (when he's
checking on the maps), then
it has one (when he asks directions of a few bikers),
then it seems to be gone
again. (00:00, 00:01)
2. Sammy retrieves his cell
phone by the river, and his
socks get pretty muddy. But
when he hears Max singing
in his apartment, the socks
have suddenly become clean.
(00:15, 00:16)

MIRROR, MIRROR, ON THE CAR . . .

Who's made this kind of blooper so far? Geez, who hasn't!

Thomas F. Wilson's car in *Back to the Future Part II*	Blooper No. 12
Alicia Silverstone's Jeep in *Clueless*	Blooper No. 5
Sylvester Stallone in *Cobra*	Blooper No. 2
David Patrick Kelly in *Commando*	Blooper No. 8
Roger Moore's taxi in *Live and Let Die*	Blooper No. 5
Billy Crystal's car in *My Giant*	Blooper No. 1
Danny DeVito's convertible in *Twins*	Blooper No. 4
Bruce Willis's car in *The Whole Nine Yards*	Blooper No. 9

3. When Sammy hangs up his cell phone after the call with Hertz, there's a distinct sound of him closing it. But after he checks the size of a footprint, the cell phone is open again. (00:15)

4. While on a bus on the Vegas strip, Sammy and Max pass by the New York, New York Hotel, then by the Riviera (reflected in the windows). Not only are these two hotels not side by side, they are on the two opposite sides of the street. (01:04)

NARROW MARGIN (4)
1990, color, 97 min.

Director: Peter Hyams

Cast: Gene Hackman (Deputy District Attorney Robert Caulfield), Anne Archer (Carol Hunnicut), James Sikking (Nelson), J.T. Walsh (Michael Tarlow), M. Emmet Walsh (Detective Sergeant Dominick Berti), Susan Hogan (Kathryn Weller), Nigel Bennett (Jack Wootton), J.A. Preston (Martin Larner), B.A. "Smitty" Smith (Keller), Codie Lucas Wilbee (Nicholas "Nick"), Antony Holland (Elderly Man), Doreen Ramos (Elderly Woman).

Special witness is moved from her hideout to where pretty much anybody can see and kill her.

Bloopers
1. Tarlow gets shot in his apartment. He falls backward onto the couch, his tie lying flat on his chest. But in the shot from the bedroom, his tie is arched. (00:10)
2. Fleeing from a mountain cabin, Caulfield shatters Carol's windshield against a large branch. When the car swerves by a cliff, the windshield is all in one piece. Then it's shattered again as they leave the main road. Then intact from the inside and shattered from the outside . . . (00:25, 00:26, 00:27)
3. To prove to little Nick that he's a cop, Caulfield produces his I.D.: he holds it with two hands, but only one when Nick is in the shot. (01:17)
4. While hanging from the train, Caulfield looks at Larner's shadow on the hill behind the train. But when Larner is walking, he has the sun almost above him. So, how can the shadow? . . . (01:28)

NIGHTMARE ON ELM STREET, A (9)
1984, color, 91 min.

Director: Wes Craven

Cast: John Saxon (Lieutenant Donald Thompson), Ronee Blakley (Marge Thompson), Heather Langenkamp (Nancy Thompson), Amanda Wyss (Tina Gray), Jsu "Nick Corri" Garcia (Rod Lane), Johnny Depp (Glen Lantz), Charles Fleischer (Dr. King), Joseph Whipp (Sergeant Parker), Robert Englund (Freddy Krueger), Lin Shaye (Teacher), Joe Unger (Sergeant Garcia), Mimi Craven (Nurse).

"One, two, Freddy's coming for you . . ."

Bloopers

1. Glen is tackled by Rod in the front yard of Tina's house. When he gets up, a grass stain is on the back of his vest—but it's gone when he kisses Nancy. (00:09, 00:10)

2. During Tina's dream sequence, she runs toward the house, and Freddy Krueger jumps out from behind a tree. His trademark glove, usually on his right hand, is on his left for some reason. (00:16)

3. After her mom leaves, Nancy rests in the bathtub, putting a cloth on her face and leaving her left hand by her left ear. In the following (mis-) matching cut, her left hand is in the middle of the tub. (00:32, 00:33)

4. Having dismissed her mom, Heather leans against the bath sink and crosses her arms. In the matching close-up, her left arm is now holding on to the collar of her robe (also, the mirror behind her is less fogged up). (00:34)

5. While under examination at the clinic, Heather manages to pull Krueger's hat out of her dream. When she goes back to sleep to bring Glen's killer to her father, she enters the boiler room in her dream. When Krueger appears behind her, he's wearing his hat. But as he starts chasing her, he doesn't (nor will he ever in this sequence). (00:51, 01:20)

6. In the kitchen with her mom, Nancy chug-a-lugs a cup of coffee without swallowing a single time. (00:51)

7. Glen is talking on the phone with Heather, and since their houses are directly across the street from each other, he lifts his bedroom's curtain in order to see her, pushing it up to his right. But when they hang up, he pulls the curtain back—from his left. (00:59, 01:00)

8. Eventually Nancy goes to sleep in her short-sleeved gown. But when she sets the alarm to her wristwatch, she's wearing a long-sleeve sweater. (01:14, 01:15)

9. After Freddy gets the sledge-

hammer in the stomach, he falls backward on the Thompson's stairs. It's possible to see a landing mattress on the steps. (01:22)

Question
Glen is killed at 12:00 midnight (or so it's said on TV); when Nancy talks to her father at the crime scene, she tells him that she's gonna get the killer, and that her dad should be at the house in twenty minutes. "It'll be exactly half past midnight." Then she rigs the house with booby traps, including a sledgehammer connected to the door and a lamp filled with gunpowder, which is activated by a wire on the floor. Fast, ain't she? (01:08, 01:10)

Fun Fact
While running away from Krueger, and aiming for the front door of her house, actress Heather Langenkamp cuts her foot: check how she hops at the door before she opens it. (00:40)

NUDE BOMB, THE (7)
1980, color, 94 min.

Director: Clive Donner

Cast: Don Adams (Maxwell Smart), Sylvia Kristel (Agent 34), Rhonda Fleming (Edith Von Secondberg), Dana Elcar (Chief), Pamela Hensley (Agent 35), Andrea Howard (Agent 22), Norman Lloyd (Carruthers), Bill Dana (Jonathan Levinson Seigte), Gary Imhoff (Jerry Krovney), Sarah Rush (Pam

Krovney), Vittorio Gassman (Sauvage / Sieeve), Vito Scotti (Italian Delegate).

Crazy fashion scientist builds a bomb that will make mankind naked. Thank God for Maxwell Smart . . .

Bloopers
1. Maxwell talks to his shoe phone while skydiving, but the phone vanishes in the long shots. By the way, doesn't it look like he's diving in bright daylight, but then when he answers the phone it's dusk? (00:04)
2. Max checks Agent 22 using the chief's rearview pipe: the reflection isn't a reflection at all: the image is not flipped (it appears as if she were driving a British car—which she is not). (00:09)
3. After recalling the Cone of Silence during the meeting with all the delegates, the Italian delegate's cone is lifted twice: the first time in the wide shot, then in his close-up. (00:23)
4. The rearview mirror on Agent 34's Mercedes vanishes when she and Maxwell talk in the car, but it reappears in the long shots. (00:52, 00:53)
5. The very strong Agent 34 pulls her car, which slides to the side . . . thanks to the two white cables that are visible near the rear left wheel. (00:53)
6. When they get cloned, there are vanishing reflections of

Sauvage (the first time he gets a double) and Maxwell Smart (the third Maxwell, as well as the original Maxwell just after "short Max"). (01:23, 01:24)

7. Right after Sauvage has become . . . four Sauvages, they all start shooting Maxwell. In the first shot behind the computers where you can see all four of them, the last Sauvage has a transparent head—you can see the lights on a computer behind him right through his forehead! (01:24)

0

OCTOPUSSY (20)
1983, color, 129 min.

Director: John Glen

Cast: Roger Moore (James Bond 007), Maud Adams (Octopussy), Louis Jourdan (Prince Kamal Khan), Kristina Wayborn (Magda), Kabir Bedi (Gobinda), Steven Berkoff (Orlov), David Meyer (Mischka, Twin One), Tony Meyer (Grischka, Twin Two), Desmond Llewelyn (Q), Robert Brown (M), Lois Maxwell (Miss Moneypenny), Michaela Clavell (Penelope Smallbone), Stuart Saunders (Major Clive), William Derrick (Thug with Yo-yo).

From India to Germany, Bond becomes both Tarzan and a clown in his thirteenth adventure.

Bloopers
1. Disguised as General Toro, 007 opens a gimmicked briefcase using his left thumb— which becomes his left index in the detail. (00:02)
2. When 007's mini-jet takes off, it flies low over a few Jeeps. From the front, its landing gear is lowered, from the back it's up. (00:05)
3. When 007 flies his mini-jet through the hangar, under the plane is a pole that connects it to its actual "engine." (00:06)

Jet Dragged by Jag

Special effects supervisor John Richardson got an XJ6 Jaguar and mounted the BD Jet on a pole connected to the car. He then drove the Jaguar into the hangar at about 75 mph . . . thus creating the illusion of flight.

---

4. While playing backgammon, Kamal asks Major Clive to raise the stakes to 100,000 rupees. From the front, Kamal is holding his dice cup; from the back, he is ges-

ticulating with the same (empty) hand. (00:30)

5. When Bond rolls the double sixes, the loaded dice on the board change positions after every shot, getting closer to his cup. (00:32)

6. Bond throws a thug on a bed of nails: the nails bend. (00:37)

7. The homing device in the Fabergé egg triggers a beep in 007's wristwatch. Beep, beep, beep . . . almost one per second when Bond tries it in Q's lab, practically facing the egg. But when he's prisoner in Kamal's residence, and Kamal is approaching in his car several yards away with the egg, the beeping suddenly speeds up. And when 007 gets closer to it in the Monsoon Palace, the beeping gets louder and quieter all by itself. Huh? (00:40, 00:49, 00:56)

8. Chased by Kamal's people, Bond walks through a cobweb, and squashes a spider on his left elbow, thus creating a quite large stained area. When the (fake) tiger pops out of the bushes, Bond's sleeve is spotless. (01:02)

9. Gobinda falls from his elephant: he holds a rifle, doesn't while falling, then does again as he lands. (01:03)

10. Bond gets rescued by a sightseeing boat. As the banner on the side of the boat says, they are the "Cincinatti Moose Lodge." Isn't it "Cincinnati"? (01:05)

11. The water surrounding Octopussy's fortress is alligator-infested (the yo-yo thug gets eaten in one second as he falls into it). But a few moments earlier, that same thug and his partners swam through the same waters with no problems at all. Not only that, but 007 crossed the same channel disguised as an alligator. (01:06, 01:16, 01:19)

12. The thug with the yo-yo slices a photo of Bond, then retrieves his weapon. In the long shot, he's placing his left hand underneath the blade, holding the safety on top with the right. In the close-up, the safety has moved to the bottom of the yo-yo. (01:12)

13. The thug with the yo-yo slices a door and enters a room, running after Bond. As the two fight and another thug gets killed by a real octopus, the yo-yo thug shows, around his left arm, a cast he didn't have before. (01:19)

14. Bond enters the Octopussy Circus in East Germany during a number by Mischka and Grischka. As he walks through the audience, Bond is holding a program with a colored clown face on it, but when he sits down and hides from Magda, he lifts the pro-

gram—which is now plain white. (01:23)

Now *That's* Dedication!

Unbeknownst to the crew, stuntman/actor William Derrick removed part of the supporting struts from the balcony of Octopussy's bedroom in the Pinewood soundstage. He fell during one take and broke an arm, but insisted on coming back to the set to complete the shooting.

15. When one of the train cars is connected to the car she's on, Octopussy looks at a glass in the middle of her table. In the following shot, the glass has moved to the left of the same table. (01:30)
16. When Bond's Mercedes is hit by a train and winds up in a lake, it "takes off" backward. Yet the front of the car lands in the water first. (01:36)
17. To get to the American military base in Berlin, Bond steals a car. As he leaves, his window is rolled halfway down. But then he fishtails in a square, and the window is rolled up. Just before a second police car enters the chase, the window is again rolled halfway down, then completely rolled down when Bond passes by Kamal and Gobinda, and again rolled down halfway when 007 enters the base. (01:48, 01:49, 01:50, 01:51)

18. One of Octopussy's acrobats, wearing a very skimpy outfit, orders an elephant to sit. But when Octopussy says, "Now!" it's the woman in the skimpy outfit who flies away on the teeter-totter, while another member of Octopussy's crew (wearing a black robe) is now commanding the elephant. (01:56)
19. Right after Gobinda climbs out of the plane, Bond is standing close to the right wing, his jacket zipped down. But after Bond avoids Gobinda's blade, his jacket is completely zipped up. (02:04)
20. Bond and Octopussy jump out of Kamal's plane just in the nick of time. She rolls off of a cliff, and Bond grabs her with his left hand, extending his right to hold on to a rock. But a shot from above reveals Bond's right arm is close to the cliff—and again, holding on to the rock. (02:06)

Questions

1. Since when was a meeting in the former Soviet Union held in English (with an accent)? (00:16)
2. While fighting, Bond and the yo-yo thug fall into the water: Bond is wearing a long-sleeve shirt, and the thug is barechested. A crocodile arrives and supposedly makes a snack of one of the two (a loud scream and waving arms make this perfectly clear). But

the waving arms belong to someone who's wearing a long-sleeve shirt—yet Bond is safe and sound, as always. Was there someone else in the pool? (01:19)

Fun Fact

At the end of the credits, it is announced that "James Bond will return in *From a View to a Kill*." As you know, the next movie is simply *A View to a Kill* (the title was changed about three months before the commencement of principal photography). (02:09)

OUT OF AFRICA (8)

1985, color, 161 min.

Director: Sidney Pollack

Cast: Robert Redford (Denys Finch Hatton), Meryl Streep (Karen Christentze "Tanne" Dinesen Blixen), Klaus Maria Brandauer (Baron Bror "Blix" Von Blixen), Michael Kitchen (Berkeley Cole), Malick Bowens (Farah Aden), Joseph Thiaka (Kamante), Stephen Kinyanjui (Kinanjui), Michael Gough (Lord "D" Delamere), Suzanna Hamilton (Felicity), Rachel Kempson (Sarah, Lady Belfield), Graham Crowden (Lord Belfield).

Indecent Proposal: The African Years

Bloopers

1. Karen is using the compass Denys gave her for the first time: she looks left and right, and spots a group of Masai warriors. She closes the compass with a loud *click,* calls Farah . . . and then closes the compass a second time. (00:49)

2. When she learns she has syphilis, Karen gets dressed in the doctor's office, and she reaches for her hat: the scarf around her neck is out of her shirt, but in the following close-up, it's tucked into the shirt. (00:59)

3. Bror is in his living room, devastated by the news Karen just told him. He produces a cigarette while sitting with his legs crossed (the right over the left); in the following cut, he's still sitting—but now the left leg is crossed over the right. (01:02)

4. It's New Year's Eve, confetti flies all over the place, and Karen kisses Denys. He kisses her back, and two streamers that are on his left shoulder vanish halfway through the kiss. They'll be back, when the whole room sings "God Save the King." (01:15, 01:16)

5. Denys peels an orange while talking with Karen. There are two oranges on the plate in the middle of the table, then one, then two again—and Denys never eats them. (01:23, 01:23)

6. Denys comes back from hunting, and Karen goes into her room at once: it's a

dreamy sequence—still she removes his tie twice before getting in bed. (01:44)

7. Berkeley passes away, and a small funeral is celebrated. At the "amen" moment, one extra (third from screen left) starts the sign of the cross . . . with his left hand. (01:50)

8. Denys invites Karen on a plane ride. She agrees, and as he's about to get on board, he hands her a pair of goggles. As she sits in her seat, he hands her the goggles again. (01:52)

P

PATRIOT, THE (6)
2000, color, 164 min.

Director: Roland Emmerich

Cast: Mel Gibson (Col. Benjamin "The Ghost" Martin), Heath Ledger (Gabriel Martin), Joely Richardson (Aunt Charlotte Putnam Selton), Jason Isaacs (Col. William Tavington), Chris Cooper (Col. Harry Burwell), Tchéky Karyo (Maj. Jean Villeneuve), Rene Auberjonois (Rev. Oliver), Lisa Brenner (Anne Patricia Howard), Tom Wilkinson (Gen. Charles Cornwallis), Donal Logue (Dan Scott), Leon Rippy (John Billings), Adam Baldwin (Capt. Wilkins), Sky McCole Bartusiak (Susan Martin).

Former soldier is turned from bystander into asskicker in the American Revolutionary War.

Bloopers
1. Benjamin goes up to put his girls to sleep, and the candles on his candelabra are about three inches long. When he comes downstairs to the boys, the candles have all grown a few inches. (00:05, 00:06)
2. Gabriel is standing in line to enlist when Benjamin approaches him from behind. When he asks, "Do you intend to enlist?" Gabriel is facing him. Then before Gabriel anwers, he turns around . . . to face him. (00:16)
3. Gabriel narrates in the letter to his brother Thomas that, " . . . my good friend Peter Cuppin fell at Elizabethtown." We then see the letter, which reads, " . . . Peter Cuppin, of whom I have written, fell at Monmouth." (00:18)
4. Gabriel comes home with a dispatch and a chest wound. Benjamin rips open Gabriel's shirt to reveal a cut on his left side, with blood all around it. In the following wide shot, the blood is gone. (00:24)
5. The straps on Colonel Mar-

tin's left shoulder change positions throughout the prisoner exchange scene with General Cornwallis. (01:29, 01:32)

6. Benjamin's youngest daughter, Susan, finally speaks and runs to him. As they embrace, her braids jump back and forth from shot to shot between being on her back and being on her chest. (01:55)

Question

Gabriel hunts down Tavington, who packs his gun with a ramrod, tosses the ramrod away, and shoots at Gabriel a first time. He then quickly reloads with a ramrod (a spare?) and tosses it away. How many ramrods does this guy keep on his belt, one for each bullet? (02:06)

PAY IT FORWARD (3)
2000, color, 123 min.

Director: Mimi Leder

Cast: Kevin Spacey (Eugene Simonet), Helen Hunt (Arlene McKinney), Haley Joel Osment (Trevor McKinney), Jay Mohr (Chris Chandler), James Caviezel (Jerry), Jon Bon Jovi (Ricki), Angie Dickinson (Grace), David Ramsey (Sidney), Gary Werntz (Thorsen), Colleen Flynn (Woman at the bridge).

"I see good people."

Bloopers

1. Trevor goes to school wearing a black-strapped wristwatch. As he walks into Professor Simonet's class, he's not wearing the watch. At his desk, he has it. When Simonet says, "This class is social studies," a shot from the back of the class reveals Trevor watchless again. After Simonet's request for class participation, the wristwatch is back, and as he says that the assignment goes all year long, the watch is missing again. (00:04, 00:05, 00:06, 00:07, 00:08, 00:10)

2. When Jerry the bum pours cereal into Trevor's bowl, the cereal goes way past the bowl's brim. But in the following shot, they're barely visible. (00:17)

3. Taping the interview, Trevor says, "But I guess it's hard for some people who are ... so used to things the way they are ... even if they're bad ... to change. And they kind of give up. And when they do, everybody kind of ... They kind of lose." When replayed by the TV news, Trevor says, "But I—I guess it's hard for some people who are ... so used to things the way they are, even if they're bad ... to change. 'Cause ... I guess they kind of give up. And ... when they do, everybody kinda ... loses." (01:50, 01:53)

PEACEMAKER, THE (5)
1997, color, 123 min.

Director: Mimi Leder

Cast: George Clooney (Thomas Devoe), Nicole Kidman (Julia Kelly), Marcel Iures (Dusan Gavrich), Aleksandr Baluyev (Aleksandr Kodoroff), Rene Medvesek (Vlado Mirich), Gary Werntz (Hamilton), Randall Batinkoff (Ken), Jim Haynie (General Garnett), Alexander Strobele (Shummaker), Holt McCallany (Appleton).

*The name is Bond . . .
George Clooney Bond.*

Bloopers

1. The hijackers short a couple of wires to move a train switch and cause the collision. The switch moves in the wrong direction (the train should have gone to the right, but an aerial shot shows it going left). (00:13)
2. Calling Dimitri on the phone, Thomas has a felt pen between the index and middle fingers of the hand that's holding the phone. In one shot, however, the pen jumps into the palm of his hand, then comes back into position. (00:31)
3. Right after the Mercedes pushes another BMW into a clothes stand, in one shot the rear-left window of the Mercedes appears to be completely down (it isn't for the entire chase up to that point),

then it's up again as Thomas hits the brakes. (00:48, 00:51, 00:52)

4. The Mercedes Thomas is driving pushes aside one BMW: on the front bumper, two grills drop open. Thomas tells Julia to move onto the front seat, and now the grills are back up in place. (00:48, 00:49)
5. Julia and Thomas find the bomb in New York City. As they open Dusan's backpack, the counter of the bomb is 02:54, 02:53 . . . and beeping. After a radio communication informs us that the bomb squad will be there in 4 minutes (or twelve beeps later) the timer says 02:48, 02:47. (01:53)

Question
At the Special Forces Command Center in Turkey, Thomas wears a green army uniform: the crossed-arrow lapel brass is right—his hat, though, isn't. The hat Thomas is wearing is Vietnam War issue—outdated for his uniform. Did he go to a garage sale to bolster his wardrobe? (00:59)

PEGGY SUE GOT MARRIED (3)
1986, color, 104 min.

Director: Francis Ford Coppola

Cast: Kathleen Turner (Peggy Sue Kelcher Bodell), Nicolas Cage (Charlie Bodell), Barry Miller (Richard Norvik), Catherine Hicks (Carol Heath), Don

YOU HAVE THE RIGHT TO REMAIN LEFT

Or right. Depending on what's left.

Christopher Lloyd's DeLorean in *Back to the Future Part II*	Blooper No. 2
Arnold Schwarzenegger's binoculars in *Commando*	Blooper No. 17
Bruce Willis's taxicab in *Die Hard With a Vengeance*	Blooper No. 4
Matthew Broderick in *Inspector Gadget*	Blooper No. 1
David Spade's car in *Joe Dirt*	Blooper No. 2
John Hannah's bus in *The Mummy Returns*	Blooper No. 8
A train in *The Peacemaker*	Blooper No. 1

Murray (Jack Kelcher), Barbara Harris (Evelyn Kelcher), Jim Carrey (Walter Getz), Wil Shriner (Arthur Nagle), Leon Ames (Barney Alvorg), Maureen O'Sullivan (Elizabeth Alvorg), Kevin J. O'Connor (Michael Fitzsimmons), Joan Allen (Maddy Nagle), Helen Hunt (Beth Bodell).

Woman goes back in time to high school to examine herself.

Bloopers

1. Peggy Sue does herself up in a mirror. The body double playing her back on the camera side of the mirror is not doing the actions in synch with Peggy Sue. Not enough rehearsal? (00:02)

2. After her "fainting spell" at the blood drive, Peggy Sue's friends give her a ride home. They take a left around the same corner twice in a row; not only is the same green car following them, but the same three cars are parked adjacent to the corner (gray, red, and light blue). (00:20)

3. Peggy Sue visits her grandparents, and after her grandfather pulls the car up to the house and they're walking away from the car, the reverse lights are on. Huh? (01:25)

PHILADELPHIA (6)

1993, color, 125 min.

Director: Jonathan Demme

Cast: Tom Hanks (Andrew Beckett), Denzel Washington (Joe Miller), Roberta Maxwell (Judge Tate), Buzz Kilman ("Crutches"), Karen Finley (Dr. Gillman), Daniel Chapman (Clinic Storyteller), Mark Sorensen Jr. (Clinic Patient), Jeffrey Williamson (Tyrone), Charles Glenn (Kenneth Killcoyne), Ron Vawter (Bob Seidman), Anna Deavere Smith (Anthea Burton), Stephanie Roth (Rachel Smilow).

Lawyer gets AIDS and fights for his rights.

Bloopers

1. After talking to Anthea, Andrew passes an envelope from his right hand to his left, in order to give a high five to another colleague. But in the over-the-shoulder shot, the envelope has zapped back into his right hand. (00:07)

2. Andrew is interrupted by Bob while he's working on two computers and eating Chinese food. The chopsticks in the container change positions during shots (they are separate, together, and separate again—when Andrew stands up). (00:09)

3. In his office, Charles sips cognac from a glass, but when Andrew says, "The faith of the participants . . ." Charles puffs from a cigar. (00:09)

4. Joe brings two bowls into the dining room and leaves them on the edge of the table; he then comes back into the kitchen, and when he returns to the dining room again, the bowls have moved on top of the two plates. (00:31)

5. In the library, Andrew slides a book in front of Joe. When Joe turns it, it's possible to see Andrew's document holder's lace: it's crumpled to the right. But when we see an overhead shot, the lace is neatly straightened across the table—to the left this time. (00:38, 00:39)

6. Before storming out of a drugstore, Joe hands his card to a young man: the man grabs the card with his right hand, but then holds it in his left. (01:00)

PICTURE PERFECT (7)
1997, color, 105 min.

Director: Glenn Gordon Caron

Cast: Jennifer Aniston (Kate Mosley), Jay Mohr (Nick), Kevin Bacon (Sam Mayfair), Olympia Dukakis (Rita Mosley), Illeana Douglas (Darcy O'Neil), Kevin Dunn (Mr. Mercer), Anne Twomey (Sela), Faith Prince (Mrs. Mercer), John Rothman (Jim Davenport), Margaret Gibson (Mrs. Davenport), Paul Cassell (Brad).

Jennifer Aniston has trouble finding love . . . a science-fiction classic.

Bloopers

1. Jim Davenport has a cigar in his mouth while Kate tells him about her "physical reaction" when she hears the Spread This slogan. Cut to Jim: the cigar is gone. (00:24)

2. Kate enters her apartment to find her mom, Rita, in it; while the two are arguing, Kate puts down the mail and her purse, which don't stand up straight and keep leaning against her back. As we cut

inside the apartment, the purse is standing perfectly straight, far away from Kate. (00:30)

3. While talking in the coffee shop, Kate and Nick get menus from a waitress. The woman places them on the table, and they are aligned when the camera is on Nick, yet askew when the camera is on Kate. (00:42)

4. Kate has a glass of ice tea (or something similar) while she's talking with Nick. As he leaves, the level of the tea has noticeably dropped, even if Kate doesn't seem to have sipped a drop. (00:43, 00:45)

5. Nick holds the script of "the big fight" with the flaps wide open when the shot is from the left, and with the right flap rolled when the shot is from the right. (00:50)

6. Nick doesn't have the cast around his right arm in the first shot of the fancy dinner with Kate's coworkers. (00:58)

7. At the restaurant, Nick places his arm around Kate twice. (01:06)

Fun Fact
Even if all through the picture he states that he "videotapes weddings," everytime we see a shot from inside Nick's videocamera, the image is in film.

PIRANHA (4)
1978, color, 93 min.

Director: Joe Dante

Cast: Bradford Dillman (Paul Grogan), Heather Menzies (Maggie McKeown), Kevin McCarthy (Dr. Robert Hoak), Keenan Wynn (Jack), Dick Miller (Buck Gardner), Barbara Steele (Dr. Mengers), Belinda Balaski (Betsy), Melody Thomas (Laura), Bruce Gordon (Colonel Waxman), Paul Bartel (Dumont), Richard Deacon (Earl Lyon), Hill Farnsworth (Water Skier).

Do you remember Jaws?
Same thing, only smaller.

Bloopers
1. Earl hands Maggie the plane ticket and she takes it, but during the exchange, the ticket turns 180 degrees in Earl's hand (check the "$5 off" writing on top of it). (00:08)

2. Dr. Hoak, wounded by the fish, is pulled onto a raft: his sweater, on the back, is ripped and shredded—then isn't. Then it is again. Wardrobe!! (00:39)

3. A water skier is practicing on the river. He's wearing an orange life jacket, but when he falls into the water, the jacket turns yellow. (01:15, 01:19)

4. Despite the fact that the boat is going full speed, when we see the two women from the water skier's POV, the rope is slack and there's no tension at all. (01:17)

Question
While they're driving to the closed testing facility, Paul and

Maggie talk in a Jeep. Is the odd reflection in the middle of the windshield a camera? (00:13)

PLANES, TRAINS AND AUTOMOBILES (3)
1989, color, 92 min.

Director: John Hughes

Cast: Steve Martin (Neal Page), John Candy (Del Griffith), Laila Robins (Susan Page), Michael McKean (State Trooper), Kevin Bacon (Taxi Racer), Dylan Baker (Owen), Carol Bruce (Joy), Olivia Burnette (Marti), Diana Douglas (Peg), Martin Ferrero (Motel Clerk), Larry Hankin (Doobie), Grant Forsberg (Brand Manager).

The best Thanksgiving movie of all time.

Bloopers
1. In the New York office, the brand manager takes off his glasses, holds them in his right hand, moves forward in his chair . . . and the glasses have jumped from his right hand into his mouth, where he holds them by one of the ear pieces. (00:01)
2. While driving and singing to a Ray Charles tune, Del steers violently, causing the car to lose one of the right hubcaps. The hubcap will come back into place a few seconds later, when the car skids at the stop sign and

then goes back onto the free-way in the wrong direction. (00:57, 00:58, 00:59)
3. Neal leaves the metro train station on the right track. Then he takes a train back to the same station. The train comes back on the same right track, but it's a reverse play of the departure shot: on the lower level sidewalk there's a pedestrian walking in reverse. And just for the sake of continuity, Neal's hair is parted on the wrong side when he gets off the train. (01:20, 01:23)

Question
At the Braidwood Inn, Neal pays with a Diner Card. Yet later on, when he reads his credit cards to Del, he says he has a Visa, a gaso-line card, and a Neiman-Marcus. What about the Diner card? (00:16, 00:32)

PLEDGE, THE (3)
2001, color, 123 min.

Director: Sean Penn

Cast: Jack Nicholson (Jerry Black), Robin Wright Penn (Lori), Helen Mirren (Doctor), Pauline Roberts (Chrissy), Benicio Del Toro (Toby Jay Wadenah), Aaron Eckhart (Stan Krolak), Sam Shepard (Eric Pollack), Tom Noonan (Gary Jackson), Vanessa Redgrave (Annalise Hansen), Mickey Rourke (Jim Olstad), Harry Dean Stanton (Floyd Cage).

Obsessed retired cop keeps looking and looking and looking and looking . . .

Bloopers
1. Jerry pulls his truck over to look at the map before making the offer on the gas station. The outside of his car is filthy. He drives 100 yards down the road to the gas station, and his car is immaculate. (00:57, 00:58)
2. Jerry offers to buy the gas station from Floyd, who's wearing reading glasses. Jerry says, "I'll tell you what," and Floyd's holding the glasses by the left ear piece. Jerry gives him his info, and asks him to "think about it," then Floyd says, "Thanks for comin' in." He's now holding his glasses by the right ear piece. (00:59, 01:00)
3. Jerry drives through a few wire fences on his "short cut" to the church, and there's a grille guard on his SUV. After he drives through the last fence he starts up the embankment, and the grille guard is gone. It's back as he reaches the top of the hill. (01:40)

POINT BREAK (10)
1991, color, 121 min.

Director: Kathryn Bigelow

Cast: Patrick Swayze (Bodhi), Keanu Reeves (Johnny "John" Utah), Gary Busey (Angelo Pappas), Lori Petty (Tyler Ann Endicott), John C. McGinley (Ben Harp), James LeGros (Roach), John Philbin (Nathanial), Bojesse Christopher (Grommet), Julian Reyes (Alvarez), Daniel Beer (Babbit), Chris Pedersen (Bunker), Jared Chandler (Pilot).

Football jock is after a surfer dude.

Bloopers
1. When Johnny places the license plate number in the system, the computer finds his lady friend: Endicott, Tyler Ann, who, according to Pappas (and after a brief glimpse of the screen) has "black hair, blue eyes." But when the computer screen is in full view, it says, under Endicott, Tyler Ann, "eyes: green—hair: blonde." The computer was right the first time. (00:17)
2. While watching Johnny on Latigo Beach with binoculars, Pappas removes his white sunglasses and places them on the dashboard. The glasses move back and forth during the whole stakeout. (00:32)
3. Bodhi, wearing a Ronald Reagan mask, is setting a gas station on fire when he's attacked by Johnny . . . or rather, by his stunt double, who

has very wet hair as a safety precaution. (01:06)

4. Johnny chases Bodhi and slides downhill before falling into an artificial channel where his left knee gives. During the slide, a white protective shirt appears underneath Johnny's shirt. The protective shirt vanishes as Johnny empties his gun at the sky. (01:09)

5. Bodhi is the first to jump from the plane, demonstrating a very skillful, aerodynamic technique. When the other four passengers jump, not only does Bodhi appear to be closer to the plane than before, but he's also totally uncoordinated. (01:18)

6. While free-falling in midair, Bodhi and his three partners join hands, and they call for Johnny to join them. As he approaches, the four skydivers appear to be separated, but in their over-the-shoulder (and following shots) they're still holding hands. (01:21)

7. Cornered at the airport, Bodhi intimates to the pilot to get on the plane, and cocks his gun. He then orders Johnny to get on the same plane—and cocks his gun. Again. (01:40)

8. Johnny grabs a gun with his left hand and jumps off the plane after Bodhi. In one shot, though, when Bodhi screams, "Go ahead, Johnny! Pull it!!" the gun has moved to his right hand. It comes back to the left hand when he lands. (01:44, 01:45)

9. During the free fall, Johnny eventually grabs Bodhi. In that same moment, Johnny has a pair of goggles on his face. (01:45)

10. On the beach with Bodhi, Johnny talks about the "fifty years storm." The two guys are under a powerful downpour, but when we see the waves, there's no rain at all. (01:44, 01:45)

Question

Johnny is attacked on the beach by four surfer dudes, and his multicolored board is snapped in half. Yet when Tyler and Johnny go surfing two mornings later (as he realizes his partners are actually bank robbers), he has the same surfboard—in one piece—underneath his arm. Does he own multiples, or was it insured? (00:34, 00:59)

POLTERGEIST (10)
    1982, color, 114 min.

Director: Tobe Hooper

Cast: Craig T. Nelson (Steve Freeling), JoBeth Williams (Diane Freeling), Beatrice Straight (Dr. Lesh), Dominique Dunne (Dana Freeling), Oliver Robins (Robbie Freeling), Heather O'Rourke (Carol Anne Freeling), Michael McManus (Ben Tuthill), Virginia Kiser (Mrs. Tuthill), Martin Casella (Marty), Richard Lawson

(Ryan), Zelda Rubinstein (Tangina).

"They're he-e-e-e-eree!"

Bloopers

1. The dog grabs a bag of potato chips by one corner; in the following shot, the dog has another corner in its mouth. (00:02)
2. Steve, in bed, has his left arm against the headrest; in the following shot, his arm is down on a pillow. (00:18)
3. The white doll carriage moves toward the closet door and falls on its side; later on, the carriage is in a totally different position, far from where it was before (now it is close to the door). (00:38)
4. Dr. Lesh wears her glasses, then she doesn't have them on; then she does, she doesn't, she does . . . Then she stands up (glasses on), and, running toward her colleagues, puts them on! (00:48, 00:50)
5. Diane has her hands one inside the other, but in the following shot, her hands are in her pants pockets. (00:49)
6. As the poltergeist enters the living room, Marty stands to Ryan's right side. When the wind blows, they instantly switch positions. (01:07)
7. The dog jumps onto the rear seat of the cab; when Robbie peeks out of the window, the dog is on the front seat. (01:09)
8. Diane walks into the kitchen, a cup in her left hand and a bottle in her right. As she sits down, the cup has moved to her right hand, and the bottle to her left. (01:10)
9. Ryan grabs a rope and rolls it around his right wrist; in the following shot, the rope is free. (01:29)
10. Robbie is attacked by the evil clown, which places its arm around the kid twice. (01:41)

Question

Talking about his family, Steve says "My wife is thirty-one . . . thirty-two. . . . My daughter is sixteen." Then when did Diane have her first daughter? (00:43)

POSTMAN, THE (4)

1997, color, 177 min.

Director: Kevin Costner

Cast: Kevin Costner (The Postman), Will Patton (General Bethlehem), Larenz Tate (Ford Lincoln Mercury), Olivia Williams (Abby), James Russo (Idaho), Daniel Von Bargen (Sheriff Briscoe), Tom Petty (Bridge City Mayor), Scott Baristow (Luke), Giovanni Ribisi (Bandit #20), Roberta Maxwell (Irene March), Joe Santos (Getty), Ron McLarty (Old George).

The story of a hero who brings hope to a future humanity is told in the same time that a letter travels from Boston to Hong Kong . . . pulled on a trailer hitch by an infant slug.

Bloopers

1. At an abandoned Unocal station, the Postman talks to Bill, his mule, while balancing on a stepladder. When he says, ".. will settle for turpentine," the Postman holds a rifle in his left hand. In the following cut, the rifle has jumped to his right hand. (00:04)

2. The prisoners are in line for lunch: the cook serves up a ladle filled with a grayish soup (with two large blobs in it) to a prisoner who's holding his skillet with his left hand. Then it's the Postman's turn: he holds his skillet with his right hand, the cook fills the ladle again (with two large blobs in the soup) and drops it into a skillet—which is being held with a left hand. The detail is exactly the same. (00:24)

3. Right after the Postman knocks a rider off of his horse, Abby fires at General Bethlehem—who has to duck and cover behind a few oil drums. The drum lying on its side gets two bullet holes, then none, then the holes are back again. . . . (01:33)

4. During a dramatic speech at Bridge City, where Abby tells the Postman that she loved her husband, the collar of the Postman's coat is lifted by the wind (when Abby has the close-up), then is resting on his shoulder (when he is in frame). (02:32)

PRESUMED INNOCENT (3)
1990, color, 127 min.

Director: Alan J. Pakula

Cast: Harrison Ford (Rusty Sabich), Brian Dennehy (Raymond Horgan), Raul Julia (Sandy Stern), Bonnie Bedelia (Barbara Sabich), Paul Winfield (Judge Larren Lyttle), Greta Scacchi (Caroline Polhemus), John Spencer (Detective Lipranzer), Joe Grifasi (Tommy Molto), Tom Mardirosian (Nico Della Guardia), Anna Maria Horsford (Eugenia), Jesse Bradford (Nat Sabich).

Accuser becomes the accused.

Bloopers

1. In Polhemus's office, Rusty squares the pictures of the murder, then squares them again before putting them away. (00:09)

2. Talking about cheating at school with his dad, Nat grabs the glass of milk but winds up holding a fork, then he lifts the glass again—but he has the fork in his hand again. (00:25)

3. When Judge Lyttle answers an objection raised by Sandy, he places his right hand on top of his left on his desk. In the over-the-shoulder shot, his left hand is free, and then his hands are crossed. (01:09)

Fun Facts

1. Talking to Rick while entering the office for the first time,

Rusty knocks down a box of doughnuts with his briefcase. He doesn't even blink. (00:04)

2. After the case is dismissed, Rusty is interviewed outside of the court; one of the tape recorders placed in front of him (in the bottom-right corner) is empty. (01:48)

PRIMARY COLORS (12)
1998, color, 140 min.

Director: Mike Nichols

Cast: John Travolta (Governor Jack Stanton), Emma Thompson (Susan Stanton), Billy Bob Thornton (Richard Jemmons), Adrian Lester (Henry Burton), Kathy Bates (Libby Holden), Maura Tierney (Daisy), Larry Hagman (Governor Fred Picker), Paul Guilfoyle (Howard Ferguson), Caroline Aaron (Lucille Kaufman), Rebecca Walker (March Cunningham), Brian Markinson (Randy), Robert Klein (Norman Asher).

The rise and triumph of a kindhearted but womanizing Southern governor running for the presidency ... hmm ... sounds familiar ...

Bloopers
1. When Henry gets dressed while arguing with his girlfriend, March, he puts on boxers, socks, pants, a shirt, and a jacket. But when he leaves, we hear the sound of shoes. (00:08, 00:09)

2. Henry is invited by Governor Stanton to go to Washington with him. Stanton has one half sandwich and a wrapped one in his left hand, but when the two turn to exit, the wrapped sandwich has jumped to Stanton's right hand. (00:12)

3. In the Washington motel, Susan takes away Henry's teacup twice. (00:16)

4. When at the airport Susan tells Henry that history is made by the first-timers, she places a hand on his shoulder. In the next shot, the hand is gone. (00:20)

5. After hearing an upsetting TV broadcast, Susan removes her left earring. But in the following shot, she's removing the right, then the left. (00:53)

6. While talking with Danny at the Krispy Kreme doughnuts shop about college games, Stanton has his hands on his coffee mug (from the back), then he raises one arm (front), then he has his hands on his coffee mug again. (00:55)

7. When Libby grabs her gun to threaten Randy, she cocks it. When she aims at Randy's crotch, she cocks the gun again. (01:07, 01:08)

8. Back at Mammoth Falls, Stanton regrets his conduct on a radio program. In the over-the-shoulder shot, his legs are crossed. (01:30)

9. They meet with Norman. As Susan takes away the plates,

he lowers his coffee cup twice. (01:37)

10. Norman suggests that "It might be a good idea to get on some TV show like Montel and Geraldo." But his mouth doesn't say "Montel." It says, "Oprah." (01:38)

11. During the television debate between Governor Stanton and Governor Picker, when we see the monitors of the live event, they are showing two of Stanton's nonsynchronized images (there's even a jump-cut in-between them). (01:43)

12. While Libby and Henry drive in the car after talking to Delgado, the reflection on the car window moves slower than the car. (01:53)

Q

QUILLS (3)
2000, color, 124 min.

Director: Philip Kaufman

Cast: Geoffrey Rush (The Marquis de Sade), Kate Winslet (Madeleine LeClerc), Joaquin Phoenix (The Abbe du Coulmier), Michael Caine (Dr. Royer-Collard), Billie Whitelaw (Madame LeClerc), Patrick Malahide (Delbené), Amelia Warner (Simone), Jane Menelaus (Renee Pelagie), Stephen Moyer (Prouix), Tony Pritchard (Valcour), Michael Jenn (Cleante), Danny Babington (Pitou).

The life and times of the Marquis de Sade. He may be daffy as a dog in heat, but it's all good, clean fun. Wait . . . strike that last phrase.

Bloopers
1. Cleante intercepts the Abbe du Coulmier as he's walking to de Sade's door. In the cage he's carrying Cleante's green bird, which jumps off its perch twice. (00:20)
2. When the marquis spits on the Bible the Abbe du Coulmier just tossed to him, the book rotates 180 degrees in his hands (look at the spine). (00:51)
3. The Abbe du Coulmier whispers a prayer in front of the dead body of Madeleine LeClerc . . . and she breathes. (01:42)

Question
The story takes place in France; when Mademoiselle Renare is beheaded, in the crowd it's possible to see banners and writings of "Fraternité" and "Mort aux tyrans." Yet, the Marquis de Sade writes his play *The Crimes of Love* in English—even the posters of the play are in English—(00:41) and his previous novel, *Justine*, appears to be in English. Why? We thought that in France they primarily spoke French . . . oh, never mind. (00:03, 00:07, 00:40)

CAN THEY PLAY "POSSUM," AT LEAST

We doubt it.

Ron Silver in *The Arrival*	Blooper No 2
Hilary Swank in *Boys Don't Cry*	Blooper No. 3
Nancy Loomis in *Halloween II*	Blooper No. 4
An orc in *Lord of the Rings: The Fellowship of the Ring*	Blooper No. 23
Kate Winslet in *Quills*	Blooper No. 3
Michael York in *Wrongfully Accused*	Blooper No. 2

R

REAR WINDOW (2)
1954, color, 112 min.

Director: Alfred Hitchcock

Cast: James Stewart (L.B. "Jeff" Jefferies), Grace Kelly (Lisa Carol Fremont), Wendell Corey (Lieutenant Thomas J. Doyle), Thelma Ritter (Stella), Raymond Burr (Mr. Lars Thorwald), Judith Evelyn (Miss Lonelyheart), Ross Bagdasarian (Songwriter), Georgine Darcy (Miss Torso, the Ballet Dancer), Sara Berner (Woman on Fire Escape), Frank Cady (Man on Fire Escape), Jesslyn Fax (Miss Hearing Aid), Rand Harper (Newlywed Man).

Crippled peeping Tom gets into hot water.

Bloopers
1. After Jeff receives the first massage from Stella, he's helped back onto his wheelchair. His pajama jacket is open but, as he sits down, one button has buttoned itself. (00:12)

2. Lisa opens her "ample enough" suitcase to show Jeff her nightgown and her slippers, which she buries underneath the gown on the side of the case before placing everything else on a desk. When Tom enters the apartment and catches a glimpse of the case, the slippers are now on top of the gown, very nicely placed. (01:10, 01:12)

Fun Fact
HITCHWATCH: Alfred Hitchcock can be seen fixing a clock in the songwriter's loft. Hey, wait a second!! That songwriter . . . why, yes! It's Ross Bagdasarian, a.k.a. Dave Seville, the father of Alvin and the Chipmunks! (00:26)

REBEL WITHOUT A CAUSE (4)
1955, color, 111 min.

Director: Nicholas Ray

Cast: James Dean (Jim Stark), Natalie Wood (Judy), Sal Mineo (Plato), Jim Backus (Mr. Stark),

Ann Doran (Mrs. Stark), Corey Allen (Buzz Gunderson), William Hopper (Judy's Father), Rochelle Hudson (Judy's Mother), Dennis Hopper (Goon), Edward Platt (Juvenile Officer Ray), Steffi Sidney (Mil), Marietta Canty (Plato's Nurse).

James Dean becomes a star, and angst-ridden teens finally find their role model.

Bloopers

1. They succeed in leaning Jim up against the wall at the police station, and he switches the windup toy from his right hand to his left, which he then places on the wall above his head. On the jump-cut to Judy behind him, his left hand holds the doll at his side. (00:02)
2. When he hears the dedication from Buzz of the song on the radio, Jim reaches through the driver's side window of his car with his left hand to turn off the radio. On the close-up, it's his right hand turning the knob. (01:09)
3. The police car patrolling near the deserted mansion rounds the corner, and it is broad daylight; the sun shines off the chrome. In the scenes both before and after this shot, it is night. (01:30)
4. Plato tries to run away from the police, Jim dives and only manages to grab his shoe. After Plato is gunned down, Jim bends down to

look and Plato is missing his left shoe. On the close-up, it's the right foot that's missing a shoe. Judy later picks up the missing shoe, which is visibly a left shoe, takes it over, and puts it back on his left foot. (01:46, 01:47, 01:48)

Fun Fact

By the way, did Jim think he unloaded the gun by removing its clip? Plato's pistol is semi-automatic, and since he already had fired it, there would still be one bullet in the chamber. (01:43)

RELIC, THE (3)

1996, color, 110 min.

Director: Peter Hyams

Cast: Penelope Ann Miller (Dr. Margo Green), Tom Sizemore (Lt. Vincent D'Agosta), Linda Hunt (Dr. Ann Cuthbert), James Whitmore (Dr. Albert Frock), Clayton Rohner (Detective Hollingsworth), Chi Moui Lo (Greg Lee), Thomas Ryan (Parkinson), Robert Lesser (Mayor Owen), Diane Robin (Mayor's Wife), Lewis Van Bergen (John Whitney), Constance Towers (Mrs. Blaisedale), Francis X. McCarthy (Mr. Blaisedale).

Quick! Pass me six thousand bottles of Raid!

Bloopers

1. A door in a museum has written on it, *"Lasciate ogni pensiero o voi che entrate."*

The correct line from Dante's *Divine Comedy* is *"Lasciate ogni speranza o voi che entrate."* (Drop every hope, oh you who are about to enter.) (00:32)

2.   There is ample use of walkie-talkies in the picture, with people interrupting one another as if they were talking on phones. (01:12)

3.   Margo steps in front of her computer to read on the screen "press 1 for result." The noise heard is of Margo pressing three keys—not just one. (01:36)

Question

Margo says that a tank filled with liquid is used to make the flesh fall off the bones of rhinoceroses. But later on, she dives into that same tank and she comes out safe and sound. How did she do that? (00:25, 01:41, 01:43)

REMEMBER THE TITANS (5)
   2000, color, 113 min.

Director: Boaz Yakin

Cast: Denzel Washington (Coach Herman Boone), Will Patton (Coach Bill Yoast), Wood Harris (Julius "Big Ju" Campbell), Ryan Hurst (Gerry Bertier), Donald Adeosun Faison (Petey Jones), Craig Kirkwood (Jerry "Rev" Harris), Ethan Suplee (Lewis Lastik), Kip Pardue (Ronnie "Sunshine" Bass), Hayden Panettiere (Sheryl Yoast), Nicole Ari Parker (Carol Boone), Kate Bosworth (Emma Hoyt), Earl Poitier (Blue Stanton), Ryan Gosling (Alan Bosley), Tim Ware (Fred Bosley).

If you can play football, it don't matter if you're black or white!

Bloopers

1.   Coach Yoast is talking about his decision to leave the team, when Mr. Bosley yells, "I say boycott T.C. Williams!" His son Alan, hands on the table, is staring at him, but in the following, matching shot, he's looking away, one hand in front of his mouth. (00:09)

2.   In the gym, Petey Jones exchanges high fives with his teammates. To the best of our recollection, the high five came around in the late seventies or early eighties . . . and certainly wasn't around in 1971. (00:10)

3.   Before entering the bar where they "have problems" with black people, Sunshine's shirt has the next to last button unbuttoned. He walks in with his two friends, and the button is now buttoned. As he's pushed onto the sidewalk, the button is unbuttoned again. (00:53, 00:54)

4.   During their spectacular 1971 championship (00:01), the Titans are dedicated a song on the radio, "Long Cool Woman in a Black Dress," by

the Hollies. Too bad that song was released in 1972, and it went up the charts during the end of the summer of that year. (01:15)

5. When his car skids after being smashed by the truck, Gerry seems to be wearing a helmet. (01:26)

RENEGADES (7)
1989, color, 106 min.

Director: Jack Sholder

Cast: Kiefer Sutherland (Buster McHenry), Lou Diamond Phillips (Hank Storm), Jami Gertz (Barbara), Robert Knepper (Marino), Bill Smitrovich (Finch), Clark Johnson (JJ), Peter MacNeill (Denny Ransom), Floyd "Red Crow" Westerman (Red Crow), Joe Griffin (Matt), John Di Benedetto (Corso), Kyra Harper (Nema), Joseph Hieu (Gang Leader).

Native American helps cop capture a gang and retrieve a sacred lance.

Bloopers
1. When Red Crow is given the Lakota sacred lance, he raises his hands and grabs it, but in the following shot he does it all over again. (00:02)

2. Buster enters Paddy's Pub, lights a cigarette, pockets the lighter and leaves the packet on the counter. When he sees a patrol car stopping another car, the lighter has moved on top of the cigarette packet, then it's gone again. And when the shooting begins, the packet is gone from the counter. (00:04, 00:05)

3. Marino, one of his henchmen, and Buster jump into a car, with Buster driving. A few gunshots from policemen pierce the windshield and smash the second headlight from the right. But when the car zigzags through traffic, the windshield appears intact, then broken again—the headlight the same. (00:22)

4. During the car chase, Buster enters a narrow train-tracked alley. At the exit of it, a white-and-yellow truck passes by, then . . . it passes by again. (00:25)

5. When Buster, Hank, and Barbara flee from the Tidal Wave Salon, a cat clock on the wall indicates it's 3:05. When they come back into the store, as Hank begins shooting, the same clock says 6:10. And then it goes back to 3:05. (01:03, 01:04)

6. Barbara is shot and killed in the middle of the street. But when Buster fires one last round at the evil guys, her body starts at the first three shots. (01:17)

7. Hank falls from a horse because of a stick someone hits him with—but mostly because of a cable that makes him jump backward. (01:37)

RETURN OF THE JEDI (35)
also Special Edition (32)
1983, color, 134 min. / 135 min.
SE

Director: Richard Marquand

Cast: Mark Hamill (Luke Skywalker), Harrison Ford (Han Solo), Carrie Fisher (Princess Leia Organa), Billy Dee Williams (Lando Calrissian), Anthony Daniels (C-3PO), Peter Mayhew (Chewbacca), Sebastian Shaw (Anakin Skywalker), Ian McDiarmid (Emperor Palpatine), Frank Oz (Yoda), James Earl Jones (Darth Vader—voice), David Prowse (Darth Vader), Alec Guinness (Ben "Obi-Wan" Kenobi), Kenny Baker (R2-D2 / Paploo), Jeremy Bulloch (Boba Fett), Caroline Blakiston (Mon Mothma), Warwick Davis (Wicket).

Who's the Jedi now, punk?!!

Bloopers
1. The pilots of the ship that approaches the main station, as well as the soldiers at the main station, are all wearing black gloves. However, the detail of a hand deactivating the shield to let the ship proceed is a bare one. (00:02)
2. C-3PO enters Jabba's room and walks down a few steps. Artoo is behind the golden robot, but it doesn't even approach the steps—yet it pops out from behind a column as we see Jabba. Quite a fast little fella, ain't he? (00:08)
3. As Artoo's hologram projection begins, Luke's light saber appears to his right. When C-3PO comments, "This can't be!" the saber has switched sides and is now to Luke's left. (00:09)
4. When Luke says, "I know that you are powerful," the shot of Jabba shows smoke going *toward* the floor and the bubbles in a bottle going down. (00:09)
5. Boba Fett draws his gun to shoot Boushh, the bounty hunter (Leia in disguise); Boba uses his left hand—but he's right-handed all through the picture. Of course, his trademark antenna swaps from his right to his left side as well. (00:12, 00:15 / 00:13, 00:15 SE)
6. Freshly defrosted, Han yells, "I can't see!" Yet when Leia crouches to let him turn to face Jabba, Han raises his right arm to clear Leia's head. Hmmm... (00:19 / 00:19, 00:20 SE)

Captain Piett was promoted to Admiral by Darth Vader in *The Empire Strikes Back*: his insignia, from three and three blocks, got upgraded to six and six. (00:23, 00:44 / also SE) In *Return*, Admiral Piett carries only three bars on his uniform. (00:54 / 00:55 SE)

7. Jabba yells, "Bring me Solo and the wookie!" After the death of the Rankor, Lando is nowhere to be seen, yet in the following shot he appears in front of Bib Fortuna. (00:27 / 00:28 SE)

8. From Jabba's vessel, Leia looks at the skiff carrying Luke, Han, and Chewbacca: the wookie's bandoleer goes from his right shoulder to his left side, while all through the picture he carries it from the left shoulder to the right side. (00:29 / 00:30 SE)

9. By the sarlacc pit, after Jabba orders, "Put him in," a soldier pushes Luke onto the plank. Lando appears in the background where Han and Chewie were standing—and where they will be again in the following shot. (00:31 / 00:32 SE)

10. Fighting with a soldier on the skiff, Lando tries not to fall into the pit by grabbing a rope with his bare hands—but in the long shot he's wearing black gloves. And then he isn't. (00:32 / 00:33 SE)

11. Luke jumps from one skiff to another; Lando, who is precariously dangling underneath the first skiff, appears in this shot quite still. (00:32 / 00:33 SE)

12. Hit by Han, Boba Fett takes off, and right after that Luke kicks a soldier—and he misses the poor guy by a mile. But the soldier falls into the pit anyway. (00:33)

13. The skiff where Han and Chewie are standing gets hit, and due to the explosion, it tilts to one side. Han flies overboard, but manages to hold on to the handrail, his feet dangling in the open. In the very next shot, he's still overboard—but this time it's head first, and Chewbacca is holding his feet. (00:33 / 00:34 SE)

14. When a tentacle of the sarlacc grabs Lando, he desperately grabs the spear that Han is offering him. But then, he doesn't seem to hold on to the spear at all. Or does he? Or doesn't he? (00:34 / 00:34, 00:35 SE)

15. C-3PO falls from Jabba's vessel. If you check out the sail behind the robot, you can see the cables that are pulling him to the ground. (00:35 / 00:36 SE)

16. Luke calls to Leia because they have to flee Jabba's vessel. He yells, "Come on!" but his mouth doesn't move. (00:35 / 00:36 SE)

17. When Luke and Leia swing from the vessel to the smaller skiff, Leia places her right arm on Luke's shoulder, but then she's holding on to the rope with her right hand, and as they land, her right arm is on Luke's right shoulder. (00:35 / 00:36)

18. Luke heads to Dagobah. Artoo's dome, which is blue and silver, appears black and silver in space. (00:36 / fixed in SE)

19. Immediately after Luke's X-wing and the *Millennium Falcon* separate, there's a shot of the Death Star and several swarming starships around. The group of four TIE fighters coming from the screen vanishes before the end of the scene. (00:36 / fixed in SE)

20. The Emperor and Darth Vader walk among the troops. The Emperor's last line ("Everything is proceeding as I have foreseen.") is said in front of a group of gray-uniformed soldiers. But in the long shot, the emperor stands in front of the white storm troopers. (00:38 / 00:39 SE)

21. In the rebel conference room, Mon Mothma shows a hologram of the Death Star and Endor. The Death Star seems to orbit around the moon from left to right (while the moon spins counterclockwise); in the following shot, the Death Star orbits from right to right (and the moon revolves clockwise). Discuss amongst yourselves. (00:48 / 00:49 SE)

22. Han and Lando talk in the hangar, when Han lends the *Falcon* to his friend, Lando's belt, the one that's crossing his chest right-to-left, flips and crosses his chest left-to-right ("Would you get going, you pirate?"). (00:50, 00:51 / 00:51, 00:52 SE)

23. At the end of the speedbike chase, before Luke and the storm trooper's bikes lock, Luke's black glove jumps from his right hand to his left and then back. (01:00 / 01:01)

24. Leia tries to attract the Ewok Wicket by offering him some food: she holds it out with her left hand, but Wicket grabs it from her right. (01:03)

25. When Wicket sits down, enjoying his treat, his spear is pointing at the sky. In his following close-up, his spear is pointing at the ground. (01:03 / 01:04 SE)

26. While the heroes are tied up at the village of the Ewoks, C-3PO and Luke discuss "magic." There is a shot of Artoo with no ropes around him, even if the robot won't be set free until a few moments later. (01:11, 01:13, 01:14 / 01:12, 01:14, 01:15 SE)

27. Vader arrives on Endor; as he walks out of his ship, his helmet goes through the upper part of the exit of the ship. (01:22)

28. When Han, Leia, and the others realize inside the bunker that they've been ambushed, an imperial officer yells, "Freeze!" Han tosses a small container at the officer, who jumps over the rail before actually getting hit by the box. (01:33)

29. After Lando yells, "Fighters comin' in!" the *Falcon* moves away from the Death Star. The first group of four TIE fighters that appear entirely from off-screen fly *through*

the *Falcon.* (01:34 / fixed in SE)

30. During the lightsaber duel between Luke and Vader, after Vader falls from the stairs, as well as in an overhead shot of the two (before Luke slices Dad's hand), it's possible to see the shadows of the light sabers on the floor. But lasers are pure energy, and shouldn't cast shadows (and never do, except now). (01:48, 01:52 / 01:49, 01:52 SE)

31. Looking for Luke, Vader walks down a small flight of stairs. The "stunt" rod that poses for the lightsaber casts a shadow on the wall to the right, but as Vader reaches the floor, he lights his saber. So when he was walking downstairs his saber was supposed to be off? And what about the shadow? (01:49 / 01:50 SE)

32. While placing bombs inside the imperial bunker, Han asks for another charge. He places it on the ceiling with his right hand, but the detail shows his left (not to mention a different part of the ceiling). (01:50 / 01:51 SE)

33. Along with all the rebels on Endor, Han runs away from the bunker before the explosion. Mysteriously, his reflection appears on the top of the screen. (01:53 / 01:54 SE)

34. When the Emperor is deep frying Luke, a close-up of Vader reveals his helmet

being dusty and opaque. But as soon as Dad steps into action, grabbing the Emperor, his helmet is as clean as a whistle. (01:55 / 01:55, 01:56 SE)

35. Luke carries his dying father near his ship, and removes his helmet, leaving the mouthpiece underneath the man's chin. When Anakin passes away, Luke bows his head: the mouthpiece is gone. (01:59, 02:00 / 02:00, 02:01 SE)

Questions

1. Luke jumps into the pit, but twirls midair and grabs the plank with one hand—or is that with two? (00:31 / 00:32 SE)

2. When Luke and Leia swing to the rebel's skiff... what is that rope attached to? (00:35 / 00:36 SE)

3. After Luke and Leia take off on a speedbike, Han yells, "Hey!" Doesn't it look like the trooper who's about to attack Han begins to stand up in the bottom-right corner, then stops waiting for his cue? (00:57 / 00:59 SE)

4. Admiral Ackbar announces to "all craft, prepare to jump into hyperspace on my mark." Lando answers, "All right, stand by"—but then jumps into hyperspace without waiting for any mark. Is this a mutiny? (01:26 / 01:27 SE)

5. Still looking for his son,

Vader tells Luke that perhaps his sister will join the dark side. Vader seems to carry, in his left hand, Luke's lightsaber. But when Luke attacks Vader, he's holding it. So... what the hell is Vader carrying around during a duel, anyway? (01:51 / 01:52 SE)

Fun Fact
Lando, in disguise, enters Jabba's place. In the first shot, he gets too close to a wall and hits it with his helmet. (00:16 / 00:17 SE)

RISING SUN (5)
1993, color, 125 min.

Director: Philip Kaufman

Cast: Sean Connery (John Connor), Wesley Snipes (Web Smith), Harvey Keitel (Tom Graham), Cary-Hiroyuki Tagawa (Eddie Sakamura), Kevin Anderson (Bob Richmond), Mako (Yoshida-san), Ray Wise (Senator John Morton), Stan Egi (Ishihara), Stan Shaw (Phillips), Tia Carrere (Jingo Asakuma), Steve Buscemi (Willy "the Weasel" Wilhelm), Tatjana Patitz (Cheryl Lynn Austin), Lauren Robinson (Zelly).

Someone did something bad, and someone else might have seen it, but nobody knows.

Bloopers
1. Web Smith enters the Nakamoto Tower with his jacket all wet because of the rain. As he walks into the building alley with Graham, his jacket is dry, but when he steps out of the elevator, it's wet again. (00:18, 00:19, 00:20)

2. After the discovery of a bedroom behind the board room, police begin the investigation around the cadaver ... which apparently is still breathing. (00:25)

3. Web, Connor, and Phillips are in the surveillance room when Connor leaves. The camera focuses on a monitor

---

SHOW ME (G)LOVE!

... and do you need a helping hand?

Roger Moore in *The Cannonball Run*	Blooper No. 12
Chris Sarandon in *Child's Play*	Blooper No. 1
Robert Englund in *A Nightmare on Elm Street*	Blooper No. 2
Mark Hamill in *Return of the Jedi*	Blooper No. 23
Alan Cummings in *Spy Kids*	Blooper No. 4
Roger Moore (again!) in *A View to a Kill*	Blooper No. 1

behind Web and Phillips, showing Connor walking along the building alley. But the image in the monitor flicks one instant before the camera focuses on it, as if it were a tape left on pause, and played *almost* at the right moment. (00:32)

4. Eddie Sakamura's car explosion is reflected in Web's windshield. Or is it? Just for fun, look again: it's not a reflection; the sequence is actually projected onto Web. (00:59)

5. Web is lying on his bed, speaking on the phone, when his daughter, Zelly, walks in. Web is holding the phone with his left hand, but in the over-the-shoulder shot, his left hand is in his pants pocket. Then Web's left hand holds the phone by the lower part, and then by the upper part—all by itself! (01:01)

ROBIN HOOD (16)
1973, color, 83 min.

Director: Wolfgang Reitherman

Cast: Roger Miller (Alan-A-Dale), Peter Ustinov (Prince John), Terry-Thomas (Sir Hiss), Brian Bedford (Robin Hood), Monica Evans (Maid Marian), Phil Harris (Little John), Andy Devine (Friar Tuck), Carole Shelley (Lady Kluck), Pat Buttram (Sheriff of Nottingham), George Lindsey (Trigger), Ken Curtis (Nutsy),

Billy Whitaker (Skippy), Pat O'Malley (Otto).

Maid Marian is a fox. For real!

Bloopers
1. Robin and Little John dodge Nottingham soldiers' arrows and hide in a tree. Once safe, Robin removes one arrow from his hat that he didn't have (also, the hole in the hat vanishes). (00:04, 00:05)

2. Hearing the sound of trumpets coming from Prince John's coach, Robin literally walks over Little John: John briefly changes color, first the stomach and arms, then the face, from a lighter to a darker brown. (00:05)

3. Prince John has three rings on his left paw, only one on his right. But when he checks himself in a mirror, wearing a crown, the reflection makes the three rings appear in his right paw. (00:06, 00:07)

4. The Prince's rings on his left paw appear and vanish all through the picture. They also jump on the right paw when Little John dresses himself as Sir Reginald. (00:06, 00:35, 00:37)

5. Robin, disguised as a gypsy, steals Prince John's right ring. But when John brings his paw to his ear, the ring is back in place, without the gem. And when he ties Sir Hiss into a knot, the ring is completely gone. (00:10, 00:11)

6. Sir Hiss has a cape that disappears when Prince John traps him in a basket, then it comes back (inside the basket!), then it vanishes again when Hiss emerges from the basket. (00:11, 01:14)

7. The sheriff's star moves from the left to the right all through the picture (e.g., check the very first two shots when he appears). (00:15)

8. He also carries a small pouch where he places the money he takes in that appears and vanishes all through the movie. (00:15, 00:16)

9. Friar Tuck gives some coins to Otto, who has his left leg in a cast. When the sheriff enters Otto's place, the cast has moved to the right leg. It'll briefly come back to the left leg during the song "The Phony King of England" (right after Robin snatches the King's underwear), and also when Otto's jailed. (00:16, 00:53, 01:10)

10. Skippy receives Robin's arrow and bow for his birthday. He tries it, and as he moves left and right, the bow's string passes through his arm. (00:19)

11. Skippy sneaks inside Prince John's backyard with his bow and arrow. Later on, when he talks with Lady Marian, he produces a sword that seems to appear out of nowhere. (00:22, 00:24)

12. Sir Hiss hisses in Prince John's ear: when John brings his paw to the ear, the ring is there but without a stone (which will appear thereafter). (00:32)

13. At the beginning of the Tournament of the Golden Arrow, Robin (disguised as a stork) wins a golden arrow. Maid Marian presents it to him, and the arrow points to her left. As she passes it to Robin, the arrow points to her right. (00:42)

14. The sheriff, singing, approaches Sir Hiss, who's keeping the count. Hiss places his orange quill down on the sheet of paper. As the sheriff reaches the desk, the quill is gone, and in the following shot is close to the inkwell. (00:54)

15. When in jail, little Skippy has a chain around his leg. But when he's freed, the chain has moved to around his neck. (00:56, 01:10)

16. After a test, the sheriff closes the hanging trapdoor: its hinges are to the right of the platform. But when Robin and Little John enter the palace, they catch a glimpse of the gallows: the trapdoor has rotated 90 degrees counterclockwise. (01:03, 01:05)

RUDY (11)
1993, color, 116 min.

Director: David Anspaugh

Cast: Sean Astin (Daniel "Rudy" Ruettiger), Jon Favreau

I DON'T LIKE YOUR HAT-TITUDE!

What's gotten into your head?

Robert Duvall's hat in *Days of Thunder*	Blooper No. 1
A stormtrooper's helmet in *The Empire Strikes Back*	Fun Fact No. 1
Robin Hood's hat in *Robin Hood*	Blooper No. 1
Timothy Olyphant's Santa hat in *Go*	Blooper No. 4
Harrison Ford's hat in *Indiana Jones and the Temple of Doom*	Blooper No. 5
A Confederate soldier's hat in *Glory*	Blooper No. 7

(D-Bob), Ned Beatty (Daniel Ruettiger), Greta Lind (Mary), Scott Benjaminson (Frank), Mary Ann Thebus (Betty), Charles Dutton (Fortune), Lili Taylor (Sherry), Christopher Reed (Pete), Robert Prosky (Father Cavanaugh), Luke Massery (13-Year-Old Rudy), Robert J. Steinmiller Jr. (13-Year-Old Pete), Jason Miller (Coach Ara Parseghian), Paul Bergan (Coach Dan Devine).

Fanatical Notre Dame football fan bugs people until they let him play. But it's heartwarming.

Bloopers

1. In his room, a young Rudy repeats word by word the plays of a football game. During his performance ("We're not gonna pass unless our secondary comes up too close!"), the boom mike gets reflected in a picture hanging on the wall. (00:05)

2. Rudy finally gets to play in 1975, after two years at Notre Dame and one at Holy Cross, which sets the beginning of the movie in 1972. In this year, Pete asks Rudy what day it is. Rudy says it's Friday, August 23. Well, August 23, 1972 was a Wednesday. And if you think the action takes place in 1971, they missed that, too: August 23, 1971 was a Monday. The closest Friday was 1974. (00:12, 01:26)

3. Pete lights a cigarette using a match, then places the match for Rudy to blow out on a small cake. The match is much more burnt when Pete is holding it than when he places it on the cake. (00:14)

4. Just before taking the bus to Notre Dame, Rudy and his dad sit at a bus station. A large poster is in the background ("Discover America. Leave the driving to us"), with a Manhattan skyline. The picture shows the World Trade Center—not yet completed in 1972. (00:21)

5. When Rudy gets run over by the Irish, he falls down and

his bag winds up by his head. In the next cut, the bag lies between Rudy's legs. (00:37)

6. At Corby's Pub, Rudy salutes a friend ("Mary, Mary, quite contrary . . .") grabbing a full glass of beer. In the over-the-shoulder shot, he grabs the same glass again. (00:48)

7. By the mailboxes at Holy Cross there's a poster that advertises an End-of-the-Year Picnic, on Saturday, December 22. Here we go again: December 22, 1972, was a Friday. (00:54)

8. After announcing to all the workers that Rudy will be going to Notre Dame, Daniel grabs a clipboard and the letter Rudy just gave him. But after a close-up of Rudy, Daniel holds the letter. Where is the clipboard? (01:05, 01:06)

9. Coach Parseghian is using a very noisy moviola (whenever he stops it and reverses the direction, there are loud *click-clacks*). He starts it counterclockwise, and after Rudy tells the coach that his father can't see him on the team, the moviola has changed direction without any other sound. (01:22)

10. All of the Irish players enter coach Devine's office to place their jerseys on the coach's desk. Jersey number 70 is tossed down twice in about ten seconds. (01:34)

11. When the team is on the field, coach Devine is surrounded by players and he gives them a final word: Rudy is in the background, behind him—yet, when the coach yells, "No excuses! Do the work!" Rudy appears right in front of him. (01:41)

Question
Rudy calls Frank on a payphone to let him know he'll be on the sidelines. The phone Rudy's using has Touch-Tone buttons. Did they exist in 1975? (01:34)

Fun Fact
The fan in a blue coat and furry collar who stands behind Rudy's parents is the real Daniel "Rudy" Ruettiger. (01:40)

S

SAVING PRIVATE RYAN (21)
1998, color, 170 min.

Director: Steven Spielberg

Cast: Tom Hanks (Captain John H. Miller), Tom Sizemore (Sergeant Michael Horvath), Edward Burns (Private Richard Reiben), Barry Pepper (Private Daniel Jackson), Adam Goldberg (Private Stanley Mellish), Vin Diesel (Private Adrian Caparzo), Giovanni Ribisi (T/4 Medic Corporal Irwin Wade), Jeremy Davies (Corporal Timothy E. Upham), Matt Damon (Private James Francis Ryan), Ted Danson (Captain Fred Hamill), Paul Giamatti (Sergeant William Hill), Dennis Farina (Lieutenant Colonel Anderson).

Troupe is assigned to endure heavy losses in saving only one guy . . . and gives him the mother of all guilt trips.

Bloopers
1. The old man walks toward the cemetery, followed by his family: a young couple (she's wearing a whitish shirt, he a blue sweater and a cap) pass by the son and walk away. In the following shot from behind the old man, the couple has still to pass by his son. (00:01)
2. Three girls follow the old man; the one in the middle carries a magazine and keeps it in front of her chest. In the following wide shot, she's holding it with one hand and toward the ground. (00:01)
3. The soldier who's almost crying in the water by Captain Miller gets killed by a bullet that goes through his jacket chest pocket. The soldier's left arm, behind Miller, pops in front of him in the next, matching cut. (00:08)
4. On the beaches of Normandy, Miller and Sergeant Horvath talk about their position; a soldier places his hand on Miller's shoulder and yells, "They're killing us! We don't have a fu**ing chance . . ." And then he van-

ishes, but we can still hear his, "And that ain't fair!" (00:16)

5. While under the fire of two MG-42s and two mortars, Miller wants to get everyone out of there. He holds his rifle with the nozzle to the sky, but when he calls three soldiers the rifle is horizontal (and his hand is gripping it in a different place), then the weapon is vertical again. (00:20)

6. Worried and upset by the news that he has to go on a mission, Corporal Upham gets his gear and knocks down a shelf with, among other things, two helmets on. When Miller tells Upham that he doesn't need a type-writer, but only a pencil, the corporal gets his helmet, now back on the shelf with-out anyone having replaced it. (00:40)

7. The eight soldiers go on the mission to save Private Ryan. During part of the mission, Private Caparzo is shot and killed, so the number of sol-diers decreases by one. After a pause and the decision to go to Ramelle, a shot of the soldiers reveals the group still made up of eight mem-bers—they go back to seven in the following shot, and re-main at seven . . . for now. (00:41, 00:55, 01:23)

8. When the wrong Ryan is called to reach Captain Miller, he runs in front of Uphal, who follows him with his eyes. When Reiben tells Horvath, "I told you he was an a**hole," Ryan passes in front of Uphal again. And again in front of Reiben and Horvath. (01:00)

9. Private Jackson and Reiben have to search through a bag of dogtags; they walk to a pile of black boxes placed as a table, with two light brown boxes as chairs on the sides. But when they get there, Jackson has to kick one of the brown boxes off of the improvised table. (01:17)

10. When Sergeant Horvath vol-unteers to go middle, then left, at the radar site, and Miller tells him to shut up, Horvath doesn't show any-thing from behind, but from the shot in front he's holding a rifle almost perfectly verti-cal. (01:26)

11. The blood spurting from Medic Corporal Wade's mouth vanishes ("Right here. I'm gonna put your hand on it.") and changes throughout the scene—and no, it's not be-cause they're cleaning his mouth with water from the canteen. Just check the amount of blood between the two shots of morphine Wade re-ceives. (01:29)

12. The blindfold Miller places over the eyes of German sol-dier "Steamboat Willie," be-comes wider as the soldier walks away. (01:37)

13. During an argument be-tween Horvath and Reiben,

private Jackson tries to get Miller's attention. When he says, "Sir, we have a situation here!" Jackson is holding his gun and aiming at Horvath. But a few moments later, he draws his gun from his belt. (01:39, 01:40)

14. When Miller informs Corporal Henderson that orders are orders and Ryan has to go home, Ryan tells them that he, too, has his own orders, the shadows on the ground go to the soldiers' right. But in the matching shot from behind, the shadows go to the left. And they'll go to the right again when Ryan realizes that "It doesn't make any sense." (01:49, 01:50)

15. Mellish and Upham walk by a few semi-destroyed buildings while waiting for the enemy tanks to arrive. On the side of them is the advertisement *"Suze—L'Ami de l'Estomach."* The proper French word for "stomach" is *"estomac"* with no *h*. (01:58)

16. While disclosing the meaning of "FUBAR" to Upham, Mellish places a belt of cartridges around his friend's neck. The belt turns 180° in Mellish's hands. (01:58)

17. During Upham's translation of the lyrics of Edith Piaf's song, Reiben's hands appear in a different position after every cut: first they are separated, then the right one is holding on to the left wrist,

then they are crossed. (02:00, 02:01)

18. Reiben is telling Mellish, Horvath, and Upham about a certain Mrs. Rachel Trombowitz. Mellish lights a cigarette, takes it with his right hand, but in the following matching cut he holds it with his left. (02:01)

19. Miller sits down with Ryan, crosses his legs, and places his right hand over his left. But then he has his left hand over his right. And back. And forth. (02:03)

20. The first soldier who tries a sticky bomb on one of the tanks has a khaki uniform— but when he blows up along with the bomb, his uniform has switched to dark green. (02:13)

21. Old Ryan stands exactly in front of Miller's tomb and salutes it. In the shot from behind, he's to the side of the cross, not in front of it anymore. But he never moved. (02:41)

Questions

1. Before Mrs. Ryan receives the sad news that three out of her four sons have died, a shot of her house shows a picture on a table of four men in uniform. Probably her sons. But a few moments later, General Marshall is informed that the four brothers were split up after all being together in the 29th Division.

And later on, private Ryan recalls that the last time the four brothers were all together was the night before Dan went off to basic, two years earlier. So . . . when exactly did the four brothers get together for the last time? (00:32, 00:33, 02:06)

2. When Miller asks in the middle of the procession of soldiers if anyone knows the whereabouts of a James Ryan from Iowa, is that a group of extras in the background, waiting for their cue to start walking? (01:20)

SAVING SILVERMAN (RATED R) (9)
2001, color, 96 min.

Director: Dennis Dugan

Cast: Steve Zahn (Wayne Furnberger), Jack Black (J.D. McNugent), Jason Biggs (Darren Silverman), Amanda Peet (Judith Fessbeggler, Ph.D.), Amanda Detmer (Sandy Perkus), R. Lee Ermey (Coach Norton), Neil Diamond (Himself), Kyle Gass (Bar Dude), Norman Armour (Minister), Colin Foo (Old Man), Chris Logan (Vageet), Esme Lambert (Raccoon Woman).

Pretty much like Saving Private Ryan . . . *but without all the laughs.*

Bloopers

1. 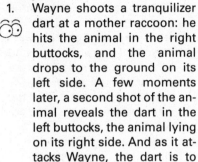 Wayne shoots a tranquilizer dart at a mother raccoon: he hits the animal in the right buttocks, and the animal drops to the ground on its left side. A few moments later, a second shot of the animal reveals the dart in the left buttocks, the animal lying on its right side. And as it attacks Wayne, the dart is to the right side again. (00:06, 00:07)

2. The Miller beer bottle turns about 180 degrees from the time Darren puts it down at Judith's table to when the magician reaches the same table. (00:10, 00:11)

3. Judith sits on "Old Ethel," J.D.'s recliner. She places her drink on the small table to her left, but as J.D. works on the lever, the glass has zapped back to her hand. And when she backflips, the glass is gone. (00:18)

4. In Judith's office, she grants Wayne and J.D. 2½ minutes. Her alarm beeps after a brief arm wrestling match. And after exactly 1 minute, 20 seconds. (00:23, 00:24)

5. When Wayne finds Judith in bed, asleep, her right hand is under the pages of a book. When she wakes up, her hand is over the pages of the same book. Sleepreading? (00:35)

6. Wayne and J.D. hold a gun in front of Judith, who's flip-

ping through a magazine. She stops at a page with the photo of a man, and she lies back on the couch. They lower the gun and leave, and when she goes back to the magazine, the open page is completely different from the one where she stopped. (00:47)

7. After saving Darren from drowning, Sandy stands up on the beach: her left leg is almost completely covered with wet sand, but after one second, she's clean as a whistle. (00:53)

8. The shape of the sandwich bun from which Wayne is feeding Judith changes from a sesame to a kaiser between shots. (01:10)

9. When Wayne's truck is driven through the jail wall, the large brick that lands on J.D.'s bed seems suspiciously lightweight (he kicks it and it rotates as if made with, well, Styrofoam). (01:22)

SCARY MOVIE (13)
2000, color, 88 min.

Director: Keenen Ivory Wayans

Cast: Jon Abrahams (Bobby Prinze), Rick Ducommun (Cindy's dad), Carmen Electra (Drew Decker), Shannon Elizabeth (Buffy Gilmore), Anna Faris (Cindy Campbell), Kurt Fuller (Sheriff Russell), Regina Hall (Brenda Meeks), Lochlyn Munro (Greg Phillippe), Cheri Oteri (Gail Hailstorm), Dave Sheridan (Deputy Doofus "Doofy" Gilmore), Marlon Wayans (Shorty Meeks), Shawn Wayans (Ray Wilkins), David L. Lander (Principal "Squiggy" Squiggman), Jayne Trcka (Miss Mann), Peter Hanlon (Suicidal Teacher).

First you Scream, *then you laugh.*

Bloopers

1. Drew has a cardboard skeleton by her entrance door; the right foot of the skeleton is higher than the door lock. However, when Drew opens the door, the detail shows that the skeleton's foot has dropped down, and now it's at the very same height as the lock. (00:02)

2. In front of the school, reporter Gail Hailstorm introduces herself. Later on, during a press conference with the sheriff, he calls her "Miss Thunderstorm." What is her name, for real? (00:10, 00:44)

3. During the flashback, Greg has a Jack Daniels bottle that is half full, then almost empty (when he gets out of the car), then half full again (when he's yelling). (00:14, 00:15)

4. Greg, inseparable from his whiskey bottle, realizes that it's not Buffy who's playing with his ass. When he yells, "Ray!" the bottle has van-

ished. But when he comes back to Buffy, he's holding the bottle again. (00:14)

5. When the radio is on, Greg climbs out of his car via the sunroof; when he leans on Cindy's seat, his Jack Daniels bottle neck bends as if made of rubber. (00:15)

6. After the car hits the fisherman, it skids and stops in the middle of a curve. The yellow line on the road goes approximately from the front-left wheel to the rear-right one—but in the shot from above, it goes from the front-*right* wheel to the rear-*left* one, and when the kids get out of the car, the line has moved once more. (00:16)

7. The kids lower the unconscious fisherman onto the deck before stripping him and throwing him into the water. "Unconscious," we said? Hmm ... look at his left hand: he moves it to ease his hitting the deck. (00:19)

8. After Miss Mann talks to the girls in the locker room, one of them (behind Buffy) removes her towel and starts putting a sweater on. But in the following shot, when everyone laughs, the girl is wearing the towel again. (00:45)

9. Cindy yells, "What are you waiting for?!" and a suicidal teacher misinterprets the message and jumps off the building. But on the top-left corner of the screen, it's pos-

sible to see the shadow of the lower scaffolds the stuntman actually jumped from. (00:50)

10. Ray and Brenda go to *Shakespeare in Love.* But the movie that they see is not in the proper sequence. (00:54, 00:56, 00:57, 00:58)

11. When Brenda leans over to pick up her food in the theater, a woman right in front of Ray turns to check on her; in the woman's close-up, Ray is missing, but he's there in the following wide shot. (00:54)

12. Ray tells Cindy how dangerous canceling TV shows is, then he grabs a knife with his left hand and stabs Bobby—but in the following shot, he's using his right hand. (01:13)

13. The killer throws Cindy against a wall: when she hits it, it wobbles (check out the shadow on top of it, behind the wooden decoration). (01:14)

Question
Buffy changes her image when she gets to school by tearing off her clothes and revealing a much more skimpy outfit. But when she and her two friends begin walking, the clothes she tossed away are nowhere to be seen. What happened to them? (00:09)

Fun Fact
Just in case you were wondering ...
When the *Amistad II* preview

starts, it is rated I for IMMATURE. The writing underneath it reads, "If you can read this you are too close"; "Pee pee poopy boogers farts butthole"; "Immature: we thought it would be funny to put this in here. Kiss our asses take it off please." (00:54)

SCARY MOVIE 2 (18)
2001, color, 83 min.

Director: Keenen Ivory Wayans

Cast: Shawn Wayans (Ray Wilkins), Marlon Wayans (Shorty Meeks), Anna Faris (Cindy Campbell), Regina Hall (Brenda Meeks), Christopher Masterson (Buddy), Kathleen Robertson (Theo), David Cross (Dwight Hartman), James Woods (Father McFeely), Tim Curry (Professor Oldman), Tori Spelling (Alex), Chris Elliott (Hanson), Andy Richter (Father Harris), Richard Moll (Hugh Kane's Ghost), Veronica Cartwright (Mrs. Voorhees), Natasha Lyonne (Megan Voorhees).

This time it's The Haunting *(and much, much more).*

Bloopers
1. Father McFeely knocks at Mrs. Voorhees's door: as he walks in, he brings his right hand to his hat to remove it, but in the next shot the hand isn't there, and in the last one the hand is on the hat again. (00:02)

2. Little Megan Voorhees is tied to her bed, her hand up by the headrest. But after Father Harris says, "Holy Lord, Almighty Father," she screams and is untied. As she sticks her tongue out, she is tied again. (00:04, 00:05)

3. Cindy is singing along with the music on her car stereo: her window is rolled halfway down, then all the way down, then again halfway down. Needless to say, she never touched it. (00:14)

4. Just before she checks the map to the house, a car drives by—but in the following shot the car is gone: you can't see it through the rear windshield. (00:14)

5. While Hanson talks to Cindy, passing his deformed hand over her face, his tie is straightened, then crooked, then straightened ("You've got the same nose"), and then crooked again. (00:16, 00:17)

6. Helping Cindy with her bag, Hanson puts her toothbrush in the left side of his mouth; as he stands up, the toothbrush has moved to the right side of his mouth—and then has vanished as the two walk into the corridor. (00:17)

7. In her room, Cindy checks out all of Caroline's dresses. The one that has been stained is lifted by Cindy's right hand—the same hand that's holding the dress by its hanger. (00:19)

8. During the dinner, Hanson squeezes Ray's cheek, leaving a spot of mashed potatoes. The potatoes are gone later on, but they're back when Ray takes a sample of a slice of cake. (00:24, 00:25, 00:26)

9. Hanson makes a dish with turkey parts, a salad, and a small, red tomato. When he places the plate down, there's pretty much only turkey on it. (00:25)

10. Buddy throws a ball to Cindy, who catches it right in the middle of her face and collapses onto a table, smashing it. The tabletop remains in one piece; however, when Cindy stands up, the tabletop is broken almost in half. (00:28)

11. The ghost uncovers a sleeping Alex, revealing her long and dirty toenails. However, as she is lifted up the wall and onto the ceiling, she's wearing socks. (00:31, 00:32)

12. Facing Mr. Kittles, Cindy apologizes for having pooped in its kitty litter (and a very eloquent shot shows the result); but when the cat scoops some of the litter at Cindy's face, the kitty litter appears poop-free. (00:34)

13. Cindy reads a diary she found in a small casket; the voice-over reads, "I can't take living with him any longer. He's becoming a monster." And then it continues, "I'm suspecting he was having an affair . . ." but on the written page it says, "Darkness is all around us." (00:38)

14. Inside the lab, while Dwight explains how to deal with the ghost, there's a clock with a large red display: it reads 2:39:44 — and counting. One minute later it reads 2:17:00 — and counting. And a few seconds later, it reads something like 14:09 (and it's stopped). (00:48, 00:49)

15. Alex is wandering through the house, looking for the ghost, wearing her goggles. When the ghost finds her, her goggles are back up on her forehead. (00:54, 00:55)

16. Just before being trapped in the freezing chamber, Buddy and Cindy are beaten by the ghost. There's a red container on the floor by the table (it's a blood bag from a deleted scene): the bag vanishes and comes back throughout the fight. (00:57)

17. Inside the freezer, Cindy is rubbing/pleasuring Buddy, whose head lies against a metal scaffolding. But when she says, "a lot of little babies," a dark green towel has appeared behind Buddy's head, then it's gone, and then it's back when he loses control. (00:59)

18. Dwight is playing "chicken" with his wheelchair and the ghost of Kane. Three white doves pass by, and one poops on Dwight's head. But

as he starts the race, the poop is gone, only to return in the following close-up. (01:02)

Questions

1. Dwight's glasses appear to be okay when he and the kids find out that they're trapped in the house; they're twisted as they all enter the laboratory; they are okay again when he tries to climb the stairs, and they're twisted again when he comes back (how, by the way, since all the entrances were closed?) to the basement. What happened to the glasses? (00:47, 00:48, 00:58, 01:08)

2. Shorty hits Hanson with his car, and the man literally takes off and lands (seen through the rear windshield of Shorty's car). But ... where did Cindy go, since she was just in front of him? (01:14)

SCREW LOOSE (5)
1999, color, 85 min.

Director: Ezio Greggio

Cast: Ezio Greggio (Bernardo Puccini), Mel Brooks (Jake Gordon), Julie Condra (Dr. Barbara Collier), Gianfranco Barra (Guido Puccini), Randi Ingerman (Sofia), John Karlsen (Dr. Caputo), Enzo Iacchetti (Factory Guard), Riccardo Miniggio (Father Superior), Claudio Parachinetto (Dr. Faccinaro), Alfio Liotta (Hotel Concierge), Massimo Artana (Dr. Linero).

An Italian chases an American in the south of France— or something like that.

Bloopers

1. It's a tight squeeze to park Bernardo's car at his factory, and the beige car to the right seems to be quite sensitive about the situation: its right rearview mirror gets folded in the shot from up above to let Bernardo's car pass more easily. The mirror will be back in position in the next shot. (00:04)

2. When Bernardo gets to the hospital, he's asked by Dr. Faccinaro, "You must be his son." When Bernardo answers, "Yes," the male nurse to the left eyes the camera. (00:13)

3. Bernardo and Dr. Collier walk up to the entrance of a Hotel in Monte Carlo: a boom mike is reflected in the glass by the door. (00:44)

4. When Bernardo gets arrested by the French gendarmes and carried to their car, a boom mike is reflected in the car's windshield. (00:47)

5. Right after Father Superior yells, "Ma vaffanculo, tié!" ("Go mind your business" but perhaps not quite so pleasant), Jake stands up from his chair. And a few seconds later, he stands up again. (01:02)

Questions

1. The movie takes place in Milan, Los Angeles, and the south of France. However, how come everyone speaks English everywhere? And, most important, how come when Jake screws up in an Italian hospital, he says "Scusi (*Sorry*)," in Italian? (00:02, 00:25, 00:45)
2. In France, Bernardo and Jake find a monastery, with a sign . . . in Italian? (00:58)

DVD Blooper

The aforementioned sign says, "Confraternita del Perpetuo Silenzio," which means "Confraternity of the Perennial Silence." The DVD captioning says, "Confraternity of Sinners Forever."

SHORT CIRCUIT (4)

1986, color, 98 min.

Director: John Badham

Cast: Ally Sheedy (Stephanie Speck), Steve Guttenberg (Newton Crosby), Fisher Stevens (Ben Jabituya), Austin Pendleton (Howard Marner), G.W. Bailey (Skroeder), Brian McNamara (Frank), Tim Blaney (Number 5), Marvin J. McIntyre (Duke), John Garber (Otis), Penny Santon (Mrs. Cepeda).

"Number Five . . . is alive!"

Bloopers

1. Ben incites Newton to join the presentation of the robots, and he puts Newton's tie around his neck. The tie is perpendicular to the ground, but when Newton says, "Just one dance!" the parts are crossed. (00:09)
2. Right after getting rid of the tracking device, Number 5 drives away while listening to the radio: on station 94.1 there's a horse race. The robot changes the station: 105.7, a preacher, 106.3, country music, and finally El DeBarge and "Who's Johnny" . . . on 94.1. What happened to the horse race?!?! (00:54)
3. Frank shoots Number 5 using a rifle. When Number 5 blocks the second bullet, it's possible to see, protruding from its right elbow, one of the rods used by the puppeteers who moved the robot in the close-ups. (01:06)
4. While crashing through the Black Lion Inn, Number 5 holds a table as a shield: the table gets riddled with bullets and even snaps in half— but appears to be in fairly good shape (and in one piece) a few moments later. (01:15)

Question

When Number 5 dances, it's to imitate John Travolta in *Saturday Night Fever*, which is playing on TV. But the movie skips a good twenty minutes, going from the song "Dancing" to "More Than a Woman." Is this version edited for TV . . . or just for *Short Circuit*? (01:00, 01:01)

Fun Fact
Newton is using a 256K Macintosh computer with a color screen. In 1986 there were no color-screened Macintosh computers. (00:08)

SILENT MOVIE (6)
1976, color, 87 min.

Director: Mel Brooks

Cast: Mel Brooks (Mel Funn), Marty Feldman (Marty Eggs), Dom DeLuise (Dom Bell), Bernadette Peters (Vilma Kaplan), Sid Caesar (Studio Chief), Harold Gould (Engulf), Ron Carey (Devour), Carol Arthur (Pregnant Lady), Liam Dunn (Newsvendor), Fritz Feld (Maître d').

Is it possible to make a silent movie in this day and age? Hell, yeah!!

Bloopers
1. Mel Funn crosses his fingers before meeting with the studio chief, but he can't uncross them anymore except when he fixes his hat and the script in the chief's office. And then they're crossed again. (00:08, 00:09)
2. After reading a dramatic telefax from New York, the studio chief holds it with his right hand and stands up . . . holding the telefax with his left hand. (00:10)
3. The newsvendor hides be-

hind his kiosk, but the Sunday edition of the *Los Angeles Chronicle* demolishes it. The detail of the newspapers, though, shows one of the walls of the kiosk on top of the newspaper bundle, not underneath it like it was in the previous shot. (00:45)
4. Mel Funn chases Paul Newman in a wheelchair. The two run side by side and there's smoke coming from the wheels. . . . Actually, on second thought, there is smoke coming back toward the wheels, since the shot is reverse play. (00:55)
5. During the Paul Newman chase, Dom Bell hits a guy in a wheelchair and sends him into the pool. Two nurses in the background remove their robes and one begins to dive. In the following shot, they remove their robes one more time and finally dive into the pool. (00:56)
6. At the end of the battle in front of the Coca-Cola machine, Mel Funn tosses a can-grenade into the middle of the lot. Devour jumps on it and there's a big explosion. Engulf bends over, lifts his partner, and the intact Coca-Cola can rolls from underneath Devour's leg—but in the following shot, the can is flat, exploded, in the middle of Devour's chest. (01:22)

SIXTEEN CANDLES (3)
1984, color, 93 min.

Director: John Hughes

Cast: Molly Ringwald (Samantha Baker), Justin Henry (Mike Baker), Michael Schoeffling (Jake Ryan), Haviland Morris (Caroline), Gedde Watanabe (Long Duk Dong), Anthony Michael Hall (The Geek— Farmer Ted), Paul Dooley (Jim Baker), Carlin Glynn (Brenda Baker), Blanche Baker (Ginny Baker Rizcheck), Edward Andrews (Howard Baker), Billie Bird (Dorothy Baker), Carole Cook (Helen).

Not all birthdays turn out to be okay . . .

Bloopers
1. The sex test Samantha is taking in class has "Confidential" spelled "Confidentail" on top of it. (00:07)
2. Jake offers Ted his father's Rolls-Royce instead of his Porsche, because Ted told Jake that he "can't drive a stick." Later on, when Jake drives by in his Porsche and catches the Geek kissing Caroline, sure enough, the Porsche has an automatic shift—not a stick. (01:01, 01:22)
3. When Jake goes to see Samantha and Long opens the door, Long's ice pack jumps from the right side of his neck to the top of his head. (01:18)

Question
Ted fails to drive Caroline home, and he falls asleep with her in the car in front of the church. He has his headgear on. Does he carry it everywhere he goes? (01:16)

Fun Fact
When the family is leaving for the ceremony, Grandma Helen asks Dorothy to let her sit first in the car. Dorothy steps out of the car, moves to the front-right door, and simply crouches down—she does *not* enter the car: she's still there when the car backs up (but she will be in the car as soon as the family sees Long passed out on the sidewalk). (01:14)

SKULLS, THE (8)
2000, color, 106 min.

Director: Rob Cohen

Cast: Joshua Jackson (Lucas "Luke" McNamara), Paul Walker (Caleb Mandrake), Hill Harper (Will Beckford), Leslie Bibb (Chloe Whitfield), Christopher McDonald (Martin Lombard), Steve Harris (Detective Sparrow), William L. Petersen (Ames Levritt), Craig T. Nelson (Litten Mandrake), David Asman (Jason Pitcairn), Scott Gibson (Travis Wheeler), Nigel Bennett (Dr. Whitney), Andrew Kraulis (McBride).

The most well-publicized Secret Society in existence goes a little too far.

Bloopers

1. Just before reaching the Skulls' building, Chloe, Will, and Lucas (and his bike) walk side by side. After Will comments, "Must be one of their rules," their positions switch and now they walk in this order: Lucas (and the bike), Will, and Chloe. (00:11)

2. After being drugged, Lucas is the first one to jump out of his coffin. And in the following shot, he jumps out again. (00:15)

3. Chloe checks the "fresh flowers" Lucas just gave her: the flowers are to her left, the stems to the right. After he closes the door, the flowers are to her right, the stems to her left. (00:30)

4. Lucas gets some cash at an ATM machine, and finds out that he has several thousand dollars more in his account. He's so happy that he walks away, apparently without retreiving his card (or the printed receipt). (00:32)

5. When Caleb discovers Will in the Ritual Room, they have an argument, and Will says, "Okay, okay, no problem, man, just calm down, you know? Here's your key, right, you can have that—but I—I got your book. I don't have it with me, though, and we can get it anytime, okay? But, uh, just calm down!" But when the tape of the incident is played back, Will says, "Here's the key . . . We'll get the book later." (00:41, 01:14)

6. Chloe stops in front of Lucas with a crumpled letter made flat again. But as she reads it, the letter appears neatly written on a new, fresh, immaculate sheet of paper—a sheet that Chloe will crumple in a few seconds. (01:08, 01:09)

7. Lucas is handcuffed with his hands behind his back and escorted out. As he exits, the handcuffs have moved in front of him. (01:21)

8. When Martin Lombard is dead, the gun he had moves closer to his body between the aerial shot and the close-up. (01:28)

SMALL SOLDIERS (4)
 1998, color, 108 min.

Director: Joe Dante

Cast: Kirsten Dunst (Christy Fimple), Gregory Smith (Alan Abernathy), Jay Mohr (Larry Benson), Phil Hartman (Phil Fimple), Kevin Dunn (Stuart Abernathy), Denis Leary (Gil Mars), David Cross (Irwin Wayfair), Ann Magnuson (Irene Abernathy), Wendy Schaal (Marion Fimple), Dick Miller (Joe), Robert Picardo (Ralph, Clean Room Technician), Alexandra Wilson (Ms. Kegel).

When Action Figures Attack.

Bloopers

1. When Larry and Irwin meet Miss Kegel in the corridor, Irwin is carrying a beige panel under his left arm, a large sheet of paper, and a black portfolio case. When they step into the meeting room, Irwin's props have turned 180 degrees and he's carrying the black portfolio, the paper, and the beige panel—now in that order. (00:03)

2. Alan picks up a box from Joe's truck, then . . . he picks it up again. (Also, it seems as though he's placing that box on top of another, but by that point in the movie he's only picked up one single box. So . . . ?) (00:12)

3. The first box Alan picks up has an orange label ("Packing List Enclosed") on the side of one of the two flaps of the box. As Alan places the box back, the label moves to the middle of the flap. (00:12)

4. Alan writes "Closed" on a piece of paper and sticks it to the door. When he removes it, "Closed" is written differently. (00:29, 00:32)

SNAKE EYES (4)
1998, color, 99 min.

Director: Brian De Palma

Cast: Nicholas Cage (Richard "Ricky"/"Rick" Santoro), Gary Sinise (Commander Kevin Dunne), John Heard (Gilbert Powell), Carla Gugino (Julia Costello), Stan Shaw (Lincoln Tyler), Kevin Dunn (Lou Logan), Michael Rispoli (Jimmy George), Joel Fabiani (Charles Kirkland), Luis Guzmán (Cyrus), David Anthony Higgins (Ned Campbell).

Cage plays a smarmy, dirty, Atlantic city cop who uncovers an even dirtier conspiracy.

Bloopers

1. In Kevin's flashback of the assassination, when the "assassin" falls, the silencer on the tip of his rifle bends like a piece of string cheese when it hits the ground. Evidently, they use fake guns in false flashbacks. (00:41)

2. Kevin pleads with Rick to vouch for him after the police van crashes into the holding area. In the close-up on Rick, when he says "You got snake eyes," we see that the latex creating the wound on Rick's left eye juts out like a diving board from his face. If it were real, he'd be bleeding like a firehose. (01:27)

3. There's a shot of a huge wave crashing over the rails as the globe rolls down the street and the police van swerves into Julia's holding cell. But in the following scene across the street, they're not flooded out, and they certainly should be.

(Apparently the original ending involved underwater sequences as a gigantic wave washed over the boardwalk. The sequence was cut for budgetary reasons.) (01:27)

4. In the last scene between Rick and Julia, he says "I keep dreaming I'm back in that tunnel, underwater. Only in my dream, I drowned. Wonder what they would've said about me then?" What tunnel? (01:31)

Questions

1. After beating up Rick, Kevin uses a handheld tracking device to follow him. The device has the exact architectural layout of the arena on it... isn't that a little sophisticated, even for the Department of Defense? (01:21)

2. When Kevin is caught in the headlights of the police van, he turns around, we assume to try the door. When he reaches for the handle, you can clearly see a large hump protruding from his left shoulder. What the heck is this? The explosive pack for the upcoming exit wound, maybe? (01:28)

Fun Fact

At the end of the credits, there's a close-up on a cement pillar, and an embedded ring sparkles at us. What is this, exactly? This is the ring Rick lost in the original underwater ending. (01:37)

SPACE COWBOYS (7)
2000, color, 130 min.

Director: Clint Eastwood

Cast: Clint Eastwood (Dr. Francis D. "Frank" Corvin), Tommy Lee Jones (William "Hawk" Hawkins), Donald Sutherland (Jerry O'Neill), James Garner (Tank Sullivan), James Cromwell (Bob Gerson), Marcia Gay Harden (Sara Holland), William Devane (Eugene Davis), Loren Dean (Ethan Glance), Courtney B. Vance (Roger Hines), Rade Serbedzija (General Vostow), Barbara Babcock (Barbara Corvin), Blair Brown (Dr. Carruthers), Eli Craig (Young Hawk Hawkins).

Who said you can't teach old dogs new tricks?

Bloopers

1. In 1958, a young Hawk sings "Fly Me to the Moon" in a very Sinatra-esque fashion. Sinatra didn't record his signature version of this song until June 9, 1964, with the Count Basie Orchestra. (00:00, 00:02)

2. Tank Sullivan is a Baptist minister, yet he recites "Hail Mary," which is not a Baptist prayer, but a Catholic one. (00:23, 01:06, 01:28)

3. Frank meets Jerry by the roller coaster. After Jerry proclaims that he's in, the two talk about Hawk. Jerry

removes his glasses, but in the over-the-shoulder shot he's still wearing them. (00:27)

4. During the second landing simulation, Hawk's microphone comes and goes (e.g., when Frank yells, "Knock it off!") (00:58)

5. Yeah, yeah, yeah, sound in space . . . (01:23)

6. Frank is inside the Russian satellite when he comments, "You don't, do you?" After that, he retracts to get out. Is that a man with no space suit standing behind him, in the upper-right area of the airlock? (01:32)

7. As the shuttle reenters the Earth's atmosphere, especially when ground control says, ". . . he's way too high, he's gonna overshoot at this rate," the shuttle has "UNITED STATES" painted on its side, with an American flag to the left, and nothing to the right. As the shuttle lands, a NASA logo suddenly appears to the right of "UNITED STATES." (01:56, 01:59)

Questions

1. Frank is about to leave the office building when a guard tells him to wait for Gerson. In the background, a man and a woman (she's wearing a light blue top and carrying a briefcase, he has a dark blue shirt) walk away from the building. When Gerson is done, Frank opens the door to leave: the same two people walk by in the same direction. Are they doing laps around the courtyard? (00:22, 00:23)

2. Is the shuttle's blown hatch back in place when the bird lands? (01:57, 01:59)

SPLASH (5)

1984, color, 111 min.

Director: Ron Howard

Cast: Tom Hanks (Allen Bauer), Daryl Hannah (Madison), Eugene Levy (Walter Kornbluth), John Candy (Freddie Bauer), Dody Goodman (Mrs. Stimler), Shecky Greene (Mr. Buyrite), Richard B. Shull (Dr. Ross), Bobby Di Cicco (Jerry), Howard Morris (Dr. Zidell), Tony DiBenedetto (Tim, The Doorman), Patrick Cronin (Michaelson), Charles Walker (Michaelson's Partner).

A man falls in love with a mermaid. One little problem: she's a real mermaid.

Bloopers

1. Mr. Stimler, Allen's secretary, holds a message from the side with her right hand, but in the following shot she's holding it from the top. (00:07, 00:08)

2. When Allen talks to Walter Kornbluth on the beach,

Walter places a hand on the crate from the front, but not from the back. (00:18)

3. Fat Jack's boat takes Allen to Cape Cod and has no engine cover. However, when Allen falls into the water and he's circled by the boat, the first time the engine shows a cover, then doesn't again. (00:19, 00:22)

4. When, by the lockers, Allen asks Freddie if he can take Madison to the dinner with the president of the U.S.A., he's wearing his letterman jacket. When Freddie bursts out laughing, the jacket is gone. (00:56)

5. Fleeing from the army, Allen's car has the side window rolled down, then up (when they cross the park with the chess players), then down again as they smash through a metal fence. (01:37, 01:38, 01:40)

SPY GAME (11)
2001, color, 126 min.

Director: Tony Scott

Cast: Robert Redford (Nathan Muir), Brad Pitt (Tom Bishop), Catherine McCormack (Elizabeth Hadley), Stephen Dillane (Charles Harker), Larry Bryggman (Troy Folger), Marianne Jean-Baptiste (Gladys Jennip), Matthew Marsh (Dr. Byars), Todd Boyce (Robert Aiken), Michael Paul Chan (Vincent Vy Ngo), Garrick

Hagon (Cy Wilson), Andrew Grainger (Andrew Unger), Bill Buell (Fred Kappler).

Old spy saves young spy's ass.

Bloopers

1. The "present day" is 1991. Yet the small cell phones and two-way pagers used are distinctively late nineties, even for the CIA. (00:00, 00:08, 00:15, 00:27)

2. An ambulance is about to leave Su Chou prison: in the monitor, the gate begins to open, then it's less open when we see it through the vehicle's windshield, and even less so when the soldiers block the exit. (00:07)

3. In his office, Nathan puts some files in a burn bag and hands it to Gladys, his secretary. The opening of the bag is folded away from the woman. As Nathan walks by her, the bag has rotated 180 degrees in her hands. (00:14)

4. Outside of Harker's office, the clocks on the sides of a large TV screen read, 7:10 and 12:10. A few moments later, Troy informs Nathan that they have 24 hours to claim Bishop back, starting now. The superimpose reads, 8:02 A.M. Hmmm . . . (00:14, 00:17)

5. At the end of the discussion on the Berlin "Fuji Film" terrace, Nathan leaves Bishop alone. The camera flies away

---

from him twice, passing in front of a large clock: the first time the clock reads 3:10, the second time, 3:05. (00:50)

6. Tom wears a San Diego Padres baseball cap in 1985 Beirut. It is blue, orange and white—colors which weren't used by the Padres until their 1991 uniform change. (01:03, 01:05)

7. When Bishop meets Nathan, who's shaving, in Beirut, Bishop underlines that it's "5 in the morning." Nathan's wristwatch, however, reads 8:00. (01:09)

8. As Nathan opens the "Imagery Analysis" folder, the top page he sees has a few photographs clipped to it. He removes that page, and the following detail shows... the very same page with photographs clipped to it. (01:40)

9. Nathan calls the London Stock Exchange to liquidate his assets, and his broker's secretary answers, "Good morning, Thomas Quinn." When he hangs up with his broker, the screen reads, "9:22 P.M." So then he was on with them at 2:22 A.M. London time. "Good morning" indeed! (01:41, 01:42)

10. When we are told by the superimpose that it's 2:55 A.M., Nathan's wristwatch reads 1:40. Ho-hum. (01:47)

11. Operation Dinner Out (the one to rescue Tom and Elizabeth from Su Chou prison) starts at 7:17 A.M. D.C. time (thus, 8:17 P.M. Su Chou time). It is dark out. The operation is over within the hour. In the chopper on the way back, dawn breaks... what, some eight hours later? But the base is only 80 miles away. It can't be morning in D.C. and China at the same time. Sorry. (01:54, 01:58)

Question

Nathan and Tom first meet in 1975, and the movie ends in 1991, 16 years later. They are certainly two handsome strapping men (played by two of the most handsome and strapping performers in film), but are we really to believe that they don't age one iota in 16 years? (00:00, 00:08, 00:20)

SPY KIDS (6)
2001, color, 88 min.

Director: Robert Rodriguez

Cast: Antonio Banderas (Gregorio Cortez), Carla Gugino (Ingrid Cortez), Alexa Vega (Carmen Cortez), Daryl Sabara (Juni Cortez), Alan Cumming (Fegan Floop), Tony Shalhoub (Mr. Alexander Minion), Teri Hatcher (Ms. Gradenko), Cheech Marin ("Uncle" Felix Gumm), Robert Patrick (Mr. Lisp), Danny Trejo (Uncle Isadore "Machete / Izzy" Cortez), Mike Judge (Donnagon / Donnamight), Richard Linklater (Cool Spy), Andy W. Bossley (Brat), Jeffrey J. Dashnaw (Brat's Dad).

Spy Kids 227

"I shall call them ... Mini-Spies."

Bloopers

1. When Juni goes to school and gets bothered by a bully, Gregorio spots the scene in the rearview mirror of the car. But the image he sees isn't a reflection at all (besides the position of the kids, the bully's jacket sports an emblem on the left side that should be reversed in the reflection). (00:11)

2. En route to the Safe House, the kids leave in the escape pod wearing their school jackets. When they pop out of the pod, they're suddenly wearing life jackets. And when they go back inside the pod, the life jackets have disappeared. Hmmm ... (00:22, 00:23, 00:24)

3. After being threatened by a Thumb-Thumb, Gregorio sits at Floop's table and passes a spoon from his right hand to his left. But in the next shot, the spoon is back in his right hand. (00:32)

4. Floop shows Gregorio a clay head of Felix, holding it with his hands (the right one wearing his glove). But as Floop starts to modify the head, the glove is suddenly gone and doesn't come back. (00:33)

5. Carmen takes a picture from her parents' wedding album, and she holds it with her right hand—but with both hands in the detail. By the way, have you noticed how the picture, in transparency, seems to be of a man wearing a white tuxedo, even if Gregorio, when we see the picture from the right side, is wearing a black one? (00:34)

6. Juni snaps the handcuff of the metal box around his right wrist; as he panics and shakes his hand in front of Carmen, the cuff has jumped onto his left wrist. And when he picks up the box and walks away, the cuff is back around his right. (00:35)

Questions

1. When in school, Juni has a doll of Fegan Floop with his trademark glove on the left hand. Yet when Fegan talks to Juni's parents, he puts his glove on his right hand. And he's wearing it on his right hand during the song he performs. Where are McFarlan Toys when you need them? (00:12, 00:32, 00:43)

2. The kids are getting ready for school. When the red alert begins, a clock behind Uncle Felix reads 7:10. But when Felix, a few moments later, checks the coordinates of Gregorio and Ingrid (they could be in "Asia or South America"), his wristwatch reads 5 minutes to 1. And he is supposed to be a spy? (00:20, 00:21)

SPY WHO LOVED ME, THE (15)
1977, color, 125 min.

Director: Lewis Gilbert

Cast: Roger Moore (James Bond
007), Barbara Bach (Major
Anya Amasova, Agent XXX),
Curd Jürgens (Karl Stromberg),
Richard Kiel (Jaws), Caroline
Munro (Naomi), Walter Gotell
(General Anatol Gogol),
Geoffrey Keen (Sir Frederick
Gray, Minister of Defense),
Bernard Lee (M), George Baker
(Captain Benson), Michael
Billington (Sergei Barzov), Olga
Bisera (Felicca), Desmond
Llewelyn (Q), Nadim Sawalha
(Azis Fekkesh), Sue Vanner
(Log Cabin Girl), Eva Reuber-
Staier (Rubelvitch).

*Tenth Bond, this time he
works on a little Russian.*

Bloopers
1. Anya's music box transmitter
plays "Lara's Theme" (from
Doctor Zhivago), music and a
movie that at the time were
banned in the Soviet Union.
(00:03)
2. In an Austrian log cabin,
Bond tries to "enlarge the vo-
cabulary" of a woman: his
hand jumps from her shoulder to her face from the
close-up to the wide shot.
(00:04)
3. Bond places a transparency
representing the tracking of a
submarine's course on a
screen: the course on the

screen and the one on the
transparency perfectly coin-
cide. But when Q explains
how to track a submarine by
its wake, the tracing of the
courses are no longer perfectly aligned. (00:13, 00:14)
4. Stromberg stops eating
when Doctor Bechmann and
Professor Markovitz enter his
dining room. He grabs his
napkin and begins wiping
his hands—but from behind,
his hands are on the chair's
armrests. Then, he's wiping
his hands again. (00:15)
5. After Fekkesh leaves his seat
in front of the sphinx show,
Bond gives him a long look,
then stands up himself. But
just before Bond does so,
there's a match cut in the
scene: look at the audience
in the background, they all
change positions. (00:28)
6. Jaws gets out of the tomb
after killing Fekkesh; he
leaves the gate open, yet
when Bond enters the same
tomb, he has to push the
gate that now is closed.
(00:30, 00:31)
7. When Jaws enters the phone
booth to kill Max Kalba, Max
drops the phone. Later, when
Bond opens the booth to find
the body, Kalba's holding the
phone. (00:36, 00:37)
8. Jaws is about to knock 007
down with a large piece of
wood that he holds close to
his head (in front) and close

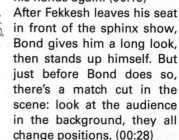

to the ground (from behind). (00:43)

9. During the explosion of the sidecar, it appears that the Materassi Sardadream truck has the steering wheel to the right. Not in Italy, for sure. (01:11)

10. When the motorcycle passes in front of the same truck, it seems that there's no driver in the cabin. (01:11)

The Sloshed Italian Who Can't Believe His Eyes

When the Lotus emerges from the sea and onto a Sardinian beach, a man who's drinking gives a long look at his bottle. (01:19) And when the gondola drives by Piazza San Marco in *Moonraker*, the *exact same man*, who's drinking again, checks his bottle. (00:40) And after the second motorcycle goes by on the chateau in *For Your Eyes Only*, once again the *same man*, and again with a glass in his hand, stands up, flabbergasted. (00:53) Who is this bizarre man who apparently lives in Italy and travels a lot? The man is Victor Tourjanky, the assistant director for the Italian crew, and having him in three different Italian locations in three different movies was an inside joke of director Lewis Gilbert and the associate producer William P. Cartlidge.

---

11. The Lotus Esprit dives from the pier into the water: as it dives, its bottom appears ordinary, but underwater it's already white and in one piece, way before Bond begins to push all the buttons he needs to turn the car into a mini-sub. (01:14)

12. The scuba diver that Bond "runs over" while underwater sinks with his arms crossed on his chest, and a lot of blood in the water. But in the next shot, he's going down with his arms separated from his body and no blood at all. (01:17)

13. The submarine *Stromberg One* receives a telex with a reprogramming code, 09276591. When the commander calls missile control for reprogramming, he gives the new code: 034285219. (01:46, 01:47)

14. While on the escape pod, XXX gets Bond's gun and threatens him with it. But when he makes her smile by saying, "Let's get out of these wet things," the gun is gone. (02:01, 02:02)

15. The closing credits announce, "James Bond will return in FOR YOUR EYES ONLY." Nope. James Bond did return, but in *Moonraker*. (02:05)

Questions

1. Why does Russian General Gogol speak English with his secretary, Rubelvitch? (00:03)

2. Jaws's disguise in Egypt is a telephone company van. The van's side reads, "Telephone Service." Since when in Egypt do they have English signs? (00:38)

Fun Fact

By the pyramids, Bond spots Jaws for the first time; he leans against a large block of stone and waits for the killer to pass. Look at Bond: doesn't he seem quite still, almost . . . flat? (00:29)

Will the More Stiff Roger Moore Please Stand Up?

Robin Browne, the optical effects cameraman, recalls that when they were editing the movie, they needed a wide shot of Bond looking at Jaws, but neither the first nor the second unit ever shot it. John Evans, the special effect coordinator, went to the Publicity Department and found a profile still of Roger Moore, which was blown up, and placed against the stone. Hey, it kinda works . . . !

STAR TREK: FIRST CONTACT (10)
1996, color, 110 min.

Director: Jonathan Frakes

Cast: Patrick Stewart (Captain Jean-Luc Picard), Jonathan Frakes (Commander William T. Riker), Brent Spiner (Lieutenant Commander Data), LeVar Burton (Lieutenant Commander Geordi La Forge), Michael Dorn (Lieutenant Commander Worf), Gates McFadden (Commander Dr. Beverly Crusher, Enterprise Medical Officer), Marina Sirtis (Counselor Deanna Troi), Alfre Woodard (Lily Sloane), James Cromwell (Dr. Zefram Cochrane), Alice Krige (Borg Queen), Michael Horton (Lieutenant Daniels), Neal McDonough (Lieutenant Hawk, Enterprise Helmsman).

The crew goes back in time to start all over again.

Bloopers

1. In the hangar of the spacecraft *Phoenix,* Data tries to handle the Lily situation, but she shoots at him, filling Data's vest with holes. A few minutes later, when Data and Picard are touching the *Phoenix,* Data's vest looks as good as new. (00:19, 00:20)

2. While Lily keeps Picard at "phaserpoint," she tells him that he better find a way out. Doing so, she moves her left thumb to the side of the weapon—but in the following shot, her thumb is still on top. (00:37)

3. Lily hands Picard the phaser in which she was keeping him in the line of fire. As he grabs it, the phaser blinks (doesn't that mean that it's firing?), yet Picard doesn't even flinch. Damned props! (00:45)

4. In describing the *Enterprise,* Captain Picard tells Lily that "There are twenty-four decks." But an officer, earlier, declared that the Borgs took control from decks twenty-six up to eleven. (00:43) Now, we imagine that there

probably isn't a Deck thirteen because of silly superstitions, however. . . . (00:49)

5. While walking outside of the *Enterprise*, Picard projects a short shadow to his right, onto Worf. But a wide shot reveals very long shadows behind the three heroes. Not only that, but when they begin the climb onto the inclined part of the craft, their shadows are shorter and to the heroes' left. (01:01, 01:05)

6. Still on the outside of the *Enterprise*, Hawk shoots a Borg, who drifts away in space. But the sparks generated by the shot fall onto the bridge. (01:08)

7. After Hawk is thrown overboard, Picard enters the travel data into the deflector computer, but the handle he has to turn is already in the vertical position. When the access is enabled, the handle is horizontal, and Picard proceeds to put it in the vertical position one more time. (01:10)

8. When Cochrane tells Riker that he built the craft only for money, Riker's right hand changes position in the grip on one of the structures of the cockpit. (01:15)

9. The computer on the *Enterprise* shows, as a destination for the escape pods, Gravett Island, in the southern hemisphere, west of South America. Once in space, the pods all seem to aim at . . . the East Coast of the United States? (01:23, 01:28)

10. Picard snaps the bionic spinal cord of the Borg Queen, then he tosses her skull onto the floor. Reflected in the skull, he can be seen standing up—but in the following shot he's still crouching down. He will stand up to help Data a few moments later. (01:38)

Question

Picard shows Lily the Earth from the *Enterprise*. He points out Australia, New Guinea, the Solomons . . . Shouldn't New Zealand be there, somewhere, or four hundred years from now does something catastrophic happen? (00:44)

STAR TREK: GENERATIONS (4)
1994, color, 123 min.

Director: David Carson

Cast: Patrick Stewart (Captain Jean-Luc Picard), Jonathan Frakes (Commander William Thomas Riker), Brent Spiner (Lieutenant Commander "Pinocchio" Data), LeVar Burton (Lieutenant Commander Geordi La Forge), Michael Dorn (Lieutenant Commander Worf, Son of Mogh), Gates McFadden (Commander Beverley Crusher nee Howard, M.D.), Marina Sirtis (Commander Deanna Troi), Malcolm McDowell (Dr.

Tolian Soran), James Doohan (Captain Montgomery "Scotty" Scott), Walter Koenig (Commander Pavel Chekov), William Shatner (Captain [retired] James Tiberius Kirk), Alan Ruck (Captain John Harriman).

When one bold and bald captain dies, you replace him with another bold and bald one.

Bloopers

1. Apparently, the fake galleon has quite realistic fresh paint on it: check Worf's knees as he's trying to climb back on board the ship. (00:21)
2. When Soran is discovered underneath a pile of debris, Worf bends over to remove a structure. And then he does it again. (00:26)
3. On Veridian III, Picard tries to convince Soran to find another way to get into nexus. They are facing each other, yet Picard has the sun to his left (hence the shadow of his head over his right shoulder). Soran, too. (01:04)

You've Seen One Exploding Klingon Ship, You've Seen 'Em All

The Klingon bird of prey explosion is a recycled sequence from *Star Trek VI: The Undiscovered Country.* (01:10)

---

4. When what's left of the *Enterprise* crash-lands, Worf is thrown over the dashboard: as he hits the floor, he almost loses his sash. In the following image, he has it firmly around his chest. (01:17)

Question

When the *Enterprise* is a holographic galleon (or something similar) in the middle of the ocean . . . is that an orange signal buoy in the open sea that appears right after Picard and Riker turn? (00:18)

STAR TREK: INSURRECTION (4)
1998, color, 103 min.

Director: Jonathan Frakes

Cast: Patrick Stewart (Captain Jean-Luc Picard), Jonathan Frakes (Commander William T. Riker), Brent Spiner (Lieutenant Commander Data), LeVar Burton (Lieutenant Commander Geordi La Forge), Michael Dorn (Lieutenant Commander Worf), Gates McFadden (Commander Beverly Crusher, M.D.), Marina Sirtis (Commander Deanna Troi, Counselor), F. Murray Abraham (Ad'har Ru'afo), Donna Murphy (Anij), Anthony Zerbe (Admiral Matthew Daugherty).

The Star Trek *crew go against Federation orders to stop a conspiracy that threatens innocents.*

Bloopers

1. A young man is wandering through the Ba'ku Village and lifts his right leg to step on a small wall on the edge of a vegetable garden. In the following, matching shot, he's lifting his left leg. (00:02)

2. After Data starts attacking the ground crew, several children flee across a stone and cement bridge, which is then hit with a laser bolt. The bridge bounces up and down. (00:04)

3. To approach the holoship in the lake, Picard, Data, and Anij use a raft: Picard paddles on the left side, Data on the right. When they reach the entrance, Data is able to open the door, but when they rise up to enter, they've switched positions: now Picard is on the right, and Data on the left. (00:32, 00:33)

4. Dr. Crusher tells Picard to check the DNA profile of one of the Son'a victims: she holds up a medscan in her left hand—yet the detail shows her holding it in her right. (01:11)

Question

Picard, Data, and Anij stand up, take three steps, and they're inside the holodeck. A few seconds later, Picard pushes Anij out of the same door, and she plummets a few yards into the lake. True, Data was emptying the lake, but not that fast. Perhaps a sudden low tide? (00:33, 00:34)

STAR TREK VI—THE UNDISCOVERED COUNTRY (12)
1992, color, 113 min.

Director: Nicholas Meyer

Cast: William Shatner (Captain James T. Kirk), Leonard Nimoy (Captain Spock), DeForest Kelley (Commander Leonard "Bones" McCoy, M.D.), James Doohan (Commander Montgomery "Scotty" Scott), Walter Koenig (Commander Pavel Chekov), Nichelle Nichols (Commander Nyota Uhura), George Takei (Captain Hikaru Sulu), Kim Cattrall (Lieutenant Valeris), Mark Lenard (Ambassador Sarek), Grace Lee Whitney (Commander Janice Rand), Brock Peters (Admiral Cartwright), Leon Russom (Chief in Command).

First time the Enterprise *meets CGI.*

Bloopers

1. Captain Sulu sips from a cup of tea, which he places in the middle of a table. Vibrations cause the cup to slide toward the edge of the table, but in the wide shot the cup is standing still in the middle of the table. It'll begin to move a few seconds later. (00:03)

2. Uhura, the black lady on the *Enterprise* crew, is credited as "Uhuru" in the closing credits. (00:12, 01:48)

3. While taping the captain's log, Kirk says, "I've never trusted Klingons ... and I

never will. I can never forgive them for the death of
my boy." However, when General Chang plays back the
same sentences during Kirk
and McCoy's trial, Kirk's voice
says, "I've never trusted Klingons . . . and I never will. I've
never been able to forgive
them for the death of my
boy." (00:14, 00:48)

4. After a formal dinner invita-
   tion is made to the Klingons,
   Captain Kirk passes by Spock.
   A clock on the bridge reads,
   "16 13:57, 58" but as Kirk
   passes by Spock ("I hope
   you're happy.") the same clock
   reads "16 13:55, 56 . . ." (00:19)

5. Lieutenant Valeris reminds
   Captain Kirk that "there's a sup-
   ply of Romulan ale aboard."
   A clock behind her states it's
   "16 14:03" (to 14:08). Cutting
   to a Spock close-up, a watch
   reads "16 14:06, 07 . . ." (00:19)

6. Spock asks for a replay of the
   torpedo attack on the Kling-

I'll Take "Klingon Anatomy" for
$1,000

During the attack on the Klingon
spacecraft, we learn that Klingon
blood is purple (00:29)—but after
the violent reaction of Soran on
board the Klingon bird of prey, in
Star Trek: Generations, we learn
that Klingon blood appears to be
red. (00:46) So . . . what's the real
color? Can we use a lifeline?

---

on spacecraft. On top of the
screen, a watch reads "10
45:46," counting up to 49.
Chekov states, "It is *Enterprise*. We fired." And Scotty
replies, "That is not possible!
All weapons visually are ac-
counted for, sir!" As we see
the clock again, it reads "10
45:50"—and counting. (00:53)

7. On Rura Penthe, Kirk faces a
   very tall alien, who seems
   sort of aggressive. McCoy no-
   tices. "He's definitely on about
   something, Jim!" His mouth
   doesn't move for the first
   half of the sentence. (00:59)

8. In order to make a point,
   Lieutenant Valeris vaporizes
   a pot in the kitchen. A female
   cook, who's carrying a tray,
   twirls to avoid the vaporizing
   beam. Twice. (01:01)

9. On Rura Penthe, the evil Kirk
   (Martia) knocks McCoy down,
   then engages in a battle with
   Kirk. The two roll on the
   ground by McCoy's feet—but
   in the following close-up of
   McCoy, they roll over him
   from his left side. Someone
   must have moved *extremely*
   fast. (01:20)

10. Spock questions (and subse-
    quently reads the mind of)
    Lieutenant Valeris. A clock in
    the background reads "05
    23:35" up to 43. A close-up of
    Scotty reveals a clock on the
    very same bridge that has
    "05 22—and something."
    (01:29, 01:30)

11. Captain Kirk asks Captain

Sulu who's on a screen, "When does this conference start?" Behind Kirk, it's possible to see—on a small monitor—a man approaching Sulu to whisper something to him. But Sulu is heard saying, "According to my information . . ." and then we cut to him, full screen. The images don't match. (01:31)

12. Quoting Hamlet's monologue just before getting hit by a torpedo, General Chang says "To be . . . or not to be . . ." and moves his head to his right. However, seen from behind, his head is pointing to his left. (01:41)

Fun Fact
Once again, a starship makes noise in the vacuum of space. Ho-hum. (00:03)

STUPIDS, THE (3)
1996, color, 94 min.

Director: John Landis

Cast: Tom Arnold (Stanley Stupid), Jessica Lundy (Joan Stupid), Bug Hall (Buster Stupid), Alex McKenna (Petunia Stupid), Scott Kraft (Policeman), Victor Ertmanis (Garbageman #1), Earl Williams (Garbageman #2), George Chiang (Chinese Waiter #1), Max Landis (Graffiti Artist), Carol Ng (Jade Palace Hostess), Arthur Eng (Chinese Waiter #2), Jennifer Dean (Meter Maid).

Family of idiots behave accordingly.

Bloopers
1. When Petunia and Buster find the Jade Palace Restaurant menu left by the door, they hold it, showing it with a long fold lengthwise. But the detail shows a menu in pristine condition and, most of all, flat as a mirror. (00:11)
2. Stanley illustrates the "pieces of the puzzle" on a white board. The first name he writes down, "Sender," changes after every cut. (00:43)
3. As Stanley enters Warehouse 21, where the illegal military operation is unfolding, he grabs the handrail on a balcony where he's standing. In the following shot, his hands have turned 180 degrees on the same handrail, without him moving them. (01:15)

SUMMER RENTAL (4)
1985, color, 86 min.

Director: Carl Reiner

Cast: John Candy (Jack Chester), Bob Wells (Stan Greene), Karen Austin (Sandy Chester), Kerri Green (Jennifer Chester), Joey Lawrence (Bobby Chester), Aubrey Jene (Laurie Chester), Richard Crenna (Al Pellet), Rip

Torn (Scully), John Larroquette (Don Moore), Richard Herd (Angus MacLachlan), Santos Morales (Cortez), Frank McCarthy (Hal).

Air-traffic controller goes on vacation and becomes a sailor.

Bloopers

1. On his way to work, Jack takes one egg and tries to peel it. The clock on the dashboard reads 8:20, but when Jack turns off the radio, the clock reads 7:40. Then it'll zoom to 8:20 again. (00:01, 00:02)

2. The windshield wipers are off while Jack drives, but when a car cuts in front of him, and Jack yells out of the window, there's all kinds of wiper action. (00:01, 00:02)

3. When Jack's family leaves to go on a speedboat with Don, Sandy grabs a plate with her left hand and two glasses with her right. But after she kisses Jack, the glasses have zapped onto the top of the plate. (00:38)

4. At the funeral home, the papers Pellet signs fold by themselves as he hands them to Jack. (00:57)

Question

Mumbling while fixing his pass, Jacks says, "I've worked here ten years . . ." When ordered to go on a vacation, his boss, Hal, says, "You've landed planes for thir-

teen years . . ." So, how long *has* Jack worked? (00:03, 00:05)

SUNSET (3)
1988, color, 107 min.

Director: Blake Edwards

Cast: Bruce Willis (Tom Mix), James Garner (Wyatt Earp), Malcolm McDowell (Alfie Alperin), Muriel Hemingway (Cheryl King), Kathleen Quinlan (Nancy Shoemaker), Jennifer Edwards (Victoria Alperin), Patricia Hodge (Christina Alperin), Richard Bradford (Captain Blackworth), M. Emmet Walsh (Chief Dibner), Joe Dallesandro (Dutch Kieffer), Andreas Katsulas (Arthur), Dann Florek (Marty Goldberg), Bing Russel (Studio Guard).

What happened when Tom Mix met (and played) Wyatt Earp. Give or take a lie or two.

Bloopers

1. On Tom Mix's movie set, Wyatt walks to Tom's trailer when he's approached by a studio guard. The shadow on the ground switches from going in front of Wyatt to going to his left. (00:13)

2. From the top of the stairs, Victoria tries to shoot Tom Mix, who's at the bottom of the same stairs. Wyatt pushes Victoria's arm to her

right, and she fires straight in front of her . . . hitting a lamp *behind* Tom. What, does she use heat-seeking bullets? (01:34)

3. The train that brings Wyatt home runs toward the San Gabriel Mountains (east of Pasadena, the departing station). There's a beautiful sunset behind these mountains, which are toward the east. Uh-huh. Right. (01:42)

SWORDFISH (7)
2001, color, 99 min.

Director: Dominic Sena

Cast: John Travolta (Gabriel Shear), Hugh Jackman (Stanley Jobson), Halle Berry (Ginger), Don Cheadle (Agent Roberts), Sam Shepard (Senator Reisman), Vinnie Jones (Marco), Drea de Matteo (Melissa), Rudolf Martin (Axl Torvalds), Zach Grenier (A.D. Joy), Camryn Grimes (Holly), Angelo Pagan (Torres), Chic Daniel (Swat Leader).

A hacker and a criminal with an interesting taste in movies join forces.

Bloopers
1. Agent Roberts enters the interrogating room, spills coffee on Axl Torvalds's lawyer, and slams him against a wall. The wall wobbles. (00:20)
2. Once alone with Axl, Roberts places his gun on the table.

Seen through the two-way mirror, he has his right hand on the gun, but as we cut inside the room ("Courtesy of the U.S. government"), Roberts's hands are crossed on his lap. (00:21)

3. Gabriel tells Stanley he has 60 seconds to enter the Department of Defense database and begins to count backward while checking his wristwatch: he announces 55 seconds after 6 seconds, 45 after 19, 20 seconds to zero after 48 seconds, 15 after 58 seconds, 10 after 1:04, and finally "3 . . . 2 . . . 1" after 1 minute and 16 seconds. (00:28)

4. To motivate Stanley to work on the database, Marco places his gun to Stanley's head. Marco alternatively holds the gun with one hand or two hands during the entire sequence. (00:28)

5. After school, little Holly is calling 411 with her cell phone when Stanley arrives; she drops the cell and runs to hug him, then as they leave he picks up her bag — but apparently, he forgets the cell. Is it still there? (00:40)

6. Stan drives Holly home; the headrest behind her is lowered. Yet when the "friend of a friend" agent jumps into the same seat, the headrest is all the way up. Needless to say, nobody touched it. (00:40, 00:42)

7. After a bone-breaking fall, Agent Roberts slams Stanley against the car at the bottom of the hill. The side of the car dents slightly. But when Stanley moves to get up, and is pushed back down, the car is just fine. (00:44, 00:45)

Question
When the rescued hostage blows up, it seems that every single pane of glass in the block shatters. Stanley lies on the floor, surrounded by splinters. Yet when Gabriel talks on the phone with Roberts, and when Stanley is shown his daughter, and for the rest of the sequence, the glass door of the bank appears to be perfectly fine. New, bomb-proof tempered glass? (00:08, 01:12, 01:13)

T

TARZAN (3)

1999, color, 88 min.

Directors: Kevin Lima and Chris Buck

Cast: Tony Goldwyn (Tarzan), Minnie Driver (Jane), Glenn Close (Kala), Alex D. Linz (Young and Baby Tarzan), Rosie O'Donnell (Terk or Terkina), Brian Blessed (Clayton), Nigel Hawthorne (Professor Porter), Lance Henriksen (Kerchak), Wayne Knight (Tantor), Taylor Dempsey (Young Tantor).

Shipwrecked boy raised in wild by apes . . . you get the picture.

Bloopers

1. Tarzan defends gorilla friends from an attack by Sabor, the cheetah. Sabor scratches Tarzan on his chest, but after a few seconds, the scratches and the blood have vanished. For good. (00:27, 00:28)
2. Tarzan offers Sabor, the cheetah, to his "father," Kerchak, by placing it on the ground in front of him. As a rifle explodes in the night and the gorillas move, the cheetah seems to have vanished without anyone grabbing it. (00:29, 00:30)
3. Before "Trashin' the Camp," Terk discovers a typewriter: the young gorilla pushes a few buttons, and the carriage moves to the right—the wrong way. After Terk incites a fellow gorilla to "rip it," and she types faster on the buttons, the carriage then moves to the left—the correct way. (00:41, 00:42)

THERE'S SOMETHING ABOUT MARY (5)

1998, color, 119 min.

Directors: Peter Farrelly and Bobby Farrelly

Cast: Cameron Diaz (Mary Jensen Matthews), Matt Dillon (Pat Healy), Ben Stiller (Ted Stroehmann), Lee Evans (Tucker / Norman Phipps), Chris Elliott (Dom

Woganowski), Lin Shaye (Magda), Jeffrey Tambor (Sully), Markie Post (Sheila Jensen), Keith David (Charlie Jensen), W. Earl Brown (Warren Jensen), Sarah Silverman (Brenda), Jonathan Richman (Jonathan), Tommy Larkins (Drummer), Steve Sweeney (Police Officer), Lenny Clarke (Fireman).

Gross-out humor goes commercial.

Bloopers

1. Jonathan's singing and guitar playing don't match with the music we hear at the beginning of the movie. (00:00)
2. After Ted gets "stuck" in the zipper, a police officer tries to help him. The officer passes his hat to a fireman, unbuttons his left sleeve and rolls it up, then does the same with the right sleeve, then unbuttons his left sleeve one more time and rolls it up—again. (00:17)
3. Ted, after digging into his wallet, holds the picture of Mary from the upper left corner in the detail, then from the bottom left in the long shot. (00:37)
4. While at the carnival, Healy tells Mary about his love for classics like *The Karate Kid* and *Harold and Maude*. During this speech, Mary's cotton candy drastically shrinks in size—even if she doesn't

take a single bite out of it. (00:56)
5. During the final confrontation scene with all of Mary's admirers and suitors, Dom desperately holds on to Mary's shoes. But every time we cut back to him they're arranged a little differently. (01:48)

THING, THE / JOHN CARPENTER'S THE THING (3)
1982, color, 109 min.

Director: John Carpenter

Cast: Kurt Russell (MacReady), Wilford Brimley (Blair), T.K. Carter (Nauls), David Clennon (Palmer), Keith David (Childs), Richard A. Dysart (Doctor Copper), Charles Hallahan (Norris), Peter Maloney (Bennings), Richard Masur (Clark), Donald Moffat (Garry), Joel Polis (Fuchs), Thomas G. Waites (Windows).

Alien parasite thaws in Antarctica and takes out a couple of outposts.

Bloopers

1. MacReady runs inside the base holding a lit flashlight. In the first shot inside the base, the flashlight is off (he could have switched it off, but he was running because someone was shooting everywhere). (00:52)
2. MacReady tapes his voice with a small recorder; he presses the Play and Record

buttons with his right hand (the one that holds the mike), and in the following shot, the hand is already up and close to his mouth. The sounds of the buttons haven't even finished yet. (01:01)

3. Childs smashes a door with an axe. After a close-up of MacReady, part of the door is intact. (01:10)

THREE TO TANGO (6)
1999, color, 98 min.

Director: Damon Santostefano

Cast: Matthew Perry (Oscar Novak), Neve Campbell (Amy Post), Dylan McDermott (Charles Newman), Oliver Platt (Peter Steinberg), Cylk Cozart (Kevin Cartwright), John C. McGinley (Strauss), Bob Balaban (Decker), Deborah Rush (Lenore), Kelly Rowan (Olivia Newman), Rick Gomez (Rick), Patrick Van Horn (Zack), David Ramsey (Bill).

An architect comes out of the closet and declares he's straight—and nobody believes him.

Bloopers

1. During their first meeting, when Oscar shakes Charles's hand, Peter's box moves from underneath his left arm to his left hand, and his briefcase moves from his right to his left hand. (00:08)

2. When Charles uses the hand sanitizer, he walks away from his desk—but when Oscar mentions the statue of Buddha, Charles is still standing in front of the sanitizer, then he walks away again. (00:08)

3. When Zack, Rick, and Bill talk about the football player nicknamed "The Ponderosa," Peter stands in the background, leaning against a column, his arms crossed. But in the matching close-up, his right hand is almost at his collar. (00:17)

4. While arguing about Egyptian toilet paper, Peter shoves Oscar, who then crosses his arms—only to have them uncrossed in the following shot. (00:33)

5. Amy steps out of the shower and Oscar pours champagne into two glasses, one green and one clear. He proceeds to hand the green one to Amy, but when she proposes a toast . . . she's holding the clear glass. (00:39)

6. Oscar sits on an easy chair holding a beer in his right hand. But when he tells his friends how the "spy operation" has gone, the bottle has jumped into his left hand. (00:44)

TOMBSTONE (12)
1993, color, 130 min.

Director: George Pan Cosmatos

Cast: Kurt Russell (Wyatt Earp), Val Kilmer (Doc Holliday), Sam

Elliott (Virgil Earp), Bill Paxton (Morgan Earp), Powers Boothe (Curly Bill Brocious), Michael Biehn (Johnny Ringo), Charlton Heston (Henry Hooker), Jason Priestley (Billy Breckinridge), Jon Tenney (John Behan, Cochise County Sheriff), Stephen Lang (Ike Clanton), Thomas Haden Church (Billy Clanton), Dana Delany (Josephine Marcus), Dana Wheeler-Nicholson ("Mattie" Blaylock Earp), Lisa Collins (Louisa Earp), Tomas Arlana (Frank Stillwell), Harry Carey, Jr. (Tombstone Marshal Fred White).

"Wyatt Earp: The Later Years."

Bloopers

1. Mattie is given some laudanum by Louisa. Then, when Wyatt is talking to Morgan and Virgil, in the background Mattie appears not to have the laudanum bottle and Louisa can be seen reaching into her purse for the same. (00:10)

2. The dollar bill Wyatt signs in The Oriental is tossed onto the table by Curly Bill. The dollar is gone when he collects $500, then it's back and it moves all across the table. (00:36, 00:37, 00:38)

3. Johnny Ringo shows his ability with a gun at the faro table. Wyatt's hands are underneath the table, but when Ringo hol-

sters the gun again, Wyatt's right hand has jumped onto the table. (00:38)

4. High on opium, Curly Bill goes on a shooting rampage: he fires over twenty gunshots without reloading (his belt doesn't have any missing bullets, either). (00:49)

5. Marshal Fred approaches Curly Bill and orders him to give up his guns. In the shots with both of them, there's a cable running from off the screen up to the marshal's left leg. (A possible connection for the explosive special effect?) (00:50, 00:51)

6. At the OK Corral, Doc fires one shot in the air with his double-barrel shotgun, then fires two shots at a man. He never reloads. (01:13)

7. Wyatt's hands are covered in fresh blood. Yet when he wipes Morgan's forehead, he doesn't leave a stain. (01:27)

8. On the pool table, Morgan dies while Wyatt hugs him. Well, "dies" is such a big word . . . check the right side of Morgan's neck: it's still pulsating. (01:28)

9. After Morgan's death, Wyatt walks out in the rain. Strangely, it's only raining in the area around him. (01:28)

10. At the train station, Wyatt kills Stillwell: his gun falls away from him, yet when Wyatt kicks it, it has moved between Stillwell's legs— and then it's away again. (01:32, 01:33)

11. When Doc Holliday confronts Johnny Ringo, Doc's coat collar keeps flipping up and down, and half up and half down thoroughout the whole scene. (01:49)
12. At the Glenwood Sanitorium, Wyatt resumes a card game with Doc. Wyatt says, "Two bits a hand. Stud?" and later asks how many cards does Doc want. But stud poker doesn't require card exchanging. (01:55)

Questions

1. Curly Bill kills everyone at a wedding, except for the bride and groom. But when he approaches the survivors, a man on the ground is breathing. Still not dead, or just a crappy extra? (00:04)
2. Isn't there a suspicious delay between Curly's shots at the window and the lamp, and the actual destruction of the aforementioned? (00:49)

TOMCATS (3)
2001, color, 95 min.

Director: Gregory Poirier

Cast: Shannon Elizabeth (Natalie Parker), Jerry O'Connell (Michael Delaney), Jake Busey (Kyle Brenner), Horatio Sanz (Steve), Jaime Pressly (Tricia), Bill Maher (Carlos), John Patrick White (Gary), David Odgen Stiers (Dr. Crawford), Soledad Alberti (Maria), Joseph D. Reitman (Dave).

Bachelor fever reaches new depths.

Bloopers

1. After the hooker incident in the interrogation room, Natalie grabs Michael's chin with her right hand: thumb to the left, other fingers to the right. As she says, "I wanna hear it," her thumb has moved to the right, the other fingers to the left. (00:27)
2. When Dr. Crawford describes a gash to be made to operate on Kyle, he wildly gestures with his left hand — but in the wide shot he lowers his right. (01:03)
3. Michael smashes a cello at an Animal Rights meeting, then he removes his foot from the instrument: he's wearing a sock because the shoe is trapped inside. But as he flees, he's wearing both shoes. (01:21)

TOOTSIE (4)
1982, color, 107 min.

Director: Sidney Pollack

Cast: Dustin Hoffman (Michael Dorsey / Dorothy Michaels), Jessica Lange (Julie Nichols), Teri Garr (Sandy), Dabney Coleman (Ron), Charles Durning (Les Nichols), Bill Murray (Jeff), Sidney Pollack (George Fields), George Gaynes (John Van Horn), Geena Davis (April), Doris

Belack (Rita), Ellen Foley (Jacqui), Peter Gatto (Rick).

Desperate actor makes a remarkable transformation, and becomes a successful . . . actress ??!

Bloopers

1. While arguing about "The Iceman Cometh," George Fields tosses a pen on the desk then, pulling himself together ("You always do this to me!"), restarts fresh with Michael. The pen is back in his hand, then on the table, then in his hand again. (00:17)

2. Julie, Ron, and Dorothy step out of the TV studio. Julie is stopped by a few fans while Ron calls a cab. When the cab arrives, on the other side of the road there is a bus with an *Evita* banner—yet the bus doesn't appear in the reflection on the doors behind Julie and Dorothy. Also, the bus is in a traffic jam, while behind Julie and Dorothy it's possible to see the cars moving. (00:40)

3. When Dorothy goes to Julie's house to help her with memorizing the lines, she brings a bunch of flowers. Julie tosses them onto the kitchen table, then . . . she tosses them again. (00:48)

4. Caught red-handed by Jeff, Michael (as Dorothy) pushes John out of the apartment. When Sandy arrives, Michael dives under the shower while Jeff hides the female disguise. And he is so fast that the wig and purse vanish from the table without anybody touching them. (01:33)

TWELVE MONKEYS (6)
1995, color, 129 min.

Director: Terry Gilliam

Cast: Bruce Willis (James Cole), Madeleine Stowe (Kathryn Railly), Brad Pitt (Jeffrey Goines), Christopher Plummer (Dr. Leland Goines), Joseph Melito (Young Cole), Joey Perillo (Detective Franki), Michael Chance (Scarface), Vernon Campbell (Tiny), H. Michael Walls (Botanist), David Morse (Dr. Peters).

Brazil meets Terminator *on acid.*

Bloopers

1. During his jump into 1990, Cole collects several bruises on his face—particularly a large one on his forehead, above his right eye. Back in his present, as he talks with the raspy voice in his room, the bruise is gone, but it's back during the interrogation that follows. (00:13, 00:38, 00:40)

2. While in jail during 1990, Cole is interviewed by Kathryn. A string of saliva drools from Cole's lower lip, it vanishes as he asks, "Why am I chained? Why are these chains

on me?" and then it comes back. (00:14)

3. While in the car, Kathryn is asked by Cole to turn the radio on. The display reads 9:29 (presumably the time, since they're driving at night) and it jumps to 103.7. Less than a minute later, Cole asks Kathryn to make the radio louder. She pushes another button, and now the radio indicates 9:33 — but with an FM in the corner, as if this were a radio station — and then it zaps again to 103.7. Hmmm... (00:50, 00:51)

4. The army of the 12 Monkeys kidnaps Dr. Goines, and his son Jeffrey removes the duct tape from the doctor's mouth and plasters it onto his forehead. The position of the tape switches back and forth all through the sequence. (01:45)

5. Cole dozes off in a theater where they are showing *Vertigo*. When he wakes up, on the screen there is a scene from *The Birds*. But when Bruce steps out of the lobby of the theater, we hear the music from *Vertigo*. And on the theater banner we learn the movies in this Hitchcock festival are *Strangers on a Train*, *North by Northwest*, *Vertigo*, and *Psycho*. Since it definitely wasn't the trailer, where did *The Birds* come from? (01:46, 01:49)

6. After he's shot in the airport, Cole is reached by Kathryn.

He raises one clean hand to caress her, and as the shot switches, Cole's hand is covered with blood. (02:02)

TWINS (8)
1988, color, 105 min.

Director: Ivan Reitman

Cast: Arnold Schwarzenegger (Julius Benedict), Danny DeVito (Vincent Benedict), Kelly Preston (Marnie Mason), Chloe Webb (Linda Mason), Bonnie Bartlett (Mary Ann Benedict), Trey Wilson (Beetroot McKinley), Marshall Bell (Webster), David Caruso (Al Greco), Hugh O'Brian (Granger), Nehemiah Persoff (Mitchell Traven), Maury Chaykin (Burt Klane).

Separated at birth, two unlikely twins are reunited.

Bloopers
1. The six fathers, two doctors, and Mary Ann pose for a picture. Doctor Garfield (the one with the van dyke) has his hands in his overcoat pocket, his thumbs sticking out. In the picture, his hands are in his pockets. No thumbs in sight. (00:01)

2. When in jail, Julius asks a guard if Vincent is really Vincent. After a close-up of Julius, one shot of Vincent, and another close-up of Julius, there's a close-up of

Vincent: the reflection shows Julius marching toward the seat, but the following shot shows Julius standing still, then moving. (00:16)

3. Vincent leaves his office to "borrow" a new Cadillac. As he closes the door of his office, in the bottom-left corner it's possible to see the reflection of a man with whitish pants moving. (00:22)

4. Vincent drives Julius in his rearview mirror–equipped car. When Vincent tells Julius that he has to pick up a car by the airport, the rearview mirror is gone. But when Julius drives the car out of the garage, the rearview mirror is back in place. (00:25, 00:28)

5. When Julius defends Vincent from Morris outside of the office, he flips Morris to the ground. Morris is wearing a backpad to protect him in the fall (the shape appears underneath his shirt). (00:28)

6. Julius shows Granger the picture taken at the beginning of the story (00:01), and once again, the picture is not the same: this time Mary Ann doesn't hold on to the hat she had. (00:43)

7. The two brothers finally dress alike and walk down the street. In the background, a blond lady with a red-and-white striped shirt keeps crossing the same road at least five times. (01:04)

8. Vincent and Julius are in a restroom; they wash their hands, grab two paper towels, use them, and toss them in a bucket. While they do this, a beer bottle jumps from Vincent's towel dispenser to Julius's, and back. (01:11)

Question
At the end of their first encounter, Vincent stands up and asks if he's on *Candid Camera*. Maybe he's right. Is that the reflection of a camera lens in the top-right corner of the glass in front of Vincent? (00:18)

BLOOPER IN A BOTTLE

Get the message?

A Miller beer bottle in *Saving Silverman*	Blooper No. 2
Arnold Schwarzenegger's beer in *Twins*	Blooper No. 8
Matthew Perry's mouthwash in *The Whole Nine Yards*	Blooper No. 13

U

UNBREAKABLE (3)
2000, color, 107 min.

Director: M. Night Shyamalan

Cast: Bruce Willis (David Dunn), Samuel L. Jackson (Elijah Price), Robin Wright Penn (Audrey Dunn), Spencer Treat Clark (Joseph Dunn), Charlayne Woodard (Elijah's Mother), Eamonn Walker (Dr. Mathison), Leslie Stefanson (Kelly), Johnny Hiram Jamison (Elijah, age 13), Michaelia Carroll (Baby-sitter), Bostin Chistopher (Comic Book Clerk), Elizabeth Lawrence (School Nurse), M. Night Shyamalan (Stadium Drug Dealer).

Two completely different lives merge into one very bizarre adventure.

Bloopers
1. Elijah's mom places a gift for her son on a bench at the playground. When Elijah sees the gift from his window, the box is almost to the end of the right side of the bench. When he walks to get the gift, the box has moved almost to the other side. (00:23)

2. David finds a folder of newspaper clippings in his closet. He opens it, and nothing can be read. But the detail shows clippings with very large headlines like "WARRIORS," or "STATS RANK #1." (00:33)

3. In Elijah's office there are three Mac G4 computers under his L-shaped working desk: two are together on one side, the last one is on the other side. After Elijah and David end their handshake, the two side-by-side computers have moved, all by themselves, under the corner of the desk. (01:38, 01:39)

Questions
1. When Dr. Mathison assists Elijah's mother with her baby, he declares that both arms and legs of the kid are broken. But doesn't it seem to be a pretty functional and

intact arm that the kid pushes his blanket with? (00:01, 00:02)

2. Joseph is channel surfing when he finds on one channel *The Powerpuff Girls,* and on the next one, an episode of *I Am Weasel* ("Where has you been, Banana?" "Now I've got you, weasel!"). But these two cartoons are both on the Cartoon Network, so how was he channel surfing on one channel? (00:09)

Fun Fact
The drug dealer at the stadium is played by *Unbreakable*'s writer/director, M. Night Shyamalan. (00:55)

V

VALENTINE (6)
2001, color, 96 min.

Director: Jamie Blanks

Cast: Marley Shelton (Kate Davies), David Boreanaz (Adam Carr), Jessica Capshaw (Dorothy Wheeler), Denise Richards (Paige Prescott), Jessica Cauffiel (Lily Voight), Katherine Heigl (Shelley Fisher), Daniel Cosgrove (Campbell Morris), Hedy Burress (Ruthie), Fulvio Cecere (Detective Vaughn), Johnny Whitworth (Max Raimi), Woody Jeffreys (Brian), Adam Harrington (Jason).

Love means never having to say, "I'm sorry I just killed you."

Bloopers

1. To unzip the bodybag where Shelley is hiding, the killer uses his left hand while holding a knife in his right hand. But when Shelley screams, the killer holds her down with his right hand (now without the knife), then he raises the knife . . . with his right hand (???), but slices her throat with his left hand. (00:12)

2. After Shelley's funeral, Adam and Kate talk by his car. Right after she discovers a tequila bottle, the sun shines only on her close-ups and not on his. (00:16)

3. Campbell arrives at Dorothy's house carrying a bag whose strap is over his jacket collar. After he says, "Cozy little place you have," the strap winds up under the collar. And after they hug and Campbell turns to leave, the strap is again over the collar. (00:20, 00:21)

4. The rose on the heart-shaped chocolate box turns 180 degrees from the time Lily sees the box to when she picks it up. (00:27)

5. Kate writes Adam "IOU— TLC" on cleaner receipt number 6443. When he takes it, the receipt number has become 6335. And when the

same note floats in a small pond, the number has become 6329. (00:49, 00:50, 01:22)

6. Paige gets electrocuted and dies in the spa, her eyes open. Later on, when her body is discovered by Kate, Paige's eyes are closed. (01:18, 01:26)

VIEW TO A KILL, A (18)
1985, color, 126 min.

Director: John Glen

Cast: Roger Moore (James Bond 007), Christopher Walken (Max Zorin), Tanya Roberts (Stacey Sutton), Grace Jones (May Day), Patrick MacNee (Sir Godfrey Tibbett), Patrick Bauchau (Scarpine), David Yip (Chuck Lee), Fiona Fullerton (Pola Ivanova), Manning Redwood (Bob Conley), Alison Doody (Jenny Flex), Willoughby Gray (Dr. Carl Mortner), Desmond Llewelyn (Q), Robert Brown (M), Joe Flood (U.S. Police Captain), Lucien Jerome (Paris Taxi Driver).

Fourteenth mission for Bond, last one for Roger Moore.

Bloopers

1. When Bond discovers the body of 003 in the snow, he's wearing white gloves. As he finds the microchip, he isn't. And when he jumps to avoid the machine gun, he's wearing them again. (00:00, 00:01)

2. Bond loses one ski and sneaks behind one soldier in order to steal his snowmobile: we catch one glimpse of Bond's boot sole; it's white. When Bond jumps off of the snowmobile, the soles of his boots are black. When he lies on the ground, and

YOU DON'T SOUND WELL

Indeed, not well at all. Have you ever had a sound check-up?

Tom Cruise in *Days of Thunder*	Blooper No. 5
The phone message in *The Fugitive*	Blooper No. 7
Jonathon Ke Quan in *Indiana Jones and the Temple of Doom*	Blooper No. 3
Jimmy Simpson in *Loser*	Blooper No. 3
Christopher Walken in *A View to a Kill*	Blooper No. 16
The passengers in *Volunteers*	Blooper No. 5
Roger Moore in *The Man With the Golden Gun*	Blooper No. 11
Mark Hamill in *Return of the Jedi*	Blooper No. 16
DeForest Kelly in *Star Trek VI: The Undiscovered Country*	Blooper No. 7
Kevin Pollak's plane in *The Whole Nine Yards*	Blooper No. 19

debris falls all around him (including the soon-to-be impromptu snowboard), the soles are white again. But they become black one more time when he loses the snowboard. Finally, in the iceberg-camouflaged launch, the soles are white with black squares and stripes. (00:02, 00:03, 00:04, 00:05)

3. On the Eiffel Tower, Bond gets his legs entangled in May Day's fishing line. She pulls him over the handrail, and as he dangles almost upside down, his legs are free. When he falls back onto the stairs, his legs are tied together. (00:18)

4. To set himself free, Bond sits down and works on the line. At that moment, 007 is holding his handgun—yet when he unhooks the line, the gun is gone. (00:18)

5. When May Day jumps from the Eiffel Tower, it's possible to see a platform sticking out from the top level of the tower. (00:18)

6. In order to follow a parachute jumper from the Eiffel Tower, Bond bullets away driving a "borrowed" taxicab. As he leaves, the boom mike is reflected in the rear window. (00:19)

7. The same window is completely rolled down as the taxi skids in the square and falls backward down the stairs. (00:19)

8. During the chase, here is what actually happens (in sequence): the taxi jumps onto the roof of a bus, then jumps down, its windshield shatters when it hits a road barrier, the bus passengers look up (as if the taxi were still on the roof), 007 zigzags through the traffic, then is back in front of the road barrier and finally the car is sliced in half by another car. (00:20)

9. From a bridge, Bond jumps onto a boat and lands in a wedding cake. But when he's carried away by two chefs, his tuxedo is perfectly clean. (00:20)

10. M talks to Bond in a car after bailing him out of jail. Bond's left arm is stretched by the window—but it isn't in the following close-up. (00:21)

11. Bond is wearing a stethoscope around his neck when he finds the horse's microchip. But when he says, "The lights!" the stethoscope is gone. It'll come back (in Bond's hand) when he closes the doors he's in front of. (00:38, 00:39)

12. In another secret room, Bond stops one boxing machine by mistake before it can pick up the lid of a crate. When two henchmen enter the same room and fight with Bond and Tibbet, the machine is still motionless, but one lid already has been picked up. And when Bond

reactivates the machine, it picks up one lid. Again. (00:39, 00:40)

13. On his racetrack, Zorin jumps the first fence and one of his men pushes the button to raise the fence. Zorin turns and waves, and the hench-man pushes the button again and nods, apparently looking at Zorin. But if you compare the position of the buttons and the man, he nods at the fence. In the following detail, the henchman pushes the button again. (00:49)

14. When May Day pushes the Rolls Royce into the lake, check the water in front of the car: you can see the cable that pulls it. (00:52)

15. The Rolls apparently sinks quite far away from shore. Yet Bond, underwater, looks up and sees Zorin and May Day as if they were no more than five feet from the car. (00:53)

16. When it's taped, Zorin says, "Main Strike's in three days. Any delays . . . I'll hold you responsible." A technician answers, "Yes, sir. Bring it up to full. Slowly." But when Bond listens to the same tape, he hears, "Main Strike's in three days. Any delays . . . I'll hold you responsible. It's essential the remaining pipe-lines are open on time." (01:03, 01:10)

17. Outside of city hall, when told that Lee's body has been found in Chinatown, Bond removes his hands from the fire truck—but the following shot of Stacey show Bond's hands still against the fire truck. (01:33)

18. Bond is dangling from the fire truck ladder and smashes a Chevron sign. A couple of crewmembers and a "caped" camera can be seen at the end of the truck. (01:36)

Questions

1. 007 steals a cab with a French driver. The guy chases the car, yelling "My car!"—in English. Why? (00:19)

2. A whole section of the horse stables is an elevator that goes underground. On the lower level, we see the floor of the elevator car going down past an upper window in the door, and then Bond crosses in immediately from the right . . . but isn't the ele-vator still in motion, even though Bond seems to be al-ready at ground level? Talk amongst yourselves. . . . (00:36)

Fun Facts

1. The movie opens with a dis-claimer stating that "Neither the name 'Zorin' nor any other name in this film is meant to portray a real com-pany or actual person" be-cause the producers found out about an actual com-pany called "Zoran" whose agenda didn't include world domination. (00:00)

2. The Rolls Royce driven by Tibbett was Albert Broccoli's, the producer of James Bond. (00:22)

3. Dolph Lundgren (of future *Rocky V* fame) appears briefly as KGB agent Venz, behind General Gogol, at Zorin's racecourse in France. (00:54)

Hold on to Your Hats . . . for a While . . .

Since after *A View to a Kill* Roger Moore bowed out of 007's scene, the movie ends with a semi-appointment: "James Bond will return." No title indicated. (02:10)

VOLUNTEERS (10)
1985, color, 107 min.

Director: Nicholas Meyer

Cast: Tom Hanks (Lawrence Bourne III), John Candy (Tom Tuttle), Rita Wilson (Beth Wexler), Tim Thomerson (John Reynolds), Gedde Watanabe (At Toon), George Plimpton (Lawrence Bourne, Jr.), Ernest Harada (Chung Mee), Allan Arbus (Albert Bardenaro), Xander Berkeley (Kent Sutcliffe), Clyde Kusatsu (Seuvanna).

Not always trying to do some good is actually the best thing.

Bloopers

1. During a card game, Lawrence lights a cigarette, but when he looks at the other players, the cigarette is unlit (and brand new). Then it's lit again. Then isn't. Then he extinguishes it in the ashtray. (00:03, 00:04)

2. Lawrence puts $1,090 on the table, the remainder of his cash. But when he checks his hidden card, a $100 bill lies by the card. (00:04)

3. Kent picks up his blanket and pillow and opens the dorm-room door. As he walks in, he's holding, under the pillow, a tie. Where did it come from? (00:07)

4. During the father-son discussion about the $28,000, a car arrives: Lawrence moves the left curtain (seen from the outside), but actually moves the right one (from the inside). (00:12)

5. While flying over Rome, the passengers are singing "Puff, the Magic Dragon." Look at their lips: they're singing an entirely different song. (00:20)

6. At Toon offers a joint to Lawrence: At Toon holds the joint between his thumb and index finger, but in the over-the-shoulder shot, he holds it between his index and middle fingers. (00:39)

7. While tied to a pole and talking to Seuvanna, Tom Tuttle's left shirt collar keeps moving under and over his jacket. (00:55)

8. Tom Tuttle lights a stick of dynamite and walks into a room, holding it in his left hand. Then it jumps into his right hand, then back into the left.... And when he mentions tuna casserole, again: right, left, right... (01:33, 01:34)

9. Seuvanna looks at the bridge with his binoculars, and even if he doesn't move, he has two different angles of sight: one from the side of the bridge, one from directly in front of it. (01:40)

10. During the mouth-to-mouth operation, Lawrence lifts his left hand from the water twice. (01:42)

W

WALL STREET (6)
1987, color, 126 min.

Director: Oliver Stone

Cast: Michael Douglas (Gordon Gekko), Charlie Sheen (Bud Fox), Daryl Hannah (Darien), Martin Sheen (Carl Fox), James Spader (Roger Barnes), Hal Holbrook (Lou Mannheim), Tamara Tunie (Carolyn), Franklin Cover (Dan), John C. McGinley (Marvin), John Capodice (Dominick), Sean Young (Kate Gekko), Terence Stamp (Sir Larry Wildman).

New kid on the financial block gets roped into insider trading and then becomes an informant. Will they never learn?

Bloopers

1. The story is set in 1985, yet Marv, speaking with Bud about Gekko's business policy, says that he was working "Thirty seconds after the Challenger blew up." The Challenger disaster occurred in 1986. (00:04, 00:08)

2. Bud's computer remembers that on Monday, May 6, it's Gekko's birthday. A-hem... May 6, 1985 was a Tuesday. (00:13)

3. Bud leaves Gekko's office. While passing through the door, his tie knot has loosened itself—without him touching it. (00:20)

4. Gekko and Bud are in a limo under the rain. Bud has no umbrella, yet when he steps out of the car, the ground is dry as a bone. (00:36)

5. When Bud goes incognito to the Marsala Company, he pulls a file from a cabinet marked "Draft." In the detail he flips two pages, but in the main shot only one page has been turned. (00:57)

6. During a meeting in Central Park, Gekko's raincoat is wet with rain, then dry ("I gave you Darien!"), and then wet again. (01:56, 01:57)

IT'S A DATE!

But often, it's the wrong date.

Sandra Bullock in *Demolition Man*	Blooper No. 2
The calendar in *The Family Man*	Blooper No. 1
A wake-up call in *Johnny Mnemonic*	Blooper No. 2
The game date in *Rudy*	Blooper No. 2
Michael Douglas's date of birth in *Wall Street*	Blooper No. 2

WAR OF THE WORLDS, THE (3)
1953, color, 85 min.

Director: Bryon Haskin

Cast: Gene Barry (Dr. Clayton Forrester), Ann Robinson (Sylvia Van Buren), Les Tremayne (General Mann), Lewis Martin (Pastor Matthew Collins), Robert Cornthwaite (Dr. Pryor), Sandro Giglio (Dr. Bilderbeck), William Phipps (Wash Perry), Paul Birch (Alonzo Hogue), Jack Kruschen (Salvatore), Vernon Rich (Col. Ralph Heffner), Houseley Stevenson, Jr. (Aide to General Mann), Ralph Dumke (Buck Mohanan).

Martians land on Earth disguised as meteors, and level everything, foregoing any attempt to communicate.

Bloopers
1. Buck hits the hollow meteor while a group of people stand by the edge of the crater. Among this group are Sylvia and Clayton. As Buck hits the meteor the final time and flees, mumbling that it's so hot that you could fry an egg, the crowd parts and Sylvia and Clayton reach the position they were in a few seconds earlier. (00:10)

2. The plane is about to drop the A-bomb on the nest of spacecrafts. The countdown is "50 seconds," 8 seconds later, "40 seconds," 10 seconds later, "30 seconds," 8 seconds later, "20 seconds," and 3.5 seconds later, "15 seconds." (01:05)

3. After blowing up a water tank, one of the alien starships is suspended by a cable while gliding down a street. (01:15)

WATERBOY, THE (8)
1998, color, 90 min.

Director: Frank Coraci

Cast: Adam Sandler (Bobby Boucher), Kathy Bates (Helen "Mama" Boucher), Henry Winkler (Coach Klein), Fairuza

Balk (Vicky Vallencourt), Jerry Reed (Red Beaulieu), Larry Gilliard, Jr. (Derek Wallace), Blake Clark (Farmer Fran), Peter Danet (Gee Grenouille), Jonathan Longhan (Lyle Robideaux), Al Whiting (Casey Bugge), Clint Howard (Paco), Allen Covert (Walter).

Good-hearted kid becomes town hero.

Bloopers

1.   Bobby Boucher gets closer to the suggestion box: a wide shot shows all the notes scattered inside the transparent box, but when Bobby's hand picks them up, they are all neatly stacked. (00:02)

2.   Bobby Boucher is struggling with an orange Gatorade cooler on his head. He takes it off just in time to see Coach Beaulieu yelling, "You're fired!!" In the following shot, the orange cooler is nowhere to be seen. (00:03)

3.   As Coach Klein has a problem breathing, he sits down and Bobby Boucher passes him a glass of water. On the blackboard, a new line has appeared close to the extra flanker behind the quarterback, and after one cut a second round line appears on the board without anybody having drawn it. (00:09)

4.   Bobby Boucher plays for the first time when Coach Klein tells him, "Third and ten,"

and then starts to explain to him what to do. During this scene, the shadows of everyone on the ground zap to the left and to the right, to the left again, to the right... (00:20)

5.   Bobby Boucher finds Vicky Vallencourt sitting and thinking about stealing L.T.'s Porsche. In the background, a red van passes twice, left to right. Or takes laps around the block, in which case it's very fast. (00:41)

6.   When Coach Klein introduces Bobby Boucher at the rally, he's holding the microphone with his left hand. As he turns, the mike has jumped into his right (and back, as he turns back again). (00:48)

7.   Vicky Vallencourt is arrested by two officers after she's threatened a player with a knife. The sheriff has a patch on his arm that reads "County Sheriff." Louisiana (where the movie takes place) doesn't have counties, it has parishes. (00:50)

8.   Bobby Boucher is studying for school when he takes a long sip from a blue thermos, which he places in front of the book he's reading. A few moments later, when he yells, "Everything is the devil to you, Mama!!" the thermos has moved to the right of the book—without anybody touching it. (00:56, 00:57)

WATERWORLD (8)
1995, color, 136 min.

Director: Kevin Reynolds (and Kevin Costner)

Cast: Kevin Costner (Mariner), Dennis Hopper (Deacon), Jeanne Tripplehorn (Helen), Tina Majorino (Enola), Michael Jeter (Old Gregor), Gerard Murphy (Nord), R.D. Call (Enforcer), Kim Coates (Drifter), John Fleck (Doctor), Robert Joy (Ledger Guy), Jack Black (Pilot), John Toles-Bey (Plane Gunner).

The future. The polar caps have melted, and the earth is covered by one huge ocean. Unfortunately, they were able to keep this lame movie afloat long enough to film it.

Bloopers

1. To amaze three kids in the atoll, the Mariner holds a mirror with four fingers on top and his thumb on the opposite side; in the next shot, they're reversed; in the following shot, they're back as they were before. (00:11)

2. The Mariner seems to have webbed feet only in the close-ups and not in the long shots. (00:21, 00:36)

3. When Old Gregor goes visiting the Mariner in the cage, the Mariner spits in the guy's face, then leans to the right side of the cage—but in the wide shot, he's leaning to the left side of it. Then, he'll be to the right side again. (00:22)

4. The Mariner climbs on top of the mast of his boat to free it from the rope attached to the seaplane. He produces a knife, then places it between his teeth and shoots the rope. He then falls into the water and emerges without the knife. But a few seconds later, he produces the knife from its holster and cuts Helen's hair. (00:56, 00:57)

5. Enola is able to hum a melody that goes "mmmh-mmmh-mmmh" while eating a fish. Huh? (01:09)

6. Talking about Enola, Helen says that "She draws what she sees. She is like a mirror." Later on, during a rant, she tells the Mariner that he has a lot of gadgets, like the "reflecting glass." Or, like a word she used earlier, a "mirror." (01:12, 01:20)

7. After the massive oil spill (and subsequent barrage of negative publicity), Exxon renamed the *Exxon Valdez* to *Sea River Mediterranean*. Therefore, the ship that sinks at the end absolutely wouldn't have "*Exxon Valdez*" on it. (01:56)

8. The Mariner ties a bungee cord to his ankles over his boots. When he jumps, he is barefoot. (01:57)

Question

The Mariner has a machine that can make urine drinkable. But urine has a much higher concentration of salt than seawater, so why not use that machine for making seawater drinkable? Does someone have a little fetish? (00:01)

WAY OF THE GUN, THE (5)
2000, color, 119 min.

Director: Christopher McQuarrie

Cast: Ryan Phillippe (Parker), Benicio Del Toro (Longbaugh), James Caan (Joe Sarno), Juliette Lewis (Robin), Taye Diggs (Jeffers), Nicky Katt (Obecks), Scott Wilson (Hale Chidduck), Dylan Kussman (Dr. Allen Painter), Kristin Lehman (Francesca Chidduck), Geoffrey Lewis (Abner), Armando Guerrero (Federale #1), Andres Orozco (Federale #2).

Strange story of friendship, kidnapping, Mexico, and other stuff.

Bloopers
1. As soon as the kidnapping has begun, while Longbaugh drives the van, Parker turns to tie up Robin. In doing so, he lets us catch a glimpse of the external rearview mirror, which is just a plain old standard rearview mirror. A few minutes later, Longbaugh rams the Jeffers and Obecks' car. Parker gets out of the van: now the rearview mirror has one of those round, smaller mirrors glued to it. (00:17, 00:21)

2. While talking to Longbaugh and Parker in the truck stop's bathroom, both the piece of toilet paper Dr. Painter places on his eyebrows and the blood stain change shape quite frequently. (00:31)

3. In Chidduck's house, the trail of blood Painter has on the right side of his face noticeably changes length—and it even gets shorter when Painter sits on one step. (00:43)

4. Francesca stops seducing Jeffers and leans back on the couch: her legs are showing, but in the wide shot they are covered by her robe. They'll return to uncovered in the following shot. (00:53)

5. Longbaugh and Parker are shot, and they both lie on the ground. The gun by Longbaugh's head changes its position without him touching it (check both when the ambulance leaves, and in the two poor saps final shot). (01:51, 01:54)

WEEKEND AT BERNIE'S (8)
1989, color, 97 min.

Director: Ted Kotcheff

Cast: Andrew McCarthy (Larry Wilson), Jonathan Silverman (Richard Parker), Catherine Mary Stewart (Gwen Saunders), Terry Kiser (Bernie Lomax), Don Calfa (Paulie), Catherine Parks (Tina), Eloise Broady (Tawny), Gregory Salata (Marty), Louis

Giambalvo (Vito), Ted Kotcheff (Jack Parker), Bruce Barbour (Beach Bum), George Cheung (Gardener).

Two friends get invited by their boss for a weekend with murder.

Bloopers

1. In Lomax's office, Larry shows a bandage around his right thumb (when he picks up a frame). As he and Richard walk out of the office, and Larry pats his partner on the shoulder, the bandage is gone. (00:13, 00:18)

2. While at home, Bernie receives a call from Paulie, and by mistake tapes it on the answering machine. When Paulie asks, "Where's your house?" Bernie answers, "It's on the point, top of the dune." And Paulie exclaims, "A-ha!" and the conversation goes on. But when Richard plays the tape, there's no "A-ha!"—but all the rest is there, even if the rhythm is a little faster. (00:30, 01:07)

3. When Paulie places the sunglasses on Bernie's face, the dead body blinks. (00:33)

4. After their first walk to the couch, Larry leaves Richard and Bernie to make some coffee. Bernie's head falls on Richard's shoulder. And then, it falls again. (00:38)

5. Upset by another of Larry's attempts to hide Bernie, a barefoot Richard goes inside the house to call the cops. After he hears the message on the answering machine, he and Larry turn the desk upside down to look for a note: Richard is wearing shoes now. When he picks up a briefcase, he's barefoot again, and when he runs away, passing through the fireplace, he is wearing shoes from the desk area, then he's barefoot in the living room. (01:06, 01:08, 01:10)

6. Richard knocks two "killers" out cold, then he and Larry decide to hide the two men in the kitchen pantry. In the pantry, the unconscious gardener lifts his legs to allow Richard to grab them easily. (01:18, 01:19)

7. On Lomax's boat, after jumping on a wave, Bernie jumps from the seat to the headrest, where "ULTRA" is written. A following close-up of Larry shows nobody sitting in the rear seat. But Bernie should be there. (01:23)

8. Paulie does the sign of the cross with his left hand after firing six bullets in Bernie's body. (01:29)

Question

After Richard sees Bernie getting ashore, he urges Gwen to leave. Richard looks fine. But as he enters the house looking for Larry, he is completely drenched. Since it was not raining, what happened? (00:54, 00:55)

WHAT DREAMS MAY COME (2)
1998, color, 113 min.

Director: Vincent Ward

Cast: Robin Williams (Chris Nielsen), Cuba Gooding, Jr. (Albert), Annabella Sciorra (Annie Nielsen), Max von Sydow (The Tracker), Jessica Brooks Grant (Marie Nielsen), Josh Paddock (Ian Nielsen), Rosalind Chao (Leona), Lucinda Jenney (Mrs. Jacobs), Maggie McCarthy (Stacey Jacobs), Wilma Bonet (Angie), Matt Salinger (Reverend Hanley), Carin Sprague (Best Friend Cindy).

A man tracks down his family in the afterlife.

Bloopers
1. As Chris enters the tunnel to help with the car wrecks, on the left side of the screen it is possible to see the shadow of the camera crane on the wall. (00:12)
2. When the painted bird poops on Chris, it covers his hair with pale green goo. In the following shot, the goo has moved to only one side of his face; the hair has no goo. (00:29, 00:30)

Question
If Chris's Heaven is a painting (at first), how come when he's underwater, everything looks real instead of painted? (00:30)

WHAT LIES BENEATH (10)
2000, color, 130 min.

Director: Robert Zemeckis

Cast: Harrison Ford (Dr. Norman Spencer), Michelle Pfeiffer (Claire Spencer), Diana Scarwid (Jody), Joe Morton (Dr. Drayton), James Remar (Warren Feur), Miranda Otto (Mary Feur), Amber Valletta (Madison Elizabeth Frank), Katharine Towne (Caitlin Spencer), Victoria Bidewell (Beatrice), Eliott Goretsky (Teddy), Wendy Crewson (Elena), Micole Mercurio (Mrs. Frank).

Ghosts can be a real pain in the neck, sometimes . . .

Bloopers
1. Claire drops a bunch of pictures and newspaper clippings from a photo album. When she picks them up, she places a clipping on top of everything—yet when she checks the stack, on top is a photo of a young Dr. Spencer and his dad. (00:11)
2. While Norman is telling Claire that he wants her to feel safe while he's at a conference, he sits on the bed: something white is sticking out of his right-back pants pocket. He doesn't do anything but remove his shoes, but when he stands up, the white thing is completely gone. (00:25, 00:26)

3. A photo frame falls from a desk and its glass shatters. Claire kneels down to remove the slivers, and she does a good job, leaving only one large triangular piece of glass to the right. But when she puts the frame back on the desk, the sliver is gone. (00:28)

4. When Claire approaches the bathtub, filled to the brim for the first time, she rolls her right sleeve up. As she gets to the faucet, she rolls the sleeve up again. (00:40)

5. Claire and Jody are in the bathroom, in front of a Ouija board: the indicator's lens is over the letter *T*, with help from neither them *nor* the spirit, it's placed on the letter *U*. (00:45)

6. Using the Vermont Missing People Database, Claire is able to find some information about Madison Elizabeth Frank: on the screen, her data appears to the left of the screen, and her picture to the right. But when she shows her husband a printout of (presumably) that very page, the photo has moved to the left and the data to the right. (01:01)

7. Claire is about to call the police on her husband while Norman is standing in front of her, trying to calm her down. She has her index finger on the dial, but in the over-the-shoulder, it's her thumb that is on the dial. And back and forth. (01:34)

8. Norman places Claire in the bathtub to drown her. She can't move because she's under the effects of a powerful anesthetic, however when she's placed down, her eyeline is at about the same level of the edge of the tub; when Norman switches from shower to faucet, her eyeline is noticeably lower; and when he calls Jody on the phone ("Could you check on her in the morning?") her eyeline is above the edge of the tub. And then it's lower again . . . (01:43, 01:44, 01:45)

9. The level of the water in the tub changes quite a few times; it's almost to the brim from the side where Claire has her feet, but then is much lower after Norman passes out for the second time. (01:46, 01:47)

10. After crashing into the water, the headlights of Claire's truck fizzle and go off as the vehicle begins to sink. Yet when its front is completely submerged, the lights are on. (01:58)

Questions

1. Claire comes home from the therapist and is about to open the door with her keys when she freezes because she spots a bag by the door. She picks up the book that is in the bag, and when she

stands up, her keys are in the door. How did she do that? (Also, when she invites her neighbor into the house for a cup of coffee, doesn't it sound like she opens the door *without* turning the keys in the lock?) (00:55, 00:56)

2. When Claire has an epiphany while standing on her husband and sees in the mirror the mental reflection of herself coming back home under the rain, the reflection is of a door with its hinges to the left. But that door's hinges are to the right. So . . . was her memory that screwed up? (01:11)

Fun Fact
It may have to do with the supernatural events in the house, but Claire's Mac sure boots up at light speed! (00:48)

WHOLE NINE YARDS, THE (20)
2000, color, 98 min.

Director: Jonathan Lynn

Cast: Bruce Willis (Jimmy "The Tulip" Tudeski), Matthew Perry (Nicholas "Oz" Oseransky), Rosanna Arquette (Sophie Oseransky), Michael Clarke Duncan (Frankie Figs), Natasha Henstridge (Cynthia Tudeski), Amanda Peet (Jill St. Claire), Kevin Pollak (Janni Gogolack), Harland Williams (Agent Steve Hanson), Carmen Ferland (Sophie's Mom), Serge Christianssens (Mr. Boulez),

Renee Madeline Le Guerrier (Waitress).

A romantic comedy about hitmen and dentists. Uh-huh . . .

Bloopers
1. Oz drives in Montreal with his headlights off—and he's the only one: since 1990, Canada requires that all cars on the road need to have their lights on (as you can see behind him). (00:03, 00:04)
2. As Oz and Jill are ordering lunch, Oz explains to the waitress that he doesn't want mayonnaise on his burger this time, and she takes the menu. He repeats his request, and she takes the menu . . . again. (00:06)
3. In the same scene, the waitress is holding a pen in her left hand and a menu in her right. As he repeats his request, the menu jumps into her left hand, and then back again. (00:06)
4. During the lunch, the level of the Pepsi in Jill's glass keeps changing throughout the scene. (00:06, 00:07)
5. Less than 1 minute passes between the ordering and the arrival of the hamburgers. (00:06, 00:07)
6. When Jill says to Oz that he should have his wife killed, she starts shaking the bottle of Tabasco sauce. She suddenly starts pouring it on her

burger without time to remove the cap. After she's done pouring, she licks the excess off the rim, and the cap instantly appears back on the bottle. (00:07)

7. Jill puts Tabasco on top of her hamburger, puts it back, and in the next shot the bun is missing. (00:07)

8. Oz first meets Jimmy, and Jimmy removes his shades and hangs them on the collar of his T-shirt with the lenses inside the shirt. In the middle of the scene, when Jimmy says, "They put mayonnaise on it?" the dark lenses are now outside his shirt, and then in the next cut they're not. (00:09)

9. Jimmy invites Oz for a drive through the town. Jimmy's car has a rearview mirror when they get in, but the mirror vanishes when they're driving. (00:12)

10. Jimmy picks Oz up and they hang out at a spot overlooking the city. At one point, Oz is sitting on the rail with his hands on the rail next to his legs ("No, I live here with my wife"). In the cut, his hands suddenly jump to his lap ("You sure you're a dentist?") and then back to the railing. (00:14)

11. When Sophie drives Oz to the airport, she gets out of the car: the crew is reflected in the door. (00:18)

12. Cynthia enters Oz's hotel room and she sits on the bed: the cigarette she's holding in her left hand zaps to her right hand and back. (00:31)

13. Oz goes into the hotel bathroom to get the vomit smell off of his breath. He brushes his teeth, uses mouthwash, then spits it out and sets the bottle down on the sink. As he walks out of the bathroom, the mouthwash bottle has vanished. Funny, because when he called room service to order scotch (00:29), the mouthwash bottle was nowhere to be seen. (00:32)

14. Frankie removes his sunglasses to hug Jimmy. But when the two hug, Frankie has his glasses back on. They vanish as the two separate. (00:41)

15. When Jimmy, Oz, and Frankie walk out of the restaurant, bystanders looking at the actors can be seen reflected in a door behind Frankie. (00:46)

16. When Oz uses the dentist's sedative on himself while talking to Jill, a tube is over his left ear and then not, depending on whether the shot is from above or from one side. (00:48)

17. In his home, Jimmy talks to a freaked-out Oz. When Jimmy tells him, "I would hate to . . ." he places his fingers on his gun trigger. Twice. (00:57)

18. Janni Gogolack's plane lands. The engine roars and slows down to a complete stop, but when Gogolack

walks out, it's possible to see that the engine is already not moving. (00:59)

19. One of the two hitmen falls down the stairs and smashes a few poles off the rail. When Frankie brings a cadaver into the house, the smashed poles are different. (01:07, 01:09)

20. When Jill peeks out of the window to distract Agent Hanson, the position of her hands changes from the wide shot and the close-up. (01:08)

Fun Fact

The second newspaper article that flashes before Oz's eyes when he recognizes "The Tulip" features a still photo from Bruce Willis's *Die Hard 2*. (00:08)

WILD AMERICA (6)

1997, color, 106 min.

Director: William Dear

Cast: Jonathan Taylor Thomas (Marshall Stouffer), Devon Sawa (Mark Stouffer), Scott Bairstow (Marty Stouffer, Jr.), Frances Fisher (Agnes Stouffer), Jamey Sheridan (Marty Stouffer, Sr.), Tracey Walter (Leon), Don Stroud (Stango), Zack Ward (D.C.), Claudia Stedelin (Carrie), Anastasia Spivey (Donna Jo), Leighanne Wallace (Tanna), Amy Lee Douglas (Julie Anne).

Three brothers go on a trip and meet EVERY SINGLE POSSIBLE CREATURE EVER CONCEIVED BY GOD, with the exception of the platypus.

Bloopers

1. Marshall cleans the toilet with Mark's and Marty's toothbrushes (one yellow and one blue)—but later on, when he's smiling while the three of them are brushing their teeth, Marshall is using one of the toothbrushes he used to clean the toilet. (00:03, 00:08)

2. After the mud race, Mark stares at two college girls who are coming at him. He is to the left of his girlfriend, but in the reverse shot he stands to her right. (00:15)

3. Chasing alligators, Mark apparently tosses the bait from the boat to the left. But when he goes to recover it, he seems to swim in front of the boat in another direction. (00:36, 00:37)

4. The kids sing "Born to Be Wild," a Steppenwolf hit from 1968. But this movie takes place during the summer of 1967. (00:49)

5. Mark breaks his right leg. The doctor gives him crutches; as the kids reach the woman's house, Mark is using only one crutch—on his left side. Going uphill, he uses one crutch—on his right side. (01:04, 01:05, 01:06)

6. The kids want to film sleeping grizzly bears. But on

September 3, bears are not hibernating at all. (01:10)

WILD WILD WEST (13)
1999, color, 107 min.

Director: Barry Sonnenfeld

Cast: Will Smith (Captain James "Jim" West), Kevin Kline (Artemus Gordon / President Ulysses S. Grant), Kenneth Branagh (Dr. Arliss Loveless), Salma Hayek (Rita Escobar), M. Emmet Walsh (Coleman, Train Engineer), Ted Levine (General "Bloodbath" McGrath, The Butcher of New Liberty), Frederique Van Der Wal (Amazonia), Musetta Vander (Munitia), Sofia Eng (Miss Lippenreider), Ling Bai (Miss East, Dr. Loveless's Personal Assistant), Garcelle Beauvais (Bell, the Girl in the Water Tower), Mike H. McGaughy (Big Reb), David Lea (Mr. Knife Guy).

Men in Black *meets James Bond meets* The Fresh Prince of Bel Air *meets blah blah blah.*

Bloopers
1. The movie takes place in 1869. When Jim West reaches the White House, in the background the Capitol Building is shown as incomplete (but it was built in 1822 and destroyed by fire on February 2, 1897). (00:00, 00:14)
2. Jim is on a carriage that has

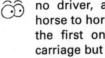 no driver, and jumps from horse to horse till he reaches the first one, stopping the carriage but winding up dangling from a cliff. When Jim tells the horses, "Back on up, now," a shot of the horses' legs reveals the right boot of a horse rider. (00:08, 00:10)
3. After Jim West and General McGrath have gone through a wall while fighting in the saloon, McGrath stands up yelling. His characteristic ear horn is missing—but it's immediately back as he exits the room. (00:13)
4. When Jim West rides his horse in front of the Capitol Building, the sunlight projects his shadow to the right. The Capitol is lit from sunlight coming from the left. Huh? (00:14)
5. In his train, Artemus shows Jim his belt buckle with a mini-gun and a mini-bullet hidden inside. The bullet has the point away from the gun. When Jim comes back to the train, he retrieves the same belt buckle and opens it. Now the bullet is pointing toward the gun. (00:25, 01:19)
6. While showing Jim his costumes, Artemus decides to 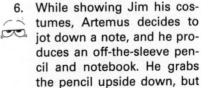 jot down a note, and he produces an off-the-sleeve pencil and notebook. He grabs the pencil upside down, but the detail shows the pencil correctly placed on the paper. (00:27)

7. When East kisses Jim and discusses his "French" knowledge, her right earring keeps popping in and out of her collar. (00:35)

8. Jim West defends himself while standing in front of a noose. In the shot from above, his hands are separated, but in the close-up he's holding his left hand on his belt buckle. And during the breakdown of the word "redneck," he lifts this right hand—but in the wide shot, he isn't. (00:39)

9. Jim has to go to Malheurex Point, so he takes the right horse of Artemus's two-horse carriage. When Artemus reaches the same place, a shot from above reveals his carriage being pulled by a horse placed in the middle. The following shot shows the horse to the left, where it was earlier. (00:41, 00:47)

10. Jim and Artemus fall into the "abysmal muck" while wearing the magnetic collars. Mud flies over Jim's hat, but as the duo walk and discuss, the hat and the collars are squeaky clean. (01:03, 01:04)

11. When the eighty-foot tarantula emerges from the canyon, its shadow covers Jim and Artemus. In the following shot, the shadow covers them again. (01:10)

12. President Grant makes Jim West and Artemus Gordon the first agents of the Secret Service. But the Secret Service was created on July 5, 1865 (four years prior to the events narrated in the movie). (01:38)

13. At the very end, Jim and Artemus ride the tarantula into the sunset while going back to Washington—which is East, actually. (01:40)

Question

Jim pushes Mr. Knife Guy off the tarantula, and the chain around his neck falls loose after him. When the tarantula stops on the edge of the cliff, Jim falls and saves himself because he grabs Mr. Knife Guy, who's hanging from the chain. What exactly happened there? (01:30, 01:37)

X

X FILES, THE (11)
1998, color, 121 min.

Director: Rob Bowman

Cast: David Duchovny (Special Agent Fox Mulder), Gillian Anderson (Special Agent Dana Scully), John Neville (The Well-Manicured Man), William B. Davis (The Cigarette-Smoking Man), Martin Landau (Dr. Alvin Kurtzweil), Mitch Pileggi (Assistant Director Walter Skinner), Jeffrey DeMunn (Dr. Ben Bronschweig), Blythe Danner (FBI Assistant Director Jana Cassidy), Terry O'Quinn (FBI Special Agent Darius Michaud), Armin Mueller-Stahl (Conrad Strughold), Lucas Black (Stevie), Christopher Fennell (2nd Boy), Glenne Headly (Barmaid).

Can one fight the future?

Bloopers
1. Trapped inside the vending room, Mulder uses his Nokia to call Scully. The detail shows a cell phone that has a nonte-lescopic antenna, yet as Mulder brings it to his ear, he pulls the antenna out. (00:15)
2. When the Barmaid asks Mulder, "Poopy day?" she is putting away glasses from the counter. One shot glass remains between her and Mulder, but in the following shot it's gone. (00:26)
3. When Mulder and Dr. Kurtzweil talk about the bomb in the building, the taxi Mulder hails arrives twice behind the duo. (00:30)
4. At the morgue, Mulder and Scully examine the body of one of the firemen who died in the bombing. She puts on latex gloves, but as she passes her hand over the corpse, she shows the white sleeve of a lab coat (which she will be wearing a few minutes later). (00:36, 00:37, 00:43)
5. Mulder enters Dr. Kurtzweil's apartment while policemen are snooping around. Casually, Mulder turns to a bookshelf on which there are a

few books, the first two with light brown spines, the next two with black spines. As he grabs the first two, there is one brown and one black. (00:39)

6. En route to the crops and the domes, Scully gets out of the car near some barbed wire: she wears black shoes with quite high heels. When she and Mulder go downhill toward the crop field, she's wearing shoes that are almost flat; and when she enters the dome, voilà: there you have the heels again! (00:58, 01:01, 01:03)

7. When Mulder opens the dome's door, a gust of air blows his tie over his right shoulder. He walks into the structure, his tie over his left shoulder. Then the tie appears to be down, then on the left shoulder again. (01:02)

8. Wilkes Land, Antarctica: Mulder is on top of a hill, keeping an eye on a secret base. He looks through his binoculars, and he sees the base from an overhead p.o.v. But the second time he looks through the binoculars, he sees the base from ground level—and he never changed his position. (01:28)

9. Walking toward the base, Mulder falls through the ice: as he lands, the hood of his jacket falls off of his head. Yet the first thing Mulder does when he stands up is remove the hood from his head. Hmmm . . . (01:29, 01:30)

10. When the Cigarette-Smoking Man comes back to the base on his snowmobile, the detail of the moving tracks is actually from Mulder's snowmobile: the Cigarette-Smoking Man's vehicle has flat tracks, while Mulder's are triangular (01:27). Exactly like the ones in the detail. (01:37)

11. After the detail of the "Fatal Hanta Virus Outbreak" article, Mulder folds his newspaper. Is it us, or does it seem that the middle pages of the paper are white? Check also when he hands the paper to Scully. (01:50)

Break Out the Prehistoric Archives

All righty, then: if anyone has photos of what north Texas looked like in 35,000 B.C., fine. If not, we won't even discuss whether or not there were mountains, or cavemen who looked like Neanderthals, or the like. There! (00:00)

Fun Fact

Mulder relieves himself in an alley, wetting a poster of *Independence Day*. (00:28)

Y

YOUNG FRANKENSTEIN (7)
1974, black & white, 98 min.

Director: Mel Brooks

Cast: Gene Wilder (Dr. Frederick Frankenstein), Peter Boyle (The Monster), Marty Feldman (Igor), Madeline Kahn (Elizabeth), Cloris Leachman (Frau Bluecher), Teri Garr (Inga), Kenneth Mars (Inspector Kemp), Richard Haydn (Herr Falkstein), Liam Dunn (Mr. Hilltop), Gene Hackman (The Blind Hermit), Mel Brooks (Voices of Werewolf and Cat Hit by Dart), Anne Beesley (Little Helga).

Grandson of mad scientist proves that creating monsters is, in fact, a laughing matter.

Bloopers
1. In Baron Von Frankenstein's castle, the clock chimes midnight . . . thirteen times. (00:03)
2. During his lecture, Professor Frankenstein draws the medulla oblongata on the blackboard—twice. (00:05)
3. Inspector Kemp has a wooden right arm and a patch over his left eye. During the monster chase, in the shot where he goes "sssssst!" the wooden arm is on the left, and the patch has moved over his right eye. (00:49, 01:34)
4. Dr. Frankenstein throws darts while talking with Inspector Kemp. The detail of the darts hitting the board doesn't match with the shot where Kemp takes the darts back from the board. (00:58, 00:59)
5. Kemp plants the darts on the board and fakes the tossing. However, when Dr. Frankenstein takes the darts back, they are in different positions than where Kemp left them. (00:59)
6. When Kemp upsets his adversary, the doctor uses only five darts (one ends up on the wall, two out the window, one hits a cat, and one is tossed behind his back),

but when the inspector's car leaves, there are at least six darts in the tires. (00:59, 01:01)

7. The monster sits on the see-saw, catapulting little Helga straight into her room. She lands on top of the bed. When her parents open the door one second later, she's completely tucked in under the covers. Also, the wire used to pull the covers up is quite visible. (01:06)

Z

ZEUS AND ROXANNE (10)
1997, color, 98 min.

Director: George Miller

Cast: Steve Guttenberg (Terrance Paul "Terry" Barnett), Kathleen Quinlan (Mary Beth Dunhill), Arnold Vosloo (Claude Carver), Dawn McMillan (Becky), Miko Hughes (Jordan Barnett), Majandra Delfino (Nora Dunhill), Jessica Howell (Mrs. Rice), Duchess Tomasello (Judith Dunhill), Shannon K. Foley (Linda), Jim R. Coleman (Phil), Alvin Farmer (Floyd), Harri James (Airline Attendant).

The strange friendship between a dog and a dolphin— a tuna-safe story.

Bloopers
1. The paper rolled up by Mrs. Rice's mailbox changes shape and position: first it gets rolled up more smoothly, then the position of the *T* in the title changes. (00:01, 00:02)
2. Terry opens the glass door to the verandah and slides a plate with a burrito on it to Zeus. When Zeus is done with the food, the glass door's blinds have been closed. But nobody did it. (00:03, 00:04)
3. Mary Beth goes to the Kemper Institute of Oceanography on her bicycle. She places a clipboard with the photo of a dolphin in one of her two bike containers and pedals happily away. When she gets to her workplace, and picks up the clipboard, the photo of the dolphin has changed. (00:07, 00:08)
4. When Mary Beth and Becky play the dolphin sound via their boat speakers, Zeus tilts his head sideways in one direction, then in the opposite direction. But from the back, his head is looking straight ahead. (00:10)
5. Kathleen sips a Coca-Cola while taking a walk with Zeus. As she sits on a bench, Zeus places a paw on the bench. In the following shot, Zeus places

his paw on the bench one more time. (00:24)

6. Looking through a gate at the police cars chasing some roller skaters, Jordan and Zeus appear to be the same height from behind. But from the front, Zeus is quite a bit shorter. (00:34)

7. Returning from one of her study trips, Mary Beth finds her two daughters waiting for her on the pier. Judith has her arms crossed (from the back), but (from the front) her left arm is along her side, and the right arm is holding on to it. (00:53)

8. After learning that they have been set up, Mary Beth and Terry sit down in front of the beach. Terry licks an ice-cream cone, holding it with his right hand. But in the matching cut, he's holding it with his left. (00:56)

9. Terry and Mary Beth talk on the phone; behind Terry is a ceiling fan, spinning rapidly. But when Terry says, "Yeah. Yeah, tomorrow'd be great," the fan is completely motion-less. And then it's spinning again. (01:10, 01:11)

10. Mary Beth is trapped in the *Delfine*, the small subma-rine. She opens the hatch to make water spill in. Her hair gets drenched, but a shot from outside the submarine reveals her hair is still per-fectly dry. In the next shot, it's wet again. (01:22, 01:23)

Questions

1. Jordan has a Nikon camera with a motor (heard after every snapshot). So . . . why does he have to rewind the film manually? (00:50, 00:51)

2. Terry goes into the kitchen to boil some water: he places the kettle under the faucet, but never removes the lid— yet the sound is of water fill-ing the container. How? (01:29)

Oops! Episode One

WHAT??? YOU NEVER BOUGHT THE FIRST BOOK?!?
Then you missed out on thousands of **bloopers, questions,**
and **fun facts** from:

Armageddon
As Good As it Gets
Austin Powers
Back to the Future
Batman
The Blues Brothers
The Brady Bunch Movie
Casablanca
Casper
Charlie's Angels
Chasing Amy
Die Hard
Dogma
Dr. No
The Emperor's New Groove
The Exorcist
Face/Off
Fast Times at Ridgemont High
Ferris Bueller's Day Off
Forrest Gump
Friday the 13th Parts I–IV
Galaxy Quest
Ghost
Ghostbusters
Good Will Hunting
Halloween
Happy Gilmore

Independence Day
It's a Wonderful Life
Jaws
Jurassic Park
King Kong
The Little Mermaid
Mary Poppins
The Matrix
Misery
Mission: Impossible
The Mummy
The Naked Gun
National Lampoon's Animal
    House
North by Northwest
Notting Hill
Parenthood
Payback
Pretty Woman
Psycho
Pulp Fiction
Quiz Show
Raiders of the Lost Ark
RoboCop
The Rock
The Rocky Horror Picture Show
Scream

Sleepy Hollow
South Park: Bigger, Longer &
  Uncut
Speed
Star Trek
Star Wars—Episodes I and IV
Superman
The Talented Mr. Ripley
The Terminator
Thunderball
Titanic

Toy Story
Twister
The Untouchables
The Usual Suspects
Wargames
Wayne's World
The Wedding Singer
Wild Things
The Wizard of Oz
X-Men
You've Got Mail

. . . and many, many more movies than you can count on a stick.

**Well . . . what are you waiting for?!?
GO PICK IT UP!!!!!!**

Oops!: Movie Mistakes
That Made the Cut

now available in fine Dumpsters everywhere